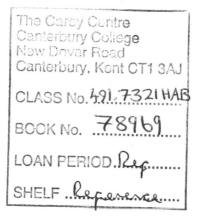
RUSSIAN-ENGLISH
ENGLISH-RUSSIAN
DICTIONARY &
PHRASEBOOK

Erika Haber

HIPPOCRENE BOOKS
New York

For information address:
HIPPOCRENE BOOKS, INC.
171 Madison Avenue
New York, New York 10016

ISBN 0-7818-1003-5

Cataloging-in-Publication Data available from the
Library of Congess.

Printed in the United States of America.

RUSSIAN-ENGLISH
ENGLISH-RUSSIAN
DICTIONARY &
PHRASEBOOK

Dictionary & Phrasebooks

Albanian
Arabic
Arabic (Eastern)
Romanized
Armenian (Eastern)
Australian
Azerbaijani
Basque
Bosnian
Breton
British
Cajun French
Chechen
Croatian
Czech
Danish
Dari *Romanized*
Esperanto
Estonian
Finnish
French
Georgian
German
Greek
Hebrew
Hindi
Hungarian
Igbo

Ilocano
Irish
Italian
Japanese *Romanized*
Lao *Romanized*
Latvian
Lingala
Lithuanian
Malagasy
Maltese
Mongolian
Nepali *Romanized*
Norwegian
Pashto *Romanized*
Pilipino (Tagalog)
Polish
Portuguese
(Brazilian)
Québécois
Romanian
Romansch
Russian
Shona
Slovak
Somali
Spanish (Latin American)
Swahili

CONTENTS

INTRODUCTION

Today over 220 million people around the world speak Russian. Despite popular misconceptions, Russian is not a difficult language. However, if you do not have the time to learn the language before your trip, try to become familiar with the Cyrillic alphabet so that you can read signs and get around a bit on your own. Unlike most other major European cities, Moscow and St. Petersburg—to say nothing of the smaller Russian cities—generally do not have signs and information posted in English.

In order to use this book most effectively, it is helpful to read the section on pronunciation. This chapter provides charts for pronunciation of the English transliteration, which allows you to "speak" Russian without knowing the Cyrillic alphabet. Once you are familiar with the pronunciation, look over the chapter Essential Expressions, which lists useful, every-day phrases. Each successive chapter covers basic words, phrases and concepts most often encountered by travelers to Russia in typical daily situations. The penultimate chapter on Numbers helps you make sense of the Russian number system and provides frequently used time expressions. The final chapter offers reference information such as holidays, weather, metric conversions and other practical information.

A unique feature of this phrasebook, the Russian-English, English-Russian Dictionary provides approximately 4,000 useful words, defined and listed with handy transliteration for easy, on-the-spot pronunciation.

ABBREVIATIONS

acc.	accusative
adj.	adjective
adv.	adverb
coll.	colloquial
comp.	comparative
conj.	conjunction
dat.	dative
f./fem.	feminine
form.	formal
gen.	genitive
instr.	instrumental
inter.	interrogative
interj.	interjection
m./masc.	masculine
n.	noun
nom.	nominative
nt./neut.	neuter
num.	numeral
par.	parenthetical
part.	particle
pl.	plural
pred.	predicate
prep.	preposition
prepl.	prepositional
pro.	pronoun
v.	verb

THE CYRILLIC ALPHABET

The Russian language is written in Cyrillic, an alphabet developed in the ninth century from ancient Greek by two monks, Saints Cyril and Methodius. Modern Russian consists of thirty-three letters total: ten vowels, twenty-one consonants and two voiceless sounds.

Russian Letter	English Sound
А/а	ah
Б/б	beh
В/в	veh
Г/г	geh
Д/д	deh
Е/е	yeh
Ё/ё	yoh
Ж/ж	zheh
З/з	zeh
И/и	ee
Й/й	y
К/к	kah
Л/л	ehl
М/м	ehm
Н/н	ehn
О/о	oh
П/п	peh
Р/р	ehr
С/с	ehs
Т/т	teh
У/у	oo
Ф/ф	ehf

Х/х	kha
Ц/ц	tseh
Ч/ч	cheh
Ш/ш	shah
Щ/щ	shchah
ъ	hard sign
ь	soft sign
ы	ih
Э/э	eh
Ю/ю	yoo
Я/я	yah

PRONUNCIATION GUIDE

Pronunciation

Like English, Russian spelling is not strictly phonetic. One letter may have more than one sound value. In the system of transliteration, each symbol is assigned a constant value. The English transliteration in this book will show you how to pronounce the Russian words even if you do not know the Cyrillic alphabet. The transliteration only approximates the Russian sounds, however, since no sound is exactly like its Russian counterpart.

Vowels

Russian vowels are shorter and purer than the English vowel sounds they resemble. Depending on where the stress falls in a word, the sound value of some Russian vowels may change. The following chart provides the approximate sounds of stressed vowels.

Russian Vowel	English Approximation	English Transliteration
а	as in **f**a**ther	*ah*
я	as in **y**ard	*yah*
э	as in **b**et	*eh*
е	as in **y**et	*yeh*
о	as in **sho**re	*oh*
ё	as in **y**ore	*yoh*
и	as in **b**ee**t	*ee*
ы	as in **p**it	*ih*
у	as in **sho**ot	*oo*
ю	as in **p**ew	*yoo*

Consonants

Russian consonants can be pronounced as either "soft" or "hard," voiced or voiceless. "Softening" (or palatalization) occurs when the letter is pronounced closer to the front of the mouth or hard palate. In Russian this occurs when consonants are followed by the vowels я, ю, и, э, ё, or the "soft sign" (ь). Sometimes the palatalization of a letter can change the meaning of a word. For instance, *брат* (braht) means "brother," whereas *брать* (braht') means "to take." Voiced consonants, those that make the vocal cords vibrate, become voiceless when they occur at the end of a word or before a voiceless consonant. For instance, "город" is phonetically represented as "gohraht," not "gohrahd" and "вчера" becomes "fchehrah," not "vchehrah." Likewise, voiceless consonants become voiced before voiced consonants. Fortunately, you do not have to learn the rules for this; all of these distinctions will be made for you in the English transliteration system provided.

Russian Consonant	English Approximation	English Transliteration
б	as in book	*b*
в	as in vote	*v*
г	as in goat	*g*
д	as in dad	*d*
ж	as in leisure	*zh*
з	as in zebra	*z*
й	as in boy	*y*
к	as in cake	*k*
л	as in lake	*l*

м	as in **m**om	*m*
н	as in **n**ap	*n*
п	as in **p**it	*p*
р	as in **r**ed	*r*
с	as in **s**ail	*s*
т	as in **t**ail	*t*
ф	as in **f**ish	*ʃ*
х	as in Ba**ch**	*kh*
ц	as in ha**ts**	*ts*
ч	as in **ch**ip	*ch*
ш	as in **sh**ip	*sh*
щ	as in fre**sh ch**eese	*shch*

Diphthongs

When two vowels occur together in Russian, they are
both pronounced. The only diphthongs in Russian are
formed by a combination of a vowel and an ee-kratkoe
(й). It is sometimes referred to as a "semi-vowel."

Russian Diphthongs	English Approximation	English Transliteration
ой	as in **toy**	*oy*
ей	as in h**ey**	*ey*
ай	as in b**ye**	*ay*
яй	like b**ye** with the **y** of "yet" preceding it	*yay*
ый	like the **i** in "pit'" followed by the **y** of "yet"	*ihy*
ий	as in may**be**	*eey*
уй	as in ph**ooey**	*ooy*

ю й	like ph**ooey** with the y of "yet" preceding it	*yooy*

Voiceless Sounds

There are two voiceless sounds in Russian. The "soft sign" or **-ь** (given as ' in transliteration) shows that the preceding consonant is soft, which means that it is pronounced closer to the front of the mouth. (i.e.: площадь)

The "hard sign" or **-ъ** (given as " in transliteration) separates a prefix ending in a consonant from a stem beginning in a vowel. (ie: отъезд)

Stress

Grammatical stress is very important in Russian. Only one syllable in each word is stressed. Secondary stresses, commonly found in English pronunciation, should be avoided. The location of the stress in a word determines the pronunciation of certain vowels. Unstressed vowels are less distinct and slightly shorter than their stressed counterparts.

For example, the first -о is not stressed in *окно,* (window) but the second one is. Thus, the first vowel is pronounced as an -а and the second one as an -о. ie: **ah**knoh not **oh**knoh. When unstressed, -е and -я sound like -и. The word *еда́* (food) is pronounced **yee**dah, not **yeh**dah, and *язы́к* (language) sounds like **yeez**ihk, not **yah**zihk.

Normally stress is not marked in Russian texts. In this book, the stressed syllable will be printed in capital letters (ie: *пустяк* poos**TYAK**).

AN INTRODUCTION TO
RUSSIAN GRAMMAR

The next few pages introduce the basics of Russian grammar. This is not meant to be a comprehensive review, but you will find here an explanation of the forms you will see in the dictionary and phrasebook. However, you can use this book perfectly well without knowing any Russian grammar at all.

Articles

There are no definite (*the*) or indefinite (*a, an*) articles in Russian. These distinctions are determined by context.

Gender

Depending on their endings, all Russian nouns are masculine, feminine or neuter. Nouns that end in any consonant, as well as -й, and sometimes -ь are considered masculine. Those that end in -a, -я, -ь are feminine. Nouns ending in -o, -e, or -мя are neuter.

masculine:	*feminine:*	*neuter:*
стол	сестра	письмо
музей	история	море
день	площадь	имя

Declension

Unlike English, Russian expresses the relations between words in a sentence by inflection. Nouns, pronouns and adjectives take different endings depending on their function in a sentence. In Russian, these functions are grouped into six different categories called cases.

Each case has its own endings. This explains why the same word may have different endings depending on its usage in a sentence.

Cases

Russian uses cases rather than word order to determine the function of words in a sentence. The endings of Russian nouns and pronouns change depending on whether they are used as subjects, direct objects or indirect objects. These changes are determined by the six cases in Russian. Each case has different endings for each gender as well as for the plural. Below you will find some of the most common uses of the cases.

The nominative case is used for the subject of the sentence. It is also the form words appear in dictionaries. *This is my dog.* Это моя **собака.**

The accusative case is used to show the direct object. It also appears after the prepositions *через, за, в, на.* *I bought a book.* Я купила **книгу.**

The dative case is used for indirect objects, for telling one's age, the complement of impersonal statements, and after the prepositions *по* and *к.*
He gave his father a gift.
Он подарил своему **отцу** подарок.

Possession is shown with the genitive case. It is also used to express the lack of something and follows the word *нет.* The genitive comes after the numbers two through four and the prepositions *для, из, от, до, после, около, без, кроме.* The genitive plural follows numbers five and higher.

That is Ivan's letter.   Это письмо **Ивана.**

The prepositional case is used to express location and
follows the prepositions *в, на, о.*
He spoke about nature.   Он говорил о **природе.**

The instrumental case appears after the prepositions *с,
между, за, над, под, перед.* It usually shows how
something is done, using what means or in what manner.
I like tea with lemon.   Я люблю чай с **лимоном.**

Adjectives
Because adjectives modify nouns, adjectives also
change their endings depending on the gender, case
and number of the noun they describe. Dictionaries
provide the nominative masculine forms of adjectives.
Masculine nominative case adjectives end in *-ый,
-ий* or *-ой:*   *грубый   близкий   большой*

Feminine nominative case adjectives end in *-ая/-яя:*
молодая   летняя

Nominative case adjectival endings for neuter nouns
are *-ое/-ее:*   *новое   синее*

Plural adjective endings do not reflect gender so they
are always either *-ые* or *-ие: добрые   хорошие*

Pronouns
Russian pronouns also change form depending on
their gender and function in the sentence. Like German and French, Russian has two forms for "you."

One is singular and informal (*ты*), the other is formal and plural (*вы*). Unless told otherwise by the person with whom you are speaking, you should always use the formal form.

Personal Pronouns

Personal pronouns are the ones used to replace nouns. Thus, they change case depending on their function in the sentence.

Sing.	I/me	you	he/it	she
Nom	я *yah*	ты *tih*	он/оно *on/ahnoh*	она *ahnah*
Acc	меня *meenyah*	тебя *tebyah*	его *yevoh*	её *yehyoh*
Gen	меня *meenyah*	тебя *tebyah*	его *yevoh*	её *yehyoh*
Dat	мне *mnyeh*	тебе *tebyeh*	ему *yehmoo*	ей *yeay*
Prepl.	мне *mnyeh*	тебе *tebyeh*	нём *nyohm*	ней *nyeay*
Instr.	мной *mnoy*	тобой *tahboy*	им *eem*	ей *yeay*

Plural	we/us	you	they
Nom.	мы *mih*	вы *vih*	они *ahnee*
Acc.	нас nahs	вас vahs	их eekh
Gen.	нас *nahs*	вас *vahs*	их *eekh*
Dat.	нам *nahm*	вам *vahm*	им *eem*

Prepl.	нас *nahs*	вас *vahs*	них *neekh*
Instr.	нами *nahmee*	вами *vahmee*	ими *eemee*

Possessive Pronouns

Unlike personal pronouns, possessive pronouns change like adjectives to modify the thing being possessed. Thus, they have different endings depending on whether the object is masculine, feminine, neuter or plural. All of these endings will also change when the object is put into a different case. The forms for his/hers/its/their do not change from case to case. Below are the nominative case forms of the possessive pronouns.

	masc.	*fem.*	*neut.*	*pl.*
my	мой *moy*	моя *maya*	мое *mayo*	мои *mayee*
your *(sg.)*	твой *tvoy*	твоя *tvaya*	твое *tvayo*	твои *tvayee*
his/hers */its*	его *yeyo*	её *yeyo*	его *yeyo*	их *eekh*
our	наш *nash*	наша *NAsha*	наше *NAshe*	наши *nashee*
your *(pl.)*	ваш *vash*	ваша *vasha*	ваше *vashe*	ваши *vashee*
their	их *eekh*	их *eekh*	их *eekh*	их *eekh*

Demonstrative Pronouns

The demonstrative pronouns are used to distinguish between "this one" or "that one." These pronouns change form depending on their function in the sentence.

masc.	этот	тот	*neut*	это	то
fem.	эта	та	*pl.*	эта	те

Although it looks similar, don't confuse these forms with this predicative form. "This/that is" in Russian is expressed with the pronouns это/то. These forms do not change for case.

This is our room.　Это наша комната.

Adverbs

Russian adverbs most commonly end in an -*o*.

быстро	*quickly*
редко	*rarely*
медленно	*slowly*

However, adverbs formed from languages and some others have an ending in -*ски*.

I speak Russian and Italian.

Я говорю по-русски и по-итальянски.

Verbs

In addition to being marked for number, person and tense, Russian verbs also have aspect. Most verbs in Russian are paired. In the pair, one verb is imperfective and the other is perfective. Imperfective verbs generally show that the action is repeated, habitual or general. Perfective verbs indicate that an action is completed, one-time or specific in nature.

The two most common forms of verb conjugations in Russian have infinitive forms that end in either -*ать* or -*ить*.

	читать/*to read*	говорить/*to speak*
я	читаю	говорю
ты	читаешь	говоришь
он/она/оно	читает	говорит
мы	читаем	говорим
вы	читаете	говорите
они	читают	говорят

Common Irregular Verbs:

Some of the verbs used most often in Russian have conjugations that do not fit into the pattern described above. Some examples are the verbs "to want," "to go," "to be able to" and "to write."

хотеть/to want

я хочу	мы хотим
ты хочешь	вы хотите
он хочет	они хотят

идти/to go (on foot)

я иду	мы идём
ты идёшь	вы идёте
он идёт	они идут

мочь/to be able to

я могу	мы можем
ты можешь	вы можете
он может	они могут

писать/to write

я пишу	мы пишем
ты пишешь	вы пишете
он пишет	они пишут

Past Tense

To form the past tense in Russian, you remove the -ть from the infinitive form and add:

-л for male:	читал	говорил
-ла for female:	читала	говорила
-ло for neuter:	читало	говорило
-ли for plural:	читали	говорили

Present Tense

The present tense of imperfective verbs is the simple conjugated form given above in *читать, говорить.* Perfective verbs have no present tense meaning. There is no present tense form of the verb "to be" in Russian.   *I am a student.*   Я студент.

Future Tense

To form the future tense of imperfective verbs, use a future tense form of the verb to be *(быть)* and the infinitive of the imperfective verb.

Я буду читать.	*I will read.*
Ты будешь читать.	*You will read.*
Он будет читать.	*He will read.*
Мы будем читать.	*We will read.*
Вы будете читать.	*You (pl.) will read.*
Они будут читать.	*They will read.*

To form the future tense of a perfective verb, use the present tense form.

Я прочитаю.   *I will finish reading.*
Ты прочитаешь.   *You will finish reading.*
Он прочитает.   *He will finish reading.*
Мы прочитаем.   *We will finish reading.*
Вы прочитаете.   *You (pl.) will finish reading.*
Они прочитают.   *They will finish reading.*

Permission

In signs you will often see the words можно (*it is permitted*) or нельзя (*it is not permitted*). These forms are followed by an infinitive verb.

Smoking is not permitted   Нельзя курить.
Smoking is permitted.   Можно курить.

Можно may also be used alone to ask permssion,
May I?   Можно?

To have/To have not

Possession in Russian is not usually expressed with a verb as in English. Instead, Russian uses a preposition *(у)* that requires the genitive case of the person doing the possessing, followed by the word *есть*. The object possessed is in the nominative case.

I have a dog.   У меня есть собака.

Есть is only used to show presence of an object. When you modify that object, you drop the есть.

I have a small dog.   У меня маленькая собака.

To say that you do not have something, you must not only use the *y* plus the genitive of the person who does not possess the item, but also the genitive of the object that is lacking. Instead of *есть*, you use *нет*.

We have no money.   У нас нет денег.

Negation

Unlike English, Russian has double negation. You not only negate the verb with the particle *не,* but also add a negative adverb.

I know nothing.   Я ничего не знаю.

Question Words

As in English, Russians usually ask questions with interrogative words at the beginning of the sentence. The basic question words in Russian are given below.

Почему	*pachehmOO*	why
Где	*gdyeh*	where
Куда	*kooDAH*	where to
Когда	*kahgDAH*	when
Как	*kahk*	how
Кто	*ktoh*	who
Что	*chtoh*	what
Сколько	*SKOHL'kah*	how many, how much

Russian-English Dictionary

A

авария ahVAHreeyah *n.f.* breakdown; accident
авеню ahveenYOO *n.m.* avenue
авиапочта ahveeahPOHCHtah *n.f.* air mail
автобус ahfTOHboos *n.m.* bus
автомат ahftahMAHT *n.m.* vending machine
автомобилист ahftahmahbeeLEEST *n.m.* motorist
автомобиль ahftahmahBEEL' *n.m.* car
автор AHFtahr *n.m.* author
адвокат ahdvahKAHT *n.m.* lawyer
адрес AHdrees *n.m.* address
азбука AHSbookah *n.f.* alphabet
аккуратный ahkooRAHTnihy *adj.* neat; tidy; punctual
акт ahkt *n.m.* act
актёр ahkTYOHR *n.m.* actor
актриса ahkTREEsah *n.f.* actress
актуальный ahktooAHL'nihy *adj.* current
акушер/акушерка ahkooSHEHR/ahkooSHEHRkah *n.m./f.* obstetrician
акцент ahkTSEHNT *n.m.* accent
алкоголь ahlkahGOHL' *n.m.* alcohol
аллергия ahleerGEEyah *n.f.* allergy
алло ahLOH *interj.* hello (on the telephone)
американец/американка ahmeereeKAHneets/ahmeereeKAHNkah *n.m./f.* American
американский ahmeereeKAHNskeey *adj.* American

ананас ahnahNAHS *n.m.* pineapple

английская булавка ahngLEEYskahyah booLAHFkah *n.f.* safety pin

английский ahngLEEYskeey *adj.* English, British

англичанин/англичанка ahngleeCHAHneen/ahngleeCHAHNkah *n.m./f.* Englishman/ Englishwoman

анкета ahnKYEHtah *n.f.* form; blank; survey

антибиотик ahnteebeeOHteek *n.m.* antibiotic

антракт ahnTRAHKT *n.m.* intermission

апельсин ahpeel'SEEN *n.m.* orange

аплодисменты ahplahdeesMYEHNtih *n.pl.* applause

аппендикс ahPYEHNdeeks *n.m.* appendix

аппендицит ahppeendeeTSEET *n.m.* appendicitis

аппетит ahpeeTEET *n.m.* appetite; **приятного аппетита!** preeYAHTnahvah ahpeeTEEtah! Hearty appetite!

аптека ahpTYEHkah *n.f.* drugstore

аптечка ahpTYEHCHkah *n.f.* first-aid kit

арбуз ahrBOOZ *n.m.* watermelon

арест ahREHST *n.m.* arrest

артерия ahrTYEHreeyah *n.f.* artery

артист ahrTEEST *n.m.* performer

артрит ahrtREET *n.m.* arthritis

архитектор ahrkheeTYEHKtahr *n.m.* architect

архитектура ahrkheeteekTOOrah *n.f.* architecture

аспирант/аспирантка ahspeeRAHNT/ ahspeeRAHNTkah *n.m./f.* graduate student

аспирин ahspeeREEN *n.m.* aspirin

астма AHSTmah *n.f.* asthma

атеизм ahtehEEZM *n.m.* atheism

атеист ahtehEEST *n.m.* atheist

атлетика ahtLYEHTeekah *n.f.* athletics
атлетический ahtleeTEEchyeskeey *adj.* athletic
афиша ahFEEshah *n.f.* poster; play bill
аэровокзал aerohvahkSAHL *n.m.* air terminal
аэропорт ahehrahPOHRT *n.m.* airport

Б

бабушка BAHbooshkah *n.f.* grandmother
багаж bahGAHSH *n.m.* baggage
баклажан bahklahzhAHN *n.m.* eggplant
балалайка bahlahLAYkah *n.f.* balalaika
балет bahLYEHT *n.m.* ballet
балкон bahlKOHN *n.m.* balcony
банан bahNAHN *n.m.* banana
банк bahnk *n.m.* bank
банка BAHNkah *n.f.* jar; can
банкомат bahnkahMAHT *n.m.* ATM
баня BAHNyah *n.f.* public bath
баранина bahRAHneenah *n.f.* mutton; lamb
бассейн bahsSEYN *n.m.* pool
батарея bahtahREEyah *n.f.* battery
башня BAHSHnyah *n.f.* tower
бегать BYEHgaht' *v.* to run
беда bceDAH *n.f.* misfortune
бедный BYEHDnihy *adj.* poor
бедро beedROH *n.nt.* hip; thigh
без byehs *prep.* without
безалкогольный beezahlkahGOHL'nihy *adj.* nonalcoholic
безбожие beezBOHzheeyeh *n.m.* atheism
безбожник beezBOHZHneek *n.m.* atheist

безвинный beezVEENnihy *adj.* innocent

безвкусный beezVKOOSnihy *adj.* tasteless

безопасно beezahPAHSnah *adv.* safely

белый BYEHlihy *adj.* white

бельё beel'YOH *n.nt.* laundry; linen

бензин beenZEEN *n.m.* gas

бензозаправочная станция beenzahzah-PRAHvahchnahyah STAHNtseeyah *n.f.* gas station

берег BYEHreek *n.m.* coast; bank; shore

берегись beereeGEES' *v.* caution

берёза beerYOHzah *n.f.* birch

беременная beeRYEHmeennahyah *adj.* pregnant

беречь beeRYEHCH' *v.* to save, keep; guard

бес byehs *n.m.* demon

беседа beeSYEHdah *n.f.* conversation

беседовать beeSYEHdahvaht' *v.* to talk, chat

бесплатный beesPLAHTnihy *adj.* free of charge

беспокоить beespahKOHeet' *v.* to worry; trouble; bother; disturb

бесполезный beespahlYEHZnihy *adj.* useless

беспосадочный beespahSAHdahchnihy *adj.* nonstop (of a flight)

беспошлинный beesPOHSHleennihy *adj.* duty-free

бессознательный beessahzNAHteel'nihy *adj.* unconscious

бессоница beesSOHNeetsah *n.f.* insomnia

бесцветный beesTSVYEHTnihy *adj.* colorless

библиотека beebleeahTYEHkah *n.f.* library

Библия BEEbleeyah *n.f.* Bible

бизнесмен beeznehsMYEHN *n.m.* businessman

билет beeLYEHT *n.m.* ticket

билетная касса beeLYEHTnahyah KAHSah *n.f.* ticket office

бинокль beeNOHKL' *n.m.* binoculars; opera glasses

бинт beent *n.m.* bandage

бить beet' *v.* to beat; to strike

биться BEETsah *v.* to fight

бифштекс beefSHTEHKS *n.m.* steak

благодарить blahgahdahREET' *v.* to thank

благодарный blahgahDAHRnihy *adj.* thankful, grateful

благополучно blahgahpahLOOCHnah *adv.* safely; without mishap

благословение blahgahslahVYEHneeyeh *n.nt.* blessing

бланк blahnk *n.m.* form; blank

бледный BLYEHDnihy *adj.* pale

ближайший bleeZHAYsheey *adj.* nearest; next

близко BLEESkah *adv.* near; close

блин bleen *n.m.* pancake

блондин/блондинка blahnDEEN/blahnDEENkah *n.m./f.* blonde

блузка BLOOSkah *n.f.* blouse

блюдо BLYOOdah *n.nt.* dish; food; course

Бог bohkh *n.m.* God

богатый bahGAHtihy *adj.* rich

богослужение bahgahslooZHEHneeyeh *n.nt.* worship service

бодрый BOHdrihy *adj.* cheerful

бок bohk *n.m.* side

более BOHleeyeh *comp.* more

болезнь bahLYEHZN' *n.f.* illness; disease

болельщик bahlYEHL'shcheek *n.m.* sports fan

болеть bahlYEHT' *v.* to be ill

болеутоляющее средство bahleeootahl-YAHyooshchehyeh SRYEHTstvah *n.nt.* painkiller

болтливый bahltLEEvihy *adj.* talkative

боль bohl' *n.f.* pain

больница bahl'NEEtsah *n.f.* hospital

больной bahl'NOY *adj.* sick

больше BOHL'sheh *comp.* larger; bigger; greater

большинство bahl'sheenstVOH *n.nt.* majority

большой bahl'SHOY *adj.* big; large; great

большой палец bahl'SHOY PAHleets *n.m.* thumb

большое спасибо bahl'SHOHyeh spahSEEbah *interj.* thanks a lot

борода bahrahDAH *n.f.* beard

борщ bohrshch *n.m.* borsch; beet soup

борьба bahr'VAH *n.f.* fight, struggle

ботанический сад bahtahNEEchehskeey saht *n.m.* botanical garden

бояться bahYAHTsah *v.* to fear, be afraid

брак brahk *n.m.* marriage

брат braht *n.m.* brother

брать braht' *v.* to take, seize

бриллиант breeleeAHNT *n.m.* diamond

бритва BREETvah *n.f.* razor

бриться BREETsah *v.* to shave; get a shave

брошь brohsh *n.f.* brooch; pin

брюки BRYOOkee *n.pl.* pants

брюнет/брюнетка bryooNYEHT/bryoo-NYEHTkah *n.m./f.* brunette

будильник booDEEL'neek *n.m.* alarm clock

будний день BOODneey dyehn' *n.m.* weekday

будущий BOOdooshcheey *adj.* future

булавка booLAHFkah *n.f.* pin
булка BOOLkah *n.f.* roll; bun
булочная BOOlahchnahyah *n.f.* bakery
бульвар bool'VAHR *n.m.* boulevard
бумага booMAHgah *n.f.* paper
бумажник booMAHZHneek *n.m.* wallet
буря BOORyah *n.f.* storm
бусы BOOsih *n.pl.* beads
бутерброд bootehrBROHT *n.m.* sandwich
бутылка booTIHLkah *n.f.* bottle
буфет boofYEHT *n.m.* snack bar
бывший BIHFsheey *adj.* former
быстро BIHStrah *adv.* fast; quickly
бюро byooROH *n.nt.* office; bureau
бюстгальтер byoozGAHL'tehr *n.f.* bra

В

в v *prep.* in, at, for, to
в один конец vahDEEN kahNYEHTS *adv.* one-way (ticket)
вагон vahGOHN *n.m.* railroad car
важность VAHZHnahst' *n.f.* importance
важный VAHZHnihy *adj.* important
валюта vahLYOOtah *n.f.* hard-currency
валютный курс vahLYOOtnihy koors *n.m.* rate of exchange
ванна VAHNnah *n.f.* bathtub
ванная VAHNnahyah *n.f.* bathroom
варенье vahRYEHN'yeh *n.nt.* jam
варить vahrEET' *v.* to cook, boil
вата VAHtah *n.f.* absorbent cotton

вверх vvyehrkh *adv.* up, upwards (destination)

вверху vveerKHOO *adv.* above; overhead (location)

вдали vdahLEE *adv.* in the distance

вдвоём vdvahYOHM *adv.* two together

вдова vdahVAH *n.f.* widow

вдовец vdahvYEHTS *n.m.* widower

вдруг vdrook *adv.* suddenly

вегетарианец/вегетарианка veegeetahreeAHNeets/veegeetahreeAHNkah *n.m./f.* vegetarian

веер VYEHeer *n.m.* fan

вежливый VYEHZHleevihy *adj.* polite; courteous

везде veezDYEH *adv.* everywhere

век vyehk *n.m.* century; age

великий veeLEEkeey *adj.* great

велосипед veelahseePYEHT *n.m.* bicycle

вена VYEHnah *n.f.* vein

вера VYEHrah *n.f.* belief; faith

верить VYEHreet' *v.* to believe, have faith

верный VYEHRnihy *adj.* true; faithful

вероятно veerahYAHTnah *adv.* probably

верх vyehrkh *adv.* top

верхний VYEHRkhneey *adj.* upper; top

вес vyehs *n.m.* weight

веселиться veeseeLEEtsah *v.* to enjoy oneself

весенний veesYEHNneey *adj.* spring

весна veesNAH *n.f.* spring

весь vyehs' *n.m.* all; the whole

ветер VYEHteer *n.m.* wind

ветреный VYEHTreenihy *adj.* windy

ветчина veetcheeNAH *n.f.* ham

вечер VYEHcheer *n.m.* evening
вечерний veeCHEHRneey *adj.* evening
вешалка VYEHshahlkah *n.f.* hanger
взгляд vzglyaht *n.m.* look; glance
взлёт vzlyoht *n.m.* takeoff (in a plane)
взрослый VZROHSlihy *n.m.* adult
взять напрокат vzyaht' nahprahKAHT *v.* to rent
вид veet *n.m.* appearance
видеть VEEdeet' *v.* to see
видно VEEDnah *adv.* visible; clear; obvious
виза VEEzah *n.f.* visa
вилка VEELkah *n.f.* fork
вина veeNAH *n.f.* guilt
вино veeNOH *n.nt.* wine
вирус VEEroos *n.m.* virus
витамин veetahMEEN *n.m.* vitamin
вишня VEESHnyah *n.f.* sour cherries
включать fklyooCHAHT' *v.* to turn, switch on
вкусный FKOOSnihy *adj.* tasty
влажный VLAHZHnihy *adj.* humid
вместе VMYEHStyeh *adv.* together
вместо VMYEHStah *prep.* instead of
вне vnyeh *adv.* outside; out of
внешний VNYEHSHneey *adj.* outward; external
вниз vnees *adv.* down; downward (destination)
внизу vneeZOO *adv.* down below (location)
внимание vneeMAHneeyeh *n.nt.* attention
внук vnook *n.m.* grandson
внутренний VNOOtreenneey *adj.* internal
внутри vnooTREE *adv.* inside
внучка VNOOCHkah *n.f.* granddaughter
вовремя VOHvreemyah *adv.* on time

вода vahDAH *n.f.* water

водитель vahDEEteel' *n.m.* driver

водка VOHTkah *n.f.* vodka

военный vahYEHNnihy *adj.* military

возвращать vahzvrahSHCHAHT' *v.* to return

воздух VOHZdookh *n.m.* air

возможность vahzMOHZHnahst' *n.f.* opportunity

возражение vahzrahZHEHneeyeh *n.nt.* objection

возраст VOHZrahst *n.m.* age

война vayNAH *n.f.* war

вокзал vahkZAHL *n.m.* train station

вокруг vahkROOK *adv.* around (location)

волноваться vahlnahVAHtsah *v.* to be worried, agitated

волосы VOHlahsih *n.pl.* hair

вольно VOHL'nah *adv.* freely; voluntarily

вольтаж vahl'TAHSH *n.m.* voltage

воля VOHLyah *n.f.* freedom

вообще vahahpSHCHEH *adv.* in general

вопрос vahpROHS *n.m.* question

вор vohr *n.m.* thief

ворота vahROHtah *n.f.* gate

воспаление vahspahLYEHneeyeh *n.nt.* inflamation

воспаление лёгких vahspahLYEHneeyeh LYOHKHkeekh *n.nt.* pneumonia

воспоминание vahspahmeeNAHneeyeh *n.nt.* memory; recollection

воспрещаться vahspreeSHCHAHtsah *v.* to be forbidden

восток vahsTOHK *n.m.* east

восточный vahsTOHCHnihy *adj.* eastern

вот voht *part.* here (is)

впервые fpeerVIHyeh *adv.* for the first time; first
вперёд fpeeRYOHT *adv.* forward; ahead
впереди fpeereeDEE *adv.* in front; ahead
впечатление fpeechahtLYEHneeyeh *n.nt.* impression
вполне fpahlNYEH *adv.* fully; completely; quite
впуск fpoosk *n.m.* admission; admittance
впускать fpoosKAHT' *v.* to admit, let in
врать vraht' *v.* to lie, tell lies
врач vrahch *n.m.* doctor
вредный VRYEHDnihy *adj.* harmful
временно VRYEHmeennah *adv.* temporarily
время VRYEHmyah *n.nt.* time
всегда fseegDAH *adv.* always
всеобщий fseeOHPshcheey *adj.* universal; general
всё-таки VSYOHtahkee *adv.* still; all the same
вслух fslookh *adv.* aloud
вставать fstahVAHT' *v.* to get, stand up
встреча FSTRYEHchah *n.f.* meeting; encounter
встречать fstreechAHT' *v.* to meet
вход fkhoht *n.m.* entrance
входить fkhahDEET' *v.* to enter
вчера fcheeRAH *n.f.* yesterday
вчерашний fcheeRAHSHneey *adj.* yesterday's
выбор VIHbahr *n.m.* choice; assortment; selection
выборы VIHbahrih *n.pl.* elections
выгодный VIHgahdnihy *adj.* profitable; favorable
выключать vihklyooCHAHT' *v.* to turn out, switch off
высокий vihSOHkeey *adj.* high; tall; lofty
выставка VIHstahfkah *n.f.* exhibition; display
выход VIHkhaht *n.m.* exit

выходить vihkhahDEET' *v.* to leave, go out, exit
выходной день vihkhahdNOY dyehn' *n.m.* day off
вышитый VIHsheetihy *adj.* embroidered

Г

гадкий GAHTkeey *adj.* nasty; foul; vile
газета gahZYEHtah *n.f.* newspaper
галстук GAHLstook *n.m.* tie
гараж gahRAHSH *n.m.* garage
гардероб gahrdeeROHP *n.m.* cloakroom
гардеробщик gahrdeeROHPshcheek *n.m.* cloakroom attendant
гастрит gahstREET *n.m.* gastritis
гастроном gahstrahNOHM *n.m.* grocery store
гвоздика gvahzDEEkah *n.f.* carnation
где gdyeh *adv.* where
где-нибудь GDYEHneeboot' *adv.* somewhere
геморрой geemahrROY *n.m.* hemorrhoids
гепатит geepahTEET *n.m.* hepatitis
герой geeROY *n.m.* hero
гид geet *n.m.* guide
гинеколог geeneeKOHlahk *n.m.* gynecologist
гипертония geepeertahNEEyah *n.f.* high blood pressure
гипс geeps *n.m.* plaster cast
гитара geeTAHrah *n.f.* guitar
главный GLAHVnihy *adj.* main; principle
глагол glahGOHL *n.m.* verb
гладить GLAHdeet' *v.* to iron
глаз glahs *n.m.* eye

гланды GLAHNdih *n.pl.* tonsils

глотать glahTAHT' *v.* to swallow

глубокий glooBOHkeey *adj.* deep; in depth

глупый GLOOpihy *adj.* stupid; silly

глухой glooKHOY *adj.* deaf

гнев gnyehf *n.m.* anger

говорить gahvahrEET' *v.* to speak, talk (about)

говядина gahvYAHDeenah *n.f.* beef

год goht *n.m.* year

голова gahlahVAH *n.f.* head

головная боль gahlahvNAHyah bohl' *n.f.* headache

голод GOHlaht *n.m.* hunger

голодный gahLOHDnihy *adj.* hungry

голос GOHlahs *n.m.* voice

голосовать gahlahsahVAHT' *v.* to vote

голубой gahlooBOY *adj.* light blue

голый GOHlihy *adj.* naked

гомосексуализм gohmahseeksooahlEEZM *n.m.* homosexuality

гора gahRAH *n.f.* mountain

гораздо gahRAHZdah *adv.* much, far

гордый GOHRdihy *adj.* proud

горе GOHRyeh *n.nt.* grief

горло GOHRlah *n.f.* throat

горничная GOHRneechnahyah *n.f.* maid

город GOHraht *n.m.* city

горох gahROHKH *n.m.* peas

горчица gahrCHEEtsah *n.f.* mustard

горький GOHR'keey *adj.* bitter

горячий gahrYAHcheey *adj.* hot (of food and drink)

господин gahspahDEEN *n.m.* Mr.

госпожа gahspahZHAH *n.f.* Mrs.

гостиница gahsTEEneetsah *n.f.* hotel

гость gohst' *n.m.* guest

государственный gahsooDAHRstveennihy *adj.*
  state; government

государство gahsooDAHRstvah *n.nt.* the State

готовить gahTOHveet' *v.* to prepare

готовый gahTOHvihy *adj.* ready

градус GRAHdoos *n.m.* degree

градусник GRAHdoosneek *n.m.* thermometer

гражданский grahzhDAHNskeey *adj.* civil;
  civilian

гражданство grahzhDAHNstvah *n.nt.* citizenship

грамм grahm *n.m.* gram

грамматика grahmMAHteekah *n.f.* grammar

грампластинка grahmplahsTEENkah *n.f.* record

гранат grahNAHT *n.m.* garnet

граница grahNEEtsah *n.f.* border

гребёнка greebYOHNkah *n.f.* comb

грейпфрут GREYPfroot *n.m.* grapefruit

грех gryehkh *n.m.* sin

грибы greeBIH *n.pl.* mushrooms

грипп greep *n.m.* flu

гроза grahZAH *n.f.* thunderstorm

грозный GROHZnihy *adj.* threatening

гром grohm *n.m.* thunder

громкий GROHMkeey *adj.* loud

грубый GROObihy *adj.* rude; course

грудь groot' *n.f.* chest; breast

грузовик groozahVEEK *n.m.* truck

группа GROOpah *n.f.* group

грустный GROOSTnihy *adj.* sad; melancholic
груша GROOshah *n.f.* pear
грязный GRYAHZnihy *adj.* dirty; filthy
грязь gryahs' *n.f.* dirt; filth
губа gooBAH *n.f.* lip
гудок gooDOHK *n.m.* horn; whistle
гулять goolYAHT' *v.* to stroll, walk
густой goosTOY *adj.* thick, dense
гусь goos' *n.m.* goose

Д

да dah *part.* yes
давай dahVAY *v./part.* let's; go ahead!
давать dahVAHT' *v.* to give
давление dahvLYEHneeyeh *n.nt.* (blood) pressure
давно dahvNOH *adv.* long ago
далее DAHleeyeh *comp.* further; farther
далеко dahleeKOH *adv.* far away
дальше DAHL'sheh *comp.* farther
дамский DAHMskeey *adj.* ladies
дарить dahrEET' *v.* to give (as a gift)
дары моря dahRIH MOHryah *n.pl.* seafood
дача DAHchah *n.f.* cottage
дверь dvyehr' *n.f.* door
движение dveeZHEHneeyech *n.nt.* movement;
  traffic
дворец dvahrYEHTS *n.m.* palace
двоюродный брат dvahYOOrahdnihy braht *n.m.*
  cousin
двоюродная сестра dvahYOOrahdnahyah
  seesTRAH *n.f.* cousin

двуспальный dvooSPAHL'nihy *adj.* double occupancy

девочка DYEHvahchkah *n.f.* little girl

девушка DYEHvooshkah *n.f.* young lady; waitress

дедушка DYEHdooshkah *n.f.* grandfather

дежурная deezhOORnahyah *n.f.* hall monitor

дезинфицировать deezeenfeeTSEErahvaht' *v.* to disinfect

дезодорант deezahdahRAHNT *n.m.* deodorant

действие DEYSTveeyeh *n.nt.* action

действительно deystVEEteel'nah *adv.* really; truly

действительный deystVEEteel'nihy *adj.* real; actual; effective

действовать DEYSTvahvaht' *v.* to act, take action

делать DYEHlaht' *v.* to do

делить deelEET' *v.* to share, divide

дело DYEHlah *n.nt.* matter; affair; business

деловой deelahVOY *adj.* business

денежный перевод DYEHneezhnihy peereeVOHT *n.m.* money order

день dyehn' *n.m.* day

день рождения dyehn' rahzhDYEHneeyah *n.m.* birthday

деньги DYEHN'gee *n.pl.* money

деревня deeRYEHVnyah *n.f.* countryside

дерево DYEHreevah *n.nt.* tree

деревянный deereevYAHnihy *adj.* wooden

держать deerZHAHT' *v.* to hold, keep, support

десерт deeSYEHRT *n.m.* dessert

детектив dehtehkTEEF *n.m.* mystery (novel/movie)

дети DYEHtee *n.pl.* children
детский DYEHTskeey *adj.* children's
дефицит deefeeTSEET *n.m.* deficit
дешёвый deeSHOHvihy *adj.* inexpensive; cheap
джинсы DZHEENsih *n.pl.* jeans
диабет deeahBYEHT *n.m.* diabetes
диагноз deeAHGnahs *n.m.* diagnosis
диван deeVAHN *n.m.* sofa
диета deeYEHtah *n.f.* diet
дикий DEEkeey *adj.* wild
директор deeRYEHKtahr *n.m.* director; manager
дирижёр deereezhOHR *n.m.* conductor (music)
дичь deech' *n.f.* wild game
длина dleeNAH *n.f.* length
длинный DLEENnihy *adj.* long (physically)
длиться DLEEtsah *v.* to last
для dlyah *prep.* for
дневной dneevNOY *adj.* daytime
до doh *prep.* to; before; until
до свидания dahsveeDAHneeyah *interj.* goodbye
доброта dahbrahTAH *n.f.* kindness
добрый DOHbrihy *adj.* good; kind
довольно dahVOHL'nah *adv.* rather; fairly
договор dahgahVOHR *n.m.* contract; agreement
дождь dohsht' *n.m.* rain
дозировка dahzeeROHFkah *n.f.* dosage
долгий DOHLgeey *adj.* long (in time)
долго DOHLgah *adv.* for a long time
должен/должна DOHLzhehn/dahlZHNA *adj.*
    m./f. should; must; ought to
долина dahLEEnah *n.f.* valley
доллар DOHlahr *n.m.* dollar

доля DOHLyah *n.f.* share; lot

дом dohm *n.m.* house; home

домохозяйка domahkhazYAYkah *n.f.* housewife

дорога dahROHgah *n.f.* road

дорогой dahrahGOY *adj.* dear; expensive; valuable

достаточно dahsTAHtahchnah *adv.* enough

достоинство dahsTOHeenstvah *n.nt.* value; worth

доступ DOHstoop *n.m.* access

доход dahKHOHT *n.m.* income

дочь dohch' *n.f.* daughter

драгоценность drahgahTSEHnahst' *n.f.* jewel

драматург drahmahTOORK *n.m.* playwright

древний DRYEHVneey *adj.* ancient

друг drook *n.m.* friend

другой drooGOY *n.m./adj.* other; another; the other

дружба DROOZHbah *n.f.* friendship

дружный DROOZHnihy *adj.* friendly; amicable

дупло doopLOH *n.nt.* cavity

дура DOOrah *n.f.* fool

дурак dooRAHK *n.m.* fool

духи dooKHEE *n.pl.* perfume

душ doosh *n.m.* shower

душа dooSHAH *n.f.* soul

душевный dooshEHVnihy *adj.* mental; emotional; sincere

душно DOOSHnah *adv.* stuffy

дым dihm *n.m.* smoke

дымный DIHMnihy *adj.* smokey

дыра dihRAH *n.f.* hole

дыхание dihKHAHneeyeh *n.nt.* breathing; respiration

дышать dihshAHT' *v.* to breath

дюжина DYOOzheenah *n.m.* dozen
дюйм dyooym *n.m.* inch
дядя DYAHdyah *n.f.* uncle

Е

еврей/еврейка yeevREY/yeevREYkah *n.m./f.*
  Jew
еврейский yeevREYskeey *adj.* Jewish; Hebrew
европеец yeevrahPYEHeets *n.m.* European
европейский yeevrahPEYskeey *adj.* European
его yeeVOH *pron.* his; its
еда yeeDAH *n.f.* food
едва yeedVAH *adv.* hardly; scarsely; barely
её yeeYOH *pron.* hers; its
ёж yohsh *n.m.* hedgehog
ежевика yeezhehVEEkah *n.f.* blackberries
ежегодный yeezhehGOHDnihy *adj.* yearly;
  annual
ежедневный yeezhehdNYEHVnihy *adj.* daily
ежемесячный yeezhehMYEHseechnihy *adj.*
  monthly
езда yeezDAH *n.f.* ride; drive
ездить YEHZdeet' *v.* to drive
ёлка YOHLkah *n.f.* spruce; Christmas tree
ермолка yeerMOHLkah *n.f.* skullcap
если YEHSlee *conj.* if; when; whereas
естественно yeestYEHSTveennah *adv.* naturally
есть yehst' *v.* to eat
ехать YEHkhaht' *v.* to drive
ещё yeeSHCHOH *adv.* still; yet; else; more; another
ещё раз yeeSHCHOH rahs *adv.* once again

Ж

жадный ZHAHDnihy *adj.* greedy
жажда ZHAHZHdah *n.f.* thirst
жалеть zhahLYEHT' *v.* to feel sorry for; pity
жалоба ZHAHlahbah *n.f.* complaint
жаль zhahl' *n.f.* pity
жар zhahr *n.m.* fever
жарить ZHAHReet' *v.* to fry, roast, broil
жаркий ZHAHRkeey *adj.* hot (of the weather)
ждать zhdaht' *v.* to wait
железа zhehleeZAH *n.f.* gland
жёлтый ZHOHLtihy *adj.* yellow
жемчуг ZHEHMchook *n.m.* pearl
жена zhehNAH *n.f.* wife
женат zhehNAHT *adj.* married (for men)
женский ZHEHNskeey *adj.* feminine; woman's
женщина ZHEHNshcheenah *n.f.* woman
жестокий zhehsTOHkeey *adj.* cruel; brutal
жечь zhehch' *v.* to burn
живопись ZHEEvahpees' *n.f.* painting
живот zheeVOHT *n.m.* stomach
животное zheeVOHTnahyeh *n.nt.* animal
жизнь zheezn' *n.f.* life
жила ZHEElah *n.f.* vein
жир zheer *n.m.* fat; grease
жирный ZHEERnihy *adj.* fatty; greasy; oily
житель ZHEEteel' *n.m.* resident
жить zheet' *v.* to live
журнал zhoorNAHL *n.m.* magazine
журналист zhoornahLEEST *n.m.* journalist

за zah *prep.* behind; beyond; past; for; in; after
заболеть zahbahLYEHT' *v.* to fall ill
забота zahBOHtah *n.f.* care; concern
забывать zahbihVAHT' *v.* to forget
забытый zahBIHTihy *adj.* forgotten
заведение zahveeDYEHneeyeh *n.nt.* institution
заведующий zahVYEHdooyooshcheey *n.m.* manager
завод zahVOHT *n.m.* factory
завтра ZAHFtrah *n.f.* tomorrow
завтрак ZAHFtrahk *n.m.* breakfast
завтракать ZAHFtrahkaht' *v.* to eat breakfast
завтрашний ZAHFtrahshneey *adj.* tomorrow's
загар zahGAHR *n.m.* sunburn; suntan
задний ZAHDneey *adj.* rear; back; hind
зажигалка zahzheeGAHLkah *n.f.* cigarette lighter
заказать zahkahzAHT' *v.* to order
заключение zahklyooCHEHneeyeh *n.nt.* conclusion
закон zahKOHN *n.m.* law
законный zahKOHNnihy *adj.* legal; legitimate
законченный zahKOHNchehnihy *adj.* finished; completed
закрытый zahKRIHtihy *adj.* closed
закуска zahKOOSkah *n.f.* appetizer; snack
закусочная zahKOOsahchnahyah *n.f.* snackbar
зал zahl *n.m.* hall
залив zahLEEF *n.m.* bay; gulf
замена zahMYEHnah *n.f.* substitution

заметка zahMYEHTkah *n.f.* note; mark; notice

замок zahMOHK *n.m.* lock

замужем ZAHmoozhehm *adv.* married (for women)

занавес ZAHnahvees *n.m.* curtain

занятие zahnYAHteeyeh *n.nt.* occupation; work; studies

занятый ZAHnyahtihy *adj.* busy; occupied

запад ZAHpaht *n.m.* west

западный ZAHpahdnihy *adj.* western

запах ZAHpahkh *n.m.* smell

записаться zahpeeSAHTsah *v.* to sign up (for)

запись ZAHpees' *n.f.* recording (record/tape)

запор zahPOHR *n.m.* constipation

запрещать zahpreeshchAHT' *v.* to forbid

заражение zahrahZHEHneeyeh *n.nt.* infection

заранее zahRAHnehyeh *adv.* in advance

заяц ZAHeets *n.m.* hare

звезда zvyehzDAH *n.f.* star

звук zvook *n.m.* sound; noise

здание ZDAHneeyeh *n.nt.* building

здесь zdyehs' *adv.* here

здоровый zdahROHvihy *adj.* healthy

здоровье zdahROHv'yeh *n.nt.* health

зеленщик zeeleenSHCHEEK *n.m.* greengrocer

зелёный zeeLYOHnihy *adj.* green

земля zeemLYAH *n.f.* ground; dirt; earth

земляника zeemleeNEEkah *n.f.* strawberries

зеркало ZYEHRkahlah *n.nt.* mirror

зерно zeerNOH *n.nt.* grain

зима zeeMAH *n.f.* winter

зимний ZEEMneey *adj.* winter

злобный ZLOHBnihy *adj.* malicious; spiteful

злой zloy *adj.* evil; wicked; mean; malicious

знак znahk *n.m.* sign; signal

знакомство znahKOHMstvah *n.nt.* acquaintance

знакомый znahKOHmihy *adj.* acquainted; familiar

знаменитый znahmeeNEEtihy *adj.* famous

знание ZNAHnccyeh *n.nt.* knowledge

знать znaht' *v.* to know

значение znahCHEHneeyeh *n.nt.* meaning; sense

значательный znahCHEEteel'nihy *adj.*
  considerable; significant

значить ZNAHcheet' *v.* to mean

значок znahCHOHK *n.m.* badge; pin

золото ZOHlahtah *n.nt.* gold

золотой zahlahTOY *adj.* gold

зонтик ZOHNteek *n.m.* umbrella

зоопарк zahahPAHRK *n.m.* zoo

зрелый ZRYEHlihy *adj.* ripe; mature

зрение ZRYEHneeyeh *n.nt.* eyesight

зритель ZREEteel' *n.m.* spectator

зуб zoop *n.m.* tooth

зубная боль zoobNAHyah bohl' *n.f.* toothache

зубная паста zoobNAHyah PAHStah *n.f.*
  toothpaste

зубная щётка zoobNAHyah SHCHOHTkah *n.f.*
  toothbrush

зубной врач zoobNOY vrahch *n.m.* dentist

зять zyaht' *n.m.* son-in-law; brother-in-law

И

и ee *conj.* and; also
иголка eeGOHLkah *n.f.* needle
игра eegRAH *n.f.* game
играть eegRAHT' *v.* to play
игрушка eegROOSHkah *n.f.* toy
идея eedYEHyah *n.f.* idea
идти eetTEE *v.* to go, walk
изба eesBAH *n.f.* peasant's hut; cabin
известие eezVYEHSteeyeh *n.nt.* news
извините eezveeNEEtyeh *v.* sorry; excuse me
извинять eezveenYAHT' *v.* to excuse, pardon
из-за eezzah *conj.* because of
излишний eezLEESHneey *adj.* excessive; superfluous
изумруд eezoomROOT *n.m.* emerald
изюм eezYOOM *n.m.* raisin
икона eekOHnah *n.f.* icon
иконостас eekahnahSTAHS *n.m.* iconostasis
икра eekRAH *n.f.* caviar
или EElee *conj.* or
именно EEMeennah *adv.* exactly; precisely
имущество eemOOSHCHehstvah *n.nt.* property
имя EEMyah *n.nt.* first name
иначе eeNAHcheh *adv.* differently; otherwise
инвалид eenvahLEET *n.m.* disabled person
инвалидность eenvahLEEDnahst' *n.f.* disability
индейка eenDEYkah *n.f.* turkey
инженер eenzheeNYEHR *n.m.* engineer
иногда eenahgDAH *adv.* sometimes

иностранец/иностранка
eenahsTRAHNeets/eenahsTRAHNkah *n.m./f.*
foreigner

иностранный eenahsTRAHNnihy *adj.* foreign

инструкция eenSTROOKtseeyah *n.f.* instructions

инсульт eenSOOL'T *n.m.* stroke

интересный eenteeRYEHSnihy *adj.* interesting

искренний EESkreeneey *adj.* sincere

искусственный eesKOOSTveenihy *adj.* artificial

искусство eesKOOSTvah *n.nt.* art; skill

испорченный eesPOHRchehnihy *adj.* spoiled; rotten; tainted

исследование eesSLYEHdahvahneeyeh *n.nt.* research

история eesTOHreeyah *n.f.* history; story

Й

йод yoht *n.m.* iodine

К

к k *prep.* to; toward

кабина kahBEEnah *n.f.* booth; cubicle

каблук kahbLOOK *n.m.* heel

каждый KAHZHdihy *adj.* every

как kahk *adv.* how

как далеко kahk dahleeKOH *adv.* how far

как долго kahk DOHLgah *adv.* how long

какао kahKAHoh *n.nt.* cocoa

какой kahKOY *adj.* which

как-то KAHKtah *adv.* somehow

календарь kahleenDAHR' *n.m.* calendar

калория kahLOHreeyah *n.f.* calorie

кальсоны kahl'SOHnih *n.pl.* long underwear

камбала KAHMbahlah *n.f.* flounder; sole

камень KAHmeen' *n.m.* rock

камера хранения KAHmeerah khrahNYEHneeyah *n.f.* baggage room

канадец/канадка kahNAHdeets/kahNAHTkah *n.m./f.* Canadian

канадский kahNAHTskeey *adj.*Canadian

канал kahNAHL *n.m.* canal

каникулы kahNEEkoolih *n.pl.* school vacation

капля KAHPlyah *n.f.* drop

капуста kahPOOStah *n.f.* cabbage

карандаш kahrahnDAHSH *n.m.* pencil

карат kahRAHT *n.m.* carat

караул kahrahOOL *n.m.* guard; sentry

карман kahrMAHN *n.m.* pocket

карманный фонарь kahrMAHNnihy fahNAHR' *n.m.* flash light

карнавал kahrnahVAHL *n.m.* carnival

карта KAHRtah *n.f.* map

картина kahrTEEnah *n.f.* picture; drawing

картофель kahrTOHfeel' *n.m.* potato

касса KAHSsah *n.f.* ticket office; cashier's booth

кассета kahsYEHtah *n.f.* cassette

кассир kahSEER *n.m.* cashier

кастрюля kahstRYOOLyah *n.f.* pot; saucepan

каток kahTOHK *n.m.* skating rink

кафе kahFEH *n.nt.* cafe

кафедра KAHfeedrah *n.f.* department

качество KAHchehstvah *n.nt.* quality

кашель KAHSHehl' *n.m.* cough
квартира kvahrTEERah *n.f.* apartment
квас kvahs *n.m.* kvass (fermented drink)
кеды KYEHdih *n.pl.* sneakers
кемпинг KYEHMpeeng *n.m.* camping
кефир keeFEER *n.m.* yogurt-like drink
килограмм keelahgRAHM *n.m.* kilogram
километр keelahMYEHTR *n.m.* kilometer
кино keeNOH *n.nt.* movie; the cinema
кинотеатр keenahteeAHTR *n.m.* movie theater
киоск keeOHSK *n.m.* kiosk
кислород keeslahROHT *n.m.* oxygen
кислый KEESlihy *adj.* sour
кишка keeshKAH *n.f.* intestine
кладбише KLAHTbeeshcheh *n.nt.* cemetery
классический klahsSEECHehskeey *adj.* classical
клей kley *n.m.* glue
климат KLEEmaht *n.m.* climate
клипсы KLEEPsih *n.pl.* clip-on earrings
клоп klohp *n.m.* bedbug
клуб kloop *n.m.* club
клюква KLYOOKvah *n.f.* cranberries
ключ klyooch *n.m.* key
книга KNEEgah *n.f.* book
книжный магазин KNEEZHnihy mahgahZEEN
   n.m. bookstore
кнопка KNOHPkah *n.f.* push button; snap
ковёр kahVYOHR *n.m.* rug
когда kahgDAH *adv.* when
кожа KOHzhah *n.m.* skin; leather
кожаный KOHzhahnihy *adj.* leather
колбаса kahlbahSAH *n.f.* sausage

колено kahLYEHnah *n.nt.* knee

колесо kahleeSOH *n.nt.* wheel

количество kahlEECHehstvah *n.nt.* quantity

колокол KOHlahkahl *n.m.* bell

команда kahMAHNdah *n.f.* sports team

командировка kahmahndeeROHFkah *n.f.* business trip; assignment

комар kahMAHR *n.m.* mosquito

комбинация kahmbeenAHTSeeyah *n.f.* slip

комедия kahMYEHdeeyah *n.f.* comedy

коммунальный kahmooNAHL'nihy *adj.* communal

комната KOHMnahtah *n.f.* room

комплект kahmpLYEHKT *n.m.* complete set

композитор kahmpahZEEtahr *n.m.* composer

компьютер kahmP'YOOteer *n.m.* computer

конверт kahnVYEHRT *n.m.* envelope

кондитерская kahnDEEteerskahyah *n.f.* confectionery shop

кондиционер kahndeetseeahNYEHR *n.m.* air conditioner

конец kahnYEHTS *n.m.* end

конечно kahnYEHSHnah *adv.* of course

конкурс KOHNkoors *n.m.* competition; contest

консервный нож kahnSYEHRVnihy nohsh *n.m.* can opener

консервы kahnSYEHRVih *n.pl.* canned goods

консульство KOHNsool'stvah *n.nt.* consulate

контактная линза kahnTAHKTnahyah LEENzah *n.f.* contact lens

контора kahnTOHrah *n.f.* office

конфеты kahnFYEHtih *n.pl.* candy

концерт kahnTSEHRT *n.m.* concert

коньки kahn'KEE *n.pl.* skates

коньяк kahn'YAK *n.m.* cognac; brandy

копейка kahPEYkah *n.f.* kopeck

корабль kahRAHBL' *n.f.* ship

корзина kahrZEEnah *n.f.* basket

корица kahREEtsah *n.m.* cinnamon

коричневый kahREECHneevihy *adj.* brown

коробка kahrOHPkah *n.f.* box

короткий kahROHTkeey *adj.* short

косметика kahsMYEHteekah *n.f.* makeup

костёр kahsTYOHR *n.m.* campfire

кость kohst' *n.f.* bone

костюм kahsTYOOM *n.m.* suit

котлета kahtLYEHtah *n.f.* cutlet

кофе KOHfyeh *n.m.* coffee

кошерный kahshEHRnihy *adj.* kosher

кошка KOHSHkah *n.f.* cat

край kray *n.m.* edge; rim; country

кран krahn *n.m.* faucet

красивый krahsEEVihy *adj.* beautiful; pretty

красный KRAHSnihy *adj.* red

красота krahsahTAH *n.f.* beauty

крахмал krahkhMAHL *n.m.* starch

кредитная карточка kreeDEETnahyah
  KAHRtahchkah *n.f.* credit card

крем kryehm *n.m.* cream; lotion

крепкий KRYEHPkeey *adj.* strong; durable

кресло KRYEHSlah *n.nt.* arm chair

крест kryehst *n.m.* cross

кривой kreeVOY *adj.* crooked

кризис KREEzees *n.m.* crisis

крик kreek *n.m.* shout; cry

кровать krahVAHT' *n.f.* bed

кровоизлияние krahvaheezleeYAHneeyeh *n.nt.* hemorrhage

кровоточить krahvahtaCHEET' *v.* to bleed

кровь krohf' *n.f.* blood

кролик KROHleek *n.m.* rabbit

кроме KROHmyeh *prep.* except for; but; besides

круг krook *n.m.* circle

круглый KROOGlihy *adj.* circular; round

круиз krooEEZ *n.m.* cruise

крыша KRIHshah *n.f.* roof

крышка KRIHshkah *n.f.* lid; cover

кстати KSTAHtee *adv.* incidentally; by the way

кто ktoh *pron.* who

кто-нибудь KTOHneeboot' *pron.* anyone; someone

куда kooDAH *adv.* where to

кукла KOOKlah *n.f.* doll; puppet

культура kool'TOOrah *n.f.* culture

купальная шапочка kooPAHL'nahyah SHAHPahchkah *n.f.* bathing cap

купальник koopAHL'neek *n.m.* bathing suit

купе kooPEH *n.nt.* train compartment

купить kooPEET' *v.* to buy

курить kooREET' *v.* to smoke

курица KOOreetsah *n.f.* chicken

курорт koorOHRT *n.m.* resort

кусок kooSOHK *n.m.* piece

кухня KOOKHnyah *n.f.* kitchen

Л

лавра LAHVrah *n.f.* monastery

лагерь LAHgeer' *n.f.* camp
ладно LAHDnah *part.* ok
лак lahk *n.m.* polish; lacquer
лампа LAHMpah *n.f.* lamp
лампочка LAHMpahchkah *n.f.* light bulb
левый LYEHvihy *adj.* left (direction)
легальный leeGAHL'nihy *adj.* legal
лёгкий LYOHKHkeey *adj.* easy
легко leekhKOH *adv.* easily
лёгкое LYOHKHkahyeh *n.nt.* lung
лёд lyoht *n.m.* ice
лезвия LYEHZveeyah *n.f.* razor blades
лекарство leeKAHRstvah *n.nt.* medicine
лекция LYEHKtseeyah *n.f.* lecture
лес lyehs *n.m.* forest
лестница LYEHSneetsah *n.f.* stairs
летний LYEHTneey *adj.* summer
лето LYEHtah *n.nt.* summer
лечение leeCHEHneeyeh *n.nt.* medical treatment
ли lee *conj.* if; whether
лимон leeMOHN *n.m.* lemon
лимонад leemahnAHT *n.m.* lemonade
липкий LEEPkeey *adj.* sticky
листок leesTOHK *n.m.* leaf; sheet (of paper)
литература leeteerahTOOrah *n.f.* literature
литр leetr *n.m.* liter
лифт leeft *n.m.* elevator
лицо leetsOH *n.nt.* face
личный LEECHnihy *adj.* personal; private
лишний LEESHneey *adj.* spare; extra
лоб lohp *n.m.* forehead
лодка LOHTkah *n.f.* boat

лодыжка lahDIHSHkah *n.f.* ankle
ложа LOHzhah *n.f.* theater box
ложка LOHSHkah *n.f.* spoon
ложный LOHZHnihy *n.m.* false
локоть LOHkaht' *n.f.* elbow
лососина lahsahSEEnah *n.f.* salmon
лошадь LOHSHaht' *n.f.* horse
лужа LOOZHah *n.f.* puddle
лук look *n.m.* onion
луна looNAH *n.f.* moon
лучше LOOCHsheh *comp.* better
лучший LOOCHsheey *adj.* better; the best
лыжи LIHzhee *n.pl.* skis
любить lyoobEET' *v.* to love
любовь lyoobOHF' *n.f.* love
любой lyoobOY *pron.* any
любопытный lyoobahPIHTnihy *adj.* curious
люди LYOOdee *n.pl.* people

M

мавзолей mahvzahLEY *n.m.* mausoleum
магазин mahgahZEEN *n.m.* store
магнитофон mahgneetahFOHN *n.m.* tape recorder
майка MAYkah *n.f.* T-shirt
мак mahk *n.m.* poppy
малахит mahlahKHEET *n.m.* malachite
маленький MAHLeen'keey *adj.* small
малина mahLEEnah *n.f.* raspberries
мало MAHlah *adv.* a little; not enough
мальчик MAHL'cheek *n.m.* boy
мандарин mahndahREEN *n.m.* tangerine

маринованный mahreeNOHvahnihy *adj.* marinated

марка MAHRkah *n.f.* stamp

маслина mahsLEEnah *n.f.* olive

масло MAHSlah *n.nt.* butter

мат maht *n.m.* check mate; obscene language

матрёшка mahtRYOHSHkah *adj.* Russian wooden nested doll

матч mahtch *n.m.* sports match

мать maht' *n.f.* mother

мачеха MAHchehkhah *n.f.* stepmother

машина mahSHEEnah *n.f.* car; machine

мебель MYEHbeel' *n.f.* furniture

мёд myoht *n.m.* honey

медленный MYEHDleenihy *adj.* slow

медсестра meedseesTRAH *n.f.* nurse

между MYEHZHdoo *prep.* between

международный meezhdoonahROHDnihy *adj.* international

мелочь MYEHlahch' *n.f.* small change

менструация meenstrooAHtseeyah *n.f.* menstruation

меньше MYEHN'sheh *comp.* less

меню meenYOO *n.m.* menu

мера MYEHrah *n.f.* measure; extent; degree

мёртвый MYOHRTvihy *adj.* dead

местный MYEHSTnihy *adj.* local

место MYEHStah *n.nt.* place; seat; site

месяц MYEHSeets *n.m.* month; moon

метр myehtr *n.m.* meter

метро meeTROH *n.nt.* subway

мех myehkh *n.m.* fur

механизм meekhahnEEZM *n.m.* mechanism

меховая шапка meekhahVAHyah SHAHPkah
  n.f. fur hat

меховой meekhahVOY *adj.* fur

мешок meeSHOHK *n.m.* bag; sack

миленький MEEleen'keey *adj.* dear; sweet

милиционер meeleetseeahNYEHR *n.m.*
  policeman

милиция meeLEEtseeyah *n.f.* the police

миллион meeleeOHN *n.m.* million

милый MEElihy *adj.* nice; sweet; dear; darling

мимо MEEmah *prep.* by; past

миндалина meenDAHleenah *n.f.* tonsil

минута meenOOTah *n.f.* minute

мир meer *n.m.* world; peace

миска MEESkah *n.f.* bowl

мишка MEESHkah *n.f.* teddy bear

младенец mlahDYEHneets *n.m.* baby; infant

младший MLAHTsheey *adj.* younger

мнение MNYEHneeyeh *n.nt.* opinion

много MNOHgah *adv.* a lot

многообразный mnahgahahbRAHZnihy *adj.*
  diverse

могила mahGEElah *n.f.* grave

могучий mahGOOcheey *adj.* powerful

мода MOHdah *n.f.* fashion; style

модный MOHDnihy *adj.* fashionable; stylish

может быть MOHZHeht biht' *adv.* maybe;
  perhaps

можно MOHZHnah *pred.* may; can

мокрый MOHKrihy *adj.* wet

молитва mahLEETvah *n.f.* prayer book

молния MOHLneeyah *n.f.* lightning; zipper

молодёжь mahlahDYOHSH' *n.m.* young people

молодой mahlahDOY *adj.* young

молоко mahlahKOH *n.nt.* milk

молочная mahLOHCHnahyah *adj.* dairy

молчание mahlCHAHneeyeh *n.nt.* silence

монастырь mahnahsTIHR' *n.f.* monastery

монета mahNYEHtah *n.f.* coin

море MOHRyeh *n.nt.* sea

морковь mahrKOHF' *n.f.* carrot

мороженое mahROHZHehnahyeh *n.nt.* ice cream

мороженный mahROHZHehnihy *adj.* frozen

мороз mahROHS *n.m.* frost

московский mahsKOHFskeey *adj.* Moscow

мост mohst *n.m.* bridge

мотор mahTOHR *n.m.* motor

мотоцикл mahtahTSEEKL *n.m.* motorcycle

мощный MOHSHCHnihy *adj.* powerful

муж moosh *n.m.* husband

мужество MOOZHehstvah *n.nt.* courage

мужской mooshSKOY *adj.* men's

мужчина mooshCHEEnah *n.f.* man

музей mooZEY *n.m.* museum

музыка MOOZihkah *n.f.* music

мука mooKAH *n.f.* flour

мультфильм mool'tFEEL'M *n.m.* cartoon

мускул MOOSkool *n.m.* muscle

мусор MOOsahr *n.m.* trash; rubbish

муха MOOkhah *n.f.* fly

мы mih *pron.* we

мыло MIHlah *n.nt.* soap

мысль mihsl' *n.f.* thought; idea

мышь mihsh *n.f.* mouse
мягкий MYAHKHkeey *adj.* soft
мясо MYAHsah *n.nt.* meat
мяч myahch *n.m.* ball

Н

на nah *prep.* on; in
набитый nahBEEtihy *adj.* tightly packed
наверно nahVYEHRnah *adv.* probably
наверх nahVYEHRKH *adv.* up; upwards (direction)
наверху nahveerKHOO *adv.* above (location)
наводнение nahvahdNYEHneeyeh *n.nt.* flood
наволочка NAHvahlahchkah *n.f.* pillowcase
навсегда nahfseegDAH *adv.* forever
награда nahGRAHdah *n.f.* reward
над naht *prep.* over; above
надгробный камень nahdGROHBnihy
    KAHmeen' *n.m.* tombstone
надежда nahDYEHZHdah *n.f.* hope
надо NAHdah *adv.* must
надпись nahtPEES' *n.f.* inscription
назад nahzAHT *adv.* back; backwards
название nahzVAHneeyeh *n.nt.* name; title
называть nahzihVAHT' *v.* to call, name
наизусть naheeZOOST' *adv.* by heart
найти nayTEE *v.* to find
наказание nahkahZAHNeeyeh *n.nt.* punishment
наконец nahkahNYEHTS *adv.* at last; finally
накрасть nahkRAHST' *v.* to steal
налево nahLYEHvah *adv.* on the left
налог nahLOHK *n.m.* tax

намерение nahMYEHreeneeyeh *n.nt.* intention

наоборот nahahbahROHT *n.m.* the other way around; on the contrary

напиток nahPEEtahk *n.m.* drink

напор nahPOHR *n.m.* pressure

направо nahPRAHvah *adv.* on the right

напрасно nahPRAIISnah *adv.* in vain; for nothing

например nahpreeMYEHR *adv.* for example; for instance

напротив nahPROHteef *adv.* opposite; facing

напряжнение nahpreeZHEHneeyeh *n.nt.* tension; stress; strain

наркоз nahrKOHS *n.m.* anesthesia

народ nahROHT *n.m.* a people

народный nahROHDnihy *adj.* national; folk

нарост nahROHST *n.m.* growth; tumor

нарочно nahROHCHnah *adv.* deliberately; on purpose

нарыв nahRIHF *n.m.* abscess

насекомое nahseeKOHmahyeh *n.nt.* insect

население nahseeLYEHneeyeh *n.nt.* population

насилие nahSEEleeyeh *n.nt.* violence

наслаждение nahslahzhDYEHneeyeh *n.nt.* enjoyment; pleasure; delight

насморк NAHsmahrk *n.m.* head cold

настоящий nahstahYAHshcheey *adj.* present; real; true

настроение nahstrahYEHneeyeh *n.nt.* mood

наушник nahOOSHneek *n.m.* earmuff; headphone

находиться nahkhahDEETsah *v.* to be found, located

национальность nahtseeahNAHL'nahst' *n.f.* nationality

нация NAHtseeyah *n.f.* nation

начало nahCHAHlah *n.nt.* beginning.

начальник nahCHAHL'neek *n.m.* chief; head; boss

начинать nahcheeNAHT' *v.* to begin, start

неблагополучный neeblahgahpahLOOCH-nihy *adj.* unfortunate; unhappy

небо NYEHbah *n.nt.* sky; heaven

небоскрёб neebahSKRYOHP *n.m.* skyscraper

небрежный neeBRYEHZHnihy *adj.* careless; negligent; sloppy; slipshod

неважный neeVAHZHnihy *adj.* unimportant

невероятный neeveerahYAHTnihy *adj.* incredible; unbelievable

невеста neeVYEHStah *n.f.* bride

невестка neeVYEHSTkah *n.f.* daughter-in-law; sister-in-law

невольный neeVOHL'nihy *adj.* unintentional; involuntary

невыгодный neeVIHgahdnihy *adj.* unprofitable; unfavorable

недавно neeDAHVnah *adv.* not long ago; recently

недалёкий needahLYOHkeey *adj.* nearby

недалеко needahleeKOH *adv.* not far; close by

неделя neeDYEHlyah *n.f.* week

недоброкачественный needahbrahKAHCH-ehstveennihy *adj.* poor-quality

недовольный needahvOHL'nihy *adj.* dissatisfied

недолго neeDOHLgah *adv.* not long; brief

недоразумение needahrahzooMYEHneeyeh *n.nt.* misunderstanding

недостаток needahsTAHtahk *n.m.* shortage; scarcity; defect; deficiency

недостаточно needahsTAHtahchnah *adv.* insufficient

недостижимый needahsteeZHEEmihy *adj.* unattainable

неестественный neeeestYEHSTveenihy *adj.* unnatural

нежный NYEHZHnihy *adj.* tender; gentle

независимость neezahVEEseemahst' *n.f.* independence

незаконный neezahKOHNnihy *adj.* illegal

незаметно neezahMYEHTnah *adv.* unnoticable

незнакомец/незнакомка neeznahKOHMeets/ neeznahKOHMkah *n.m./f.* stranger

незнакомый neeznahKOHmihy *adj.* unfamiliar

незрелый neezRYEHlihy *adj.* unripe; not mature

неизвестный neeeezVYEHSnihy *adj.* unknown

нейтральный neytRAHL'nihy *adj.* neutral

некрасивый neeKRAHSeevihy *adj.* ugly

неловкий neeLOHFkeey *adj.* awkward; clumsy

нельзя neel'ZYAH *adv.* impossible; one cannot

немец/немка NEHMeets/NEHMkah *n.m./f.* German

немецкий nehMYETSskeey *adj.* German

немного neemNOHgah *adv.* a little; not much

необходимый neeahpkhahDEEmihy *adj.* necessary; essential

необыкновенный neeahbihknahVYEHNihy *adj.* unusual; uncommon

неопределённый neeahpreedeeLYOHNihy *adj.* vague; indefinite

неопытный neeOHpihtnihy *adj.* inexperienced

неохотно neeahKHOHTnah *adv.* reluctantly

непонятный neepahnYAHTnihy *adj.*
incomprehensible; unintelligible

неправда neePRAHVdah *n.f.* untruth; lie

неправильный neePRAHveel'nihy *adj.* wrong;
incorrect

неприличный neepreeLEECHnihy *adj.* improper;
indecent

неприятный neepreeYAHTnihy *adj.* unpleasant;
disagreeable

нерв nyehrf *n.m.* nerve

нервный NYEHRVnihy *adj.* nervous; irritable

несгораемый шкаф neezgahRAHeemihy
shkahf *n.m.* safe

несколько neeSKOHL'kah *adv.* a few; some;
several

неслышный neeSLIHSHnihy *adj.* inaudible

несправедливый neesprahveedLEEvihy *adj.*
unfair; injust

несчастный neeSHCHAHSnihy *adj.* unhappy;
unfortunate

несчастный случай neeSHAHSTnihy
SLOOchay *n.m.* accident

не nyeh *part.* not

нет nyeht *part.* no

нетерпение neeteerPYEHneeyeh *n.nt.* impatience

неудобный neeooDOHBnihy *adj.* uncomfortable

неуспешный neeoosPYEHSHnihy *adj.*
unsuccessful

нечестный neeCHEHSnihy *adj.* dishonest

нечистый neeCHEEStihy *adj.* unclean; dirty

неясный neeYAHSnihy *adj.* unclear

нижнее бельё NEEZHneeyeh beel'YOH *n.nt.*
underwear

нижний NEEZHnihy *adj.* lower
никак neeKAHK *adv.* no way
никогда neekahgDAH *adv.* never
никто neekTOH *pron.* no one
нитка NEETkah *n.f.* thread
ничего neecheeVOH *adv.* nothing
но noh *conj.* but; however
новый NOHvihy *adj.* new
Новый год NOHvihy goht *n.m.* New Year
нога nahGAH *n.f.* leg; foot
нож nohsh *n.m.* knife
ножницы NOHZHneetsih *n.pl.* scissors
ноль nohl' *n.f.* zero
номер NOHmeer *n.m.* hotel room; number; issue
номерок nahmeeROHK *n.m.* (coat-check) ticket
нормальный nohrMAHL'nihy *adj.* normal
нос nohs *n.m.* nose
носилки nahSEELkee *n.m.* stretcher
носильщик nahSEEL'shcheek *n.m.* porter
носки nahsKEE *n.pl.* socks
ночь nohch *n.f.* night
нравиться NRAHveetsah *v.* to enjoy
нравы NRAHvih *n.pl.* customs
ну noo *interj.* well; well then
нужда noozhDAH *n.f.* need
нужно NOOZHnah *adv.* (one) must, has to

О

о oh *prep.* about
оба OHbah *num.* both
обед ahBYEHT *n.m.* lunch

обедать ahBYEHdaht' *v.* to have lunch

обезболивание ahbeesBOHleevahneeyeh *n.nt.* anesthesia

обещание ahbeeSHCHAHneeyeh *n.nt.* promise

обида ahBEEdah *n.f.* offense; insult

область OHblahst' *n.f.* region; area; field; domain

обман ahbMAHN *n.m.* fraud; deception

обмен ahbMYEHN *n.m.* exchange

обменять ahbmeenYAHT' *v.* to exchange

образ OHbrahs *n.m.* image; way; mode; manner

образец ahbrahzYEHTS *n.m.* sample; model; pattern

образование ahbrahzahVAHneeyeh *n.nt.* education

обратный ahbRAHTnihy *adj.* return; opposite

обстановка ahbstahNOHFkah *n.f.* situation; setting

обувь OHboof *n.f.* shoes

обход ahpKHOHT *n.m.* detour

общежитие ahpshchehZHEEteeyeh *n.nt.* dormitory

общество OHPshchehstvah *n.nt.* society; company

общий OHPshcheey *adj.* general; common

объявление ahb"yahvLYEHneeyeh *n.nt.* announcement

объяснение ahb"yahsNYEHneeyeh *n.nt.* explanation

обычно ahBIHCHnah *adv.* usually

обязательный ahbeeZAHteel'nihy *adj.* obligatory; mandatory

овёс ahVYOHS *n.m.* oats

овощи OHvahshchee *n.pl.* vegetables

овсянка ahfSYAHNkah *n.f.* oatmeal

огурцы ahgoorTSIH *n.pl.* cucumbers

одежда ahDYEHZHdah *n.f.* clothes

одеяло ahdeeYAHlah *n.nt.* blanket

одинаковый ahdeeNAHkahvihy *adj.* identical

однажды ahdNAHZHdih *adv.* once; one day

однако ahdNAHkah *conj.* however; but

одновременный ahdnahVRYEHmeennihy *adj.*
  simultaneous

ожерелье ahzheeRYEHL'yeh *n.nt.* necklace

озеро OHzeerah *n.nt.* lake

океан ahkeeAHN *n.m.* ocean

окно ahkNOH *n.nt.* window

около OHkahlah *prep.* around; approximately; about

окончание ahkahnCHAHneeyeh *n.nt.*
  completion; end

окраска ahKRAHSkah *n.f.* dye; hair coloring

оленина ahLYEHneenah *n.f.* venison

он ohn *pron.* he

она ahNAH *pron.* she

они ahNEE *pron.* they

опоздать ahpahzDAHT' *v.* to be late

опасный ahPAHSnihy *adj.* dangerous

опера OHpeerah *n.f.* opera

описание ahpeeSAHneeyeh *n.nt.* description

опоздание ahpahzDAHneeyeh *n.nt.* delay;
  tardiness

определённый ahpreedeeLYOHNnihy *adj.*
  definite; set; certain

оптик OPteek *n.m.* optician

опыт OHpiht *n.m.* experience; experiment

опять ahPYAHT' *adv.* again

оранжевый ahRAHNzhehvihy *adj.* orange

орех ahRYEHKH *n.m.* nut

оркестр ahrKYEHSTR *n.m.* orchestra

оса ahSAH *n.f.* wasp

осень OHseen' *n.f.* fall

осложнение ahslahzhNYEHneeyeh *n.nt.*
complication

осмотр ahsMOHTR *n.m.* examination; checkup

основа ahsNOHvah *n.f.* basis

особенно ahSOHbeenah *adv.* especially

остановка ahstahnOHFkah *n.f.* bus stop

остаток ahsTAHtahk *n.m.* remainder

осторожно ahstahROHZHnah *adv.* beware; careful

остров OHStrahf *n.m.* island

острый OHStrihy *adj.* sharp; pungent; keen

от oht *prep.* from

ответ ahtVYEHT *n.m.* answer

отдел ahdDYEHL *n.m.* section; department

отдельно ahdDYEHL'nah *adv.*
separately; individually

отдых OHDdihkh *n.m.* rest

отец ahTYEHTS *n.m.* father

отечество ahTYEHCHehstvah *n.nt.* fatherland

отказ ahtKAHS *n.m.* refusal

открытка ahtKRIHTkah *n.f.* postcard

открытый ahtKRIHtihy *adj.* open

отлёт ahtLYOHT *n.m.* departure (airplane)

отношение ahtnahSHEHneeyeh *n.nt.* attitude;
relationship; connection

отопление ahtahpLYEHneeyeh *n.nt.* heating

отпуск OHTpoosk *n.m.* vacation from work

отрава ahtRAHvah *n.f.* poison

отрицательный ahtreeTSAHteel'nihy *adj.*
negative

отрывок ahtRIHvahk *n.m.* passage; excerpt

отсутствие ahtSOOTSTveeyeh *n.nt.* absence
отход ahtKHOHT *n.m.* departure (train)
отчество OHtyehehstvah *n.nt.* patronymic
отчим OHTcheem *n.m.* step-father
отъезд aht"YEHST *n.m.* detour
официант ahfeetseeAHNT *n.m.* waiter
официантка ahfeetseeAHNTkah *n.f.* waitress
оформление ahfahrmLYEHneeyeh *n.nt.*
  processing (of documents)
охота ahKHOHtah *n.f.* wish; desire
очевидный ahchehVEEDnihy *adj.* obvious
очень OHcheen' *adv.* very
очередь OHCHehreet' *n.f.* line
очки ahchKEE *n.pl.* glasses
ошибка ahshEEPkah *n.f.* mistake

П

падеж pahDYEHSH *n.m.* grammatical case
пакет pahKYEHT *n.m.* packet; package
палатка pahLAHTkah *n.f.* tent
палец PAHleets *n.m.* finger
пальто pahl"TOH *n.nt.* coat
памятник PAHMeetneek *n.m.* monument
память PAHMeet' *n.f.* memory
пара PAHrah *n.f.* pair
пареный PAHreenihy *adj.* steamed
парикмахер pahreekMAHkheer *n.m.* barber
парилка pahREELkah *n.f.* steam room
парк pahrk *n.m.* park
пароход pahrahKHOHT *n.m.* ship
пасмурный PAHsmoornihy *adj.* overcast

паспорт PAHSpahrt *n.m.* passport
пассажир pahsahZHEER *n.m.* passenger
Пасха PAHSkhah *n.f.* Easter; Passover
паук pahOOK *n.m.* spider
пахнуть PAHKHnoot' *v.* to smell
пациент pahtseeEHNT *n.m.* patient
пачка PAHCHkah *n.f.* pack; bundle
певец peevYEHTS *n.m.* singer
педиатр peedeeAHTR *n.m.* pediatrician
пенициллин peeneetseelLEEN *n.m.* penicillin
пепельница PYEHpeel'neetsah *n.f.* ashtray
первоначальный peervahnahCHAHL'nihy *adj.*
  original
перевести peereeveesTEE *v.* to translate
перевод peereeVOHT *n.m.* translation
переводчик peereeVOHTcheek *n.m.* translator;
  interpreter
перевязка peereeVYAHSkah *n.f.* bandaging;
  dressing
переговоры peereegahVOHrihy *n.pl.* negotiations
перед PYEHreet *prep.* before; in front of
передача peereeDAHchah *n.f.* broadcast;
  transmission
передний peeRYEHDneey *adj.* front
переносный peereeNOHSnihy *adj.* portable
переписка peereePEESkah *n.f.* correspondence
перерыв peereeRIHF *n.m.* break; recess
пересадка peereeSAHTkah *n.f.* change; transfer
  (on planes, trains, buses etc)
переулок peereeOOLahk *n.m.* side street
переход peereeKHOHT *n.m.* place to cross;
  crosswalk
перец PYEHreets *n.m.* pepper

персик PYEHRseek *n.m.* peach
перцовка peerTSOHFkah *n.f.* pepper vodka
перчатки peerCHAHTkee *n.pl.* gloves
песня PYEHSnyah *n.f.* song
песок peeSOHK *n.m.* sand
петрушка peeTROOSHkah *n.f.* parsley
печальный peeCHAHL'nihy *adj.* sad
печёнка peechOHNkah *n.f.* liver (food)
печень PYEHchehn' *n.f.* liver (anatomy)
печенье peeCHEHN'yeh *n.nt.* cookie; pastry
печь pyehch *n.f.* stove
пешком peeshKOHM *adv.* on, by foot
пиво PEEvah *n.nt.* beer
пиджак peedZHAHK *n.m.* man's suit jacket
пижама peeZHAHMah *n.f.* pyjamas
пилав peeLAHF *n.m.* pilaf
пилюля peeLYOOlyah *n.f.* pill
пинцет peenTSEHT *n.m.* tweezers
пирог peeROHK *n.m.* pie
пирожное peeROHZHnahyeh *n.nt.* pastry
писатель peeSAHteel' *n.m.* writer
писать peeSAHT' *v.* to write
письменно PEES'meennah *adv.* in writing
письмо pees'MOH *n.nt.* letter
пить peet' *v.* to drink
пишущая машинка PEESHooshchahyah
  mahSHEENkah *n.f.* typewriter
пища PEEshchah *n.f.* food
плавать PLAHvaht' *v.* to swim
плакат plahKAHT *n.m.* poster
план plahn *n.m.* city map
платить plahTEET' *v.* to pay

платок plahTOHK *n.m.* kerchief

платье PLAHT'yeh *n.nt.* dress

плацкартный plahtsKAHRTnihy *adj.* reserved (on a train)

плащ plahshch *n.m.* raincoat

племянник pleemYAHNneek *n.m.* nephew

племянница pleemYAHNeetsah *n.f.* niece

плёнка PLYOHNkah *n.f.* film

плечо pleeCHOH *n.nt.* shoulder

плитка PLEETkah *n.f.* (chocolate) bar

пломба PLOHMbah *n.f.* (tooth) filling

плохо PLOHkhah *adv.* badly

плохой plahKHOY *adj.* bad; poor

площадь PLOHshchaht' *n.f.* area; square

пляж plyahzh *n.m.* beach

по poh *prep.* along; about; according to

по крайней мере pah KRAYnyeh MYEHreh *adv.* at least

победа pahBYEHdah *n.f.* victory

повар POHvahr *n.m.* cook

повторить pahftahREET' *v.* to repeat

погода pahGOHdah *n.f.* weather

под poht *prep.* under; beneath

подарок pahDAHrahk *n.m.* present; gift

подгузник pahdGOOZneek *n.m.* diaper

подмётка pahdMYOHTkah *n.f.* sole (of a shoe)

подписать pahtpeeSAHT' *v.* to sign

подпись POHTpees' *n.f.* signature

подробность pahdROHBnahst' *n.f.* detail

подтверждение pahttveerzhDYEHneeyeh *n.nt.* confirmation

подушка pahDOOSHkah *n.f.* pillow

поезд POHeest *n.m.* train

пожалуйста pahZHAHLstah *part.* please

пожар pahZHAHR *n.m.* fire

пожатие pahZHAHteeyeh *n.nt.* handshake

пожилой pahzheeLOY *adj.* elderly

позавчера pahzahfcheeRAH *adv.* day before
  yesterday

позвонить pahzvahNEET' *v.* to call (on the phone)

поздний POHZDneey *adj.* late

поздравлять pahzdrahvLYAHT' *v.* to
  congratulate.

позже POHZHzheh *adv.* later

познакомить pahznahKOHmeet' *v.* to introduce

пока pahKAH *adv.* meanwhile; bye *(interj./coll.)*

показать pahkahZAHT' *v.* to show

покупатель pahkooPAHteel' *n.m.* customer

покупка pahKOOPkah *n.f.* purchase

полдень POHLdeen' *n.m.* noon

поле POHLyeh *n.nt.* field; area

полезный pahLYEHZnihy *adj.* useful; helpful

полёт pahLYOHT *n.m.* flight

поликлиника pahleeKLEEneekah *n.f.* clinic

политика pahLEEteekah *n.f.* politics

полка POHLkah *n.f.* berth; shelf

полночь POHLnahch' *n.f.* midnight

полный POHLnihy *adj.* full; complete

половина pahlahVEEnah *n.f.* half

положение pahlahZHEHneeyeh *n.nt.* situation;
  condition

положительный pahlahZHEEteel'nihy *adj.*
  positive; affirmative

полотенце pahlahTYEHNtseh *n.nt.* towel

полтора pahltahRAH *num.* one and a half

полчаса pahlcheeSAH *n.m.* half hour

польза POHL'zah *n.f.* use; benefit

помидор pahmeeDOHR *n.m.* tomato

помощь POHmahshch' *n.f.* help

понимать pahneeMAHT' *v.* to understand

понос pahNOHS *n.m.* diarrhea

пончик POHNcheek *n.m.* doughnut

понятный pahnYAHTnihy *adj.* understandable

поправка pahPRAHFkah *n.f.* correction; adjustment

пора pahRAH *adv.* it's time

порох POHrahkh *n.m.* powder

порт pohrt *n.m.* port

портрет pahrtRYEHT *n.m.* portrait

портфель pahrtFYEHL' *n.m.* briefcase

порядок pahRYAHdahk *n.m.* order; sequence

посадка pahSAHTkah *n.f.* landing

послать pahsLAHT' *v.* to send

после POHSlee *prep.* after

последний pahsLYEHDneey *adj.* last; latest

послезавтра pahsleeZAHFtrah *adv.* day after tomorrow

пословица pahsLOHveetsah *n.f.* proverb

посоветовать pahsahVYEHtahvaht' *v.* to recommend

посольство pahSOHL'stvah *n.nt.* embassy

постепенно pahsteePYEHNnah *adv.* gradually

постоянный pahstahYAHnihy *adj.* constant; continuous

посуда pahSOOdah *n.f.* dishes

посылка pahSIHLkah *n.f.* package

пот poht *n.m.* sweat

потерять pahtyehRYAHT' *v.* to lose (sth.)

потолок pahtahLOHK *n.m.* ceiling

потом pahTOHM *adv.* then; next; afterwards

потому что pahtahMOOshtah *conj.* because

похожий pahKHOHzheey *adj.* similar; like

поцелуй pahtseeLOOY *n.m.* kiss

почему pahcheeMOO *inter.* why

почему-то pahcheeMOOtah *adv.* for some reason

почка POHCHkah *n.f.* kidney

почта POHCHtah *n.f.* mail; post office

почтамт pohchTAHMT *n m* main post office

почти pahchTEE *adv.* almost

почтовый ящик pahchTOHvihy YAHshcheek
n.m. mailbox

пошлина POHSHleenah *n.f.* duty (customs)

поэзия pahEHzeeyah *n.f.* poetry

поэт pahEHT *n.m.* poet

поэтому pahEHtahmoo *conj.* therefore

пояс POHees *n.m.* belt; waist

правда PRAHVdah *n.f.* truth

правило PRAHveelah *n.nt.* rule

правильный PRAHVeel'nihy *adj.* correct; right

правительство prahVEEteel'stvah *n.nt.*
government

православный prahvahSLAHVnihy *adj.*
orthodox

правый PRAHvihy *adj.* right (direction)

праздник PRAHZneek *n.m.* holiday

пребывание preebihVAHneeyeh *n.nt.* stay

предложение preedlahZHEHneeyeh *n.nt.* offer;
proposal; suggestion

предмет preedMYEHT *n.m.* subject

предприятие preedpreeYAHteeyeh *n.nt.*
undertaking; venture

предупреждение preedoopreezhDYEHneeyeh
n.nt. warning

прежде PRYEHZHdyeh *adv.* before; formerly

прежний PRYEHZHneey *adj.* former; previous

презерватив preezeervahTEEF *n.m.*
contraceptive; condom

прекрасный preeKRAHSnihy *adj.* wonderful

преподаватель preepahdahVAHteel' *n.m.*
teacher

преподавательница
preepahdahVAHteelneetsah *n.f.* teacher

препятствие preePYAHTStveeyeh *n.nt.*
hindrance

преступление preestoopLYEHneeyeh *n.nt.* crime

преувеличение preeooveeleeCHEHneeyeh *n.nt.*
exaggeration

при pree *prep.* before

привет preeVYEHT *interj.* hi *(coll.)*

привычка preeVIHCHkah *n.f.* habit

приглашение preeglahSHEHneeyeh *n.nt.*
invitation

пригород PREEgahraht *n.m.* suburb

приезд preeYEHST *n.m.* arrival

приём preeYOHM *n.m.* reception

прилёт preeLYOHT *n.m.* arrival (on a plane)

приличный preeLEESHnihy *adj.* proper; civilized

пример preeMYEHR *n.m.* example

принимать preeneeMAHT' *v.* to accept

природа preeROHdah *n.f.* nature

пристань PREEstahn' *n.f.* dock; pier; wharf

причёска preeCHOHSkah *n.f.* hair-do

причина preeCHEEnah *n.f.* reason

приятный preeYAHTnihy *adj.* pleasant

про proh *prep.* about

проблема prahBLYEHmah *n.f.* problem

прогноз prahgNOHS *n.m.* prognosis; forecast

продавец prahdahVYEHTS *n.m.* salesman

продажа prahDAHzhah *n.f.* sale

продать prahDAHT' *v.* to sell

продолжение prahdahlZHEHneeyeh *n.nt.*
  continuation

произношение praheeznahSHEHneeyeh *n.nt.*
  pronunciation

происхождение praheeskhahzhDYEHneeyeh
  n.nt. origin

пролив prahLEEF *n.m.* strait; channel

прописка prahPEESkah *n.f.* registration

пропуск PROHpoosk *n.m.* admission; admittance

простите prahsTEEtyeh *v.* sorry; excuse me

просто PROHstah *adv.* simply

простой prahsTOY *adj.* simple; easy

простуда prahsTOOdah *n.f.* head cold

простыня prahstihnYAH *n.f.* bed sheet

просьба PROZ'bah *n.f.* request

протез (зубной) prahTYEHS zoopNOY *n.m.*
  denture

против PROHteef *prep.* against

профессия prahFYEHseeyah *n.f.* profession

профессор prahFYEHsahr *n.m.* professor

прошлый PROHSHlihy *adj.* past

прощай prahSHCHAY *interj.* farewell

проявление praheevLYEHneeyeh *n.nt.* (film) development

пруд proot *n.m.* pond

прямой preeMOY *adj.* straight

птица PTEEtsah *n.f.* bird

пуговица POOgahveetsah *n.f.* button

пуловер poolOHveer *n.m.* sweater

пункт poonkt *n.m.* point; station; center

пустой poosTOY *adj.* empty; vacant

путеводитель pooteevahDEEteel' *n.m.* guidebook

путешественник pooteeshEHSTveeneek *n.m.* traveler

путешествие pooteeSHEHSTveeyeh *n.nt.* trip

путь poot' *n.f.* trip; way; path

пшеница pshehNEEtsah *n.f.* wheat

пьеса P'YEHsah *n.f.* play; drama

пьяный P'YAHnihy *adj.* drunk; intoxicated

пьяница PYAHneetsah *n.f.* drunkard

пятно peetNOH *n.nt.* spot; stain

P

работа rahBOHtah *n.f.* work

работать rahBOHtaht' *v.* to work

рабочий rahBOHcheey *n.m.* worker

раввин rahvVEEN *n.m.* rabbi

равнодушный rahvnahDOOSHnihy *adj.* indifferent

равный RAHVnihy *adj.* equal

рагу *n.m.* rahGOO stew

рад raht *adj.* glad; pleased

радио RAHdeeoh *n.nt.* radio

радиостанция rahdeeahSTAHNtseeyah *n.f.* radio station

радостный RAHdahstnihy *adj.* joyful; joyous

раз rahs *num.* time; once; one

разве RAHZveh *part.* really?; is that so?

развитие rahzVEEteeyeh *n.nt.* development

развлечение rahzvleeCHEHneeyeh *n.nt.* amusement; entertainment

разговор rahzgahVOHR *n.m.* conversation

разговорник rahzgahVOHRneek *n.m.* phrasebook

разговорный rahzgahVOHRnihy *adj.* conversational; colloquial

раздевалка rahzdeeVAHLkah *n.f.* cloakroom

раздражение rahzdrahZHEHneeyeh *n.nt.* irritation

раздутый rahzDOOtihy *adj.* swollen; puffed up

размер rahzMYEHR *n.m.* size

разница RAHSneetsah *n.f.* difference; distinction

разный RAHZnihy *adj.* different

разрешение rahzreeSHEHneeyeh *n.nt.* permission; permit

разумно rahzOOMnah *adv.* sensibly; rationally

рак rahk *n.m.* crayfish; cancer

раковина RAHkahveenah *n.f.* (bathroom) sink

рана RAHnah *n.f.* wound

раненый RAHNecnihy *adj.* wounded, injured

ранний RAHNneey *adj.* early

раньше RAHN'sheh *comp.* earlier; sooner

расписание rahspeeSAHneeyeh *n.nt.* schedule; timetable

распродано rahsPROHdahnah *adv.* sold out

рассвет rahsSVYEHT *n.m.* dawn; daybreak

рассказ rahsKAHS *n.m.* story; tale; account

расстояние rahstahYAHneeyeh *n.nt.* distance

расстройство желудка rahsTROYstvah zhehLOOTkah *n.nt.* indigestion

растение rahsTYEHneeyeh *n.nt.* plant

растяжение rahsteeZHEHneeyeh *n.nt.* strain; sprain

расходы rahsKHOHdih *n.pl.* expenses

рваный RVAHnihy *adj.* torn; ripped

ребёнок reeBYOHnahk *n.m.* child

ребро reebROH *n.nt.* rib

ревматизм reevmahTEEZM *n.m.* rheumatism

редиска reeDEESkah *n.f.* radish

редкий RYEHTkeey *adj.* rare; infrequent

редко RYEHTkah *adv.* rarely

режиссёр reezheeSYOHR *n.m.* (theater) director

резаный RYEHZahnihy *adj.* cut; sliced

резиновый reeZEEnahvihy *adj.* rubber

рейс reys *n.m.* trip; flight

река reeKAH *n.f.* river

реклама reeKLAHmah *n.f.* advertisement; sign

рельс ryehl's *n.m.* rail; track

ремонт reeMOHNT *n.m.* repair

ремонт обуви reeMOHNT OHboovee *n.m.* shoe repair

рентген reenGYEHN *n.m.* X ray

репа RYEHpah *n.f.* turnip

ресница reesNEEtsah *n.f.* eyelash

республика reesPOObleekah *n.f.* republic

ресторан reestahRAHN *n.m.* restaurant

рецепт reeTSEHPT *n.m.* prescription

речь ryehch' *n.f.* speech

решение reeSHEHneeyeh *n.nt.* decision

рис rees *n.m.* rice

рисование reesahVAHneeyeh *n.nt.* drawing

рифма REEFmah *n.f.* rhyme

робкий ROHPkeey *adj.* timid; shy

родина ROHdeenah *n.f.* homeland

родители rahDEEteelee *n.pl.* parents

родной rahdNOY *adj.* native

родственники ROHTSTveeneekee *n.pl.* relatives

рождение rahzhDYEHneeyeh *n.nt.* birth

Рождество rahzheestVOH *n.nt.* Christmas

рожь rohsh *n.f.* rye

роза ROHzah *n.f.* rose

розетка rahzYEHTkah *n.f.* electrical socket

роль rohl' *n.f.* role; part

роман rahMAHN *n.m.* novel

роса rahSAH *n.f.* dew

роскошный rahsKOHSHnihy *adj.* luxurious

российский rahSEEYskeey *adj.* Russian

рост rohst *n.m.* growth; height

ростбиф ROHSTbeef *n.m.* roast beef

рот roht *n.m.* mouth

рубашка rooBAHSHkah *n.f.* shirt

рубин rooBEEN *n.m.* ruby

рубль roobl' *n.m.* ruble

рука rooKAH *n.f.* hand; arm

рукав rooKAHF *n.m.* sleeve

рукавица rookahVEEtsah *n.f.* mitten

руководство rookahVOHTstvah *n.nt.* leadership

рукопись ROOkahpees' *n.f.* manuscript

рулет rooLYEHT *n.m.* meat loaf

русский/русская ROOSkeey/ROOSkahyah
   n.m./f./adj. Russian

ручка ROOCHkah *n.f.* pen
рыба RIHBah *n.f.* fish
рынок RIHNahk *n.m.* market
рюкзак ryookZAHK *n.m.* backpack
ряд ryaht *n.m.* row; file
рядом RYAHdahm *adv.* alongside; beside; next to

C

с s *prep.* with; off; since
сад saht *n.m.* garden
салат sahLAHT *n.m.* salad
салфетка sahlFYEHTkah *n.f.* napkin
самовар sahmahVAHR *n.m.* samovar
самолёт sahmahLYOHT *n.m.* airplane
самообслуживание sahmahahpSLOOzheevah-
    neeyeh *adj.* self-service
самостоятельный sahmahstahYAHteel'nihy *adj.*
    independent
самоубийство sahmahooBEEYstvah *n.nt.* suicide
самоуверенный sahmahooVYEHreenihy *adj.*
    self-confident
сандалии sahnDAHleeee *n.pl.* sandals
санки SAHNkee *n.pl.* sleigh; sled
сапоги sahpahGEE *n.pl.* boots
сапфир sahpFEER *n.m.* saphire
сарказм sahrKAHZM *n.m.* sarcasm
сатира sahTEErah *n.f.* satire
сахар SAHkhahr *n.m.* sugar
сахарин sahkhahREEN *n.m.* saccharin
сбор zbohr *n.m.* collection; gathering
сборник ZBOHRneek *n.m.* anthology; collection
свадьба SVAHT'bah *n.f.* wedding

свежий SVYEHzheey *adj.* fresh

свёкла SVYOHKlah *n.f.* beets

сверх svyehrkh *adv.* over and above; in excess of

свет svyeht *n.m.* light

светло- SVYEHTlah- *adj.* light-(color)

светлый SVYEHTlihy *adj.* light; bright

светофор sveetahFOHR *n.m.* traffic light

свеча sveeCHAH *n.f.* candle

свидание sveeDAHneeyeh *n.nt.* appointment;
   meeting

свинина sveeNEEnah *n.f.* pork

свинья sveen'YAH *n.f.* pig

свобода svahBOHdah *n.f.* freedom

свободный svahBOHDnihy *adj.* free; vacant

святой sveeTOY *adj.* holy; sacred

священник sveeSHCHEHneek *n.m.* priest;
   clergyman

сдача ZDAHchah *n.f.* change

север SYEHveer *n.m.* north

северный SYEHveernihy *adj.* northern

сегодня seeVOHdnyah *adv.* today

сегодняшний seeVOHdnyahshneey *adj.* today's

сейчас seeCHAHS *adv.* now

сейф seyf *n.m.* safe (bank)

секретарь seekreeTAHR' *n.f.* secretary

секунда seekOONdah *n.f.* second (time measure)

секция SYEHKtseeyah *n.f.* section

село seeLOH *n.nt.* village

семья seem'YAH *n.f.* family

сервиз seerVEES *n.m.* set (of dishes or silverware)

сердечный припадок seerDYEHCHnihy
   preePAHdahk *n.m.* heart attack

сердитый seerDEEtihy *adj.* angry
сердце SYEHRseh *n.nt.* heart
серебро seereeBROH *n.nt.* silver
серебряный seeRYEHBreenihy *adj.* silver
середина seereeDEEnah *n.f.* middle
серёжки seerYOHSHkee *n.pl.* earrings
серьги SYEHR'gee *n.pl.* earrings
серый SYEHrihy *adj.* gray
серьёзный seer'YOHZnihy *adj.* serious
сестра seesTRAH *n.f.* sister
сигара seeGAHrah *n.f.* cigar
сигарета seegahRYEHtah *n.f.* cigarette
сила SEElah *n.f.* strength
сильный SEEL'nihy *adj.* strong
синагога seenahGOHgah *n.f.* synagogue
синий SEEneey *adj.* dark blue
синяк seenYAHK *n.m.* bruise
сирень seeRYEHN' *n.f.* lilac
система seesTYEHmah *n.f.* system
сказка SKAHSkah *n.f.* tale
скамейка skahMEYkah *n.f.* bench
сквозь skvohs' *prep.* through
скидка SKEETkah *n.f.* sale
сковорода skahvahrahDAH *n.f.* frying pan
скользкий SKOHL'skeey *adj.* slippery
сколько SKOHL'kah *adv.* how much; how many
скорая помощь SKOHrahyah POHmahshch *n.f.*
  ambulance; first aid; emergency room
скорее skahRYEHeh *adv.* quickly
скорлупа skahrlooPAH *n.f.* (egg) shell
скорость SKOHrahst' *n.f.* speed
скорый SKOHrihy *adj.* quick; rapid; fast

скромный SKROHMnihy *adj.* modest

скрытый SKRIHtihy *adj.* hidden; secret

скульптура skool'pTOOrah *n.f.* sculpture

скучный SKOOCHnihy *adj.* boring

слабительное slahBEEteel'nahyeh *n.nt.* laxative

слабый SLAHbihy *adj.* weak

слава SLAHvah *n.f.* glory

сладкий SLAHTkeey *adj.* sweet

сладкое (на) SLAHTkahyeh (nah) *n.nt.* (for) dessert

следствие SLYEHTstveeyeh *n nt.* result; consequence; investigation

следующий SLYEHdooyooshcheey *adj.* next

слёзы SLYOHzih *n.pl.* tears

сливки SLEEFkee *n.pl.* cream

слишком SLEESHkahm *adv.* too

словарь slahVAHR' *n.m.* dictionary

слово SLOHvah *n.nt.* word

сложный SLOHZHnihy *adj.* complex; difficult

сломать slahMAHT' *v.* to break

служба SLOOSHbah *n.f.* church service

случай SLOOchay *n.m.* incident

случайно slooCHAYnah *adv.* accidentally

слышный SLIHSHnihy *adj.* audible

смелый SMYEHlihy *adj.* brave; courageous

смерть smychrt' *n.f.* death

сметана smeeTAHnah *n.f.* sour cream

смех smyehkh *n.m.* laughter

смешной smeeshNOY *adj.* funny

смотреть smahTRYEHT' *v.* to look

смущение smooSHCHEHneeyeh *n.nt.* embarrassment

сначала snahCHAHlah *adv.* at first; in the beginning

снег snyehk *n.m.* snow

собака sahBAHkah *n.f.* dog

собор sahBOHR *n.m.* cathedral

собрание sahBRAHneeyeh *n.nt.* meeting

событие sahBIHTeeyeh *n.nt.* event

совет sahVYEHT *n.m.* advice

совпадение sahfpahDYEHneeyeh *n.nt.* coincidence

современный sahvreemMYEHNnihy *adj.* contemporary

согласный sahGLAHSnihy *adj.* in agreement

сок sohk *n.m.* juice

сокращение sahkrahSHCHEHneeyeh *n.nt.* abbreviation.

солдат sahlDAHT *n.m.* soldier

солёный sahlYOHnihy *adj.* salted

солнечный SOHLneechnihy *adj.* sunny

солнце SOHNtseh *n.nt.* sun

соль sohl' *n.f.* salt

сомнение sahmNYEHneeyeh *n.nt.* doubt

сон sohn *n.m.* sleep; dream

сообщать sahahpSHCHAHT' *v.* to notify, inform

соревнование sahreevnahVAHneeyeh *n.nt.* competition; sports match

сорт sohrt *n.m.* kind; sort

сосед sahSYEHT *n.m.* neighbor

соска SOHSkah *n.f.* pacifier

состояние sahstahYAHneeyeh *n.nt.* condition

сотый SOHTihy *num.* hundredth

соус SOHoos *n.m.* sauce; gravy

сочетание sahchehTAHneeyeh *n.nt.* combination

сочувствие sahCHOOSTveeyeh *n.nt.* sympathy

союз sahYOOS *n.m.* union

спальня SPAHL'nyah *n.f.* bedroom

спасибо spahSEEbah *interj.* thank you

спать spaht' *v.* to sleep

спектакль speekTAHKL' *n.m.* performance; play

специальность speetseeAHL'nahst' *n.f.* specialty

спешный SPYEHSHnihy *adj.* hurried; rushed

спина speeNAH *n.f.* back; spine

список SPEEsahk *n.m.* list

спичка SPEECHkah *n.f* match

спокойный spahKOYnihy *adj.* calm; tranquil

спор spohr *n.m.* argument

спорный SPOHRnihy *adj.* controversial

справка SPRAHFkah *n.f.* reference; information; certificate

средний SRYEHDneey *adj.* middle; average

средство от комаров SRYEHTstvah aht kahmahROHF *n.nt.* mosquito repellent

срок srohk *n.m.* (period of) time; date; deadline

срочный SROHCHnihy *adj.* urgent

стадион stahdeeOHN *n.m.* stadium

стакан stahKAHN *n.m.* (drinking) glass

станция STAHNtseeyah *n.f.* station

старший STAHRsheey *adj.* older; elder; senior

старый STAHrihy *adj.* old

стекло steekLOH *n.nt.* glass

стена steeNAH *n.f.* wall

степень STYEHpeen' *n.f.* degree; extent

стирка STEERkah *n.f.* washing; laundry

стол stohl *n.m.* table

столетие stahLYEHteeyeh *n.nt.* century

столица stahLEEtsah *n.f.* capital (of a state)

столовая stahLOHvahyah *n.f.* dining hall

стоп stohp *interj.* stop

сторона stahrahNAH *n.f.* side

стоянка stahYAHNkah *n.f.* (bus, taxi) stop

стоянка для машин stahYAHNkah dlyah mahSHEEN *n.f.* parking lot

страна strahNAH *n.f.* country

страница strahNEEtsah *n.f.* page

странный STRAHNnihy *adj.* strange; odd

страстный STRAHSnihy *adj.* passionate

страх strahkh *n.m.* fear

страшный STRAHSHnihy *adj.* horrible; terrifying

стрижка STREESHkah *n.f.* haircut; trim

строгий STROHgeey *adj.* strict; harsh; severe

студент stooDYEHNT *n.m.* student

стук stook *n.m.* knock

стул stool *n.m.* chair

стыд stiht *n.m.* shame

стюардесса styooahrDYEHsah *n.f.* stewardess

сувенир sooveeNEER *n.m.* souvenir

судьба soot'BAH *n.f.* fate

сумасшедший soomahshEHTsheey *adj.* crazy; mad; insane

суп soop *n.m.* soup

супруг soopROOK *n.m.* husband

супруга soopROOgah *n.f.* wife

сутки SOOTkee *n.pl.* twenty-four-hour period; day

сухой sooKHOY *adj.* dry

счастливый shahsLEEvihy *adj.* happy; lucky

счёт shchoht *n.m.* check; bill

сын sihn *n.m.* son

сыр sihr *n.m.* cheese
сырой sihROY *adj.* raw
сытый SIHTihy *adj.* full (of food)

T

табак tahBAHK *n.m.* tobacco
таблетка tahbLYEHTkah *n.f.* pill; tablet
также TAHKzheh *adv.* as well; also
такси tahkSEE *n.pl.* taxi
талон tahLOHN *n.m.* coupon
там tahm *adv.* there
таможенник tahMOHZHehneek *n.m.* customs
   official
таможня tahMOHZHnyah *n.f.* customs
тампон tahmPOHN *n.m.* tampon
танец TAHneets *n.m.* dance
тапочки TAHPahchkee *n.pl.* slippers
таракан tahrahKAHN *n.m.* cockroach
тарелка tahRYEHLkah *n.f.* plate
твёрдый TVYOHRdihy *adj.* hard
творог tvahROHK *n.m.* cottage cheese
творчество TVOHRchehstvah *n.nt.* creative work
театр teeAHTR *n.m.* theater
телевизор teeleeVEEzahr *n.m.* television
телеграмма *n.f.* teeleeGRAHmah telegram
телеграф teeleeGRAHF *n.m.* telegraph office
телефон teeleeFOHN *n.m.* telephone
телефон-автомат teeleeFOHNahftahMAHT *n.m.*
   pay phone
телефонистка teeleefahnEESTkah *n.f.* operator
тело TYEHlah *n.nt.* body

телятина teelYAHteenah *n.f.* veal

тёмные очки TYOHMnihyeh ahchKEE *n.pl.* sunglasses

тёмный TYOHMnihy *adj.* dark

температура teempeerahTOOrah *n.f.* temperature

теннис TYEHnees *n.m.* tennis

тень tyehn' *n.f.* shadow

теперь teePYEHR' *adv.* now

тёплый TYOHPlihy *adj.* warm

термос TYEHRmahs *n.m.* thermos

терпеливый teerpeeLEEvihy *adj.* patient

тесный TYEHSnihy *adj.* crowded

тетрадь teeTRAHT' *n.f.* notebook

тётя TYOHtyah *n.f.* aunt

тефтели TEHFteelee *n.pl.* meatballs

тихий TEEKHeey *adj.* quite

ткань tkahn' *n.f.* fabric

товар tahVAHR *n.m.* merchandise

тогда tahgDAH *adv.* then

тоже TOHzheh *conj.* also; too

толпа tahlPAH *n.f.* crowd

толстый TOHLstihy *adj.* fat

только TOHL'kah *adv.* only

тонкий TOHNkeey *adj.* thin

топаз tahPAHS *n.m.* topaz

тормоза tahrmahZAH *n.f.* brakes (car)

торт tohrt *n.m.* cake

тот toht *pron.* that (one)

точно TOHCHnah *adv.* exactly

тошнота tashnahTAH *n.f.* nausea

трава trahVAH *n.f.* grass

трагедия trahGYEHdeeyah *n.f.* tragedy

трамвай trahmVAY *n.m.* street car
трасса TRAHsah *n.f.* highway
треска treesKAH *n.f.* cod
трогать TROHgaht' *v.* to touch
троллейбус trahLEYboos *n.m.* trolley bus
тротуар trahtooAHR *n.m.* sidewalk
трубка TROOPkah *n.f.* pipe
трудный TROODnihy *adj.* difficult
трусы trooSIH *n.pl.* underpants
туалет tooahLYEHT *n.m.* toilet
туалетная бумага tooahLYEHTnahyah
  booMAHgah *n.f.* toilet paper
туда tooDAH *adv.* that way
туда и обратно tooDAH ee ahbRAHTnah *adv.*
  roundtrip (ticket)
туман tooMAHN *n.m.* fog
тунец tooNYEHTS *n.m.* tuna
турист tooREEST *n.m.* tourist
тут toot *adv.* here
туфли TOOFlee *n.pl.* shoes
тысяча TIHseechah *num.* thousand
тюрьма tyoor'MAH *n.f.* prison
тяжёлый teezhOHLihy *adj.* difficult; heavy

У

у oo *prep.* at
убийство ooBEEYSTvah *n.nt.* murder
убийца ooBEEYtsah *n.f.* murderer
уборная ooBOHRnahyah *n.f.* bathroom
уборщик ooBOHRshcheek *n.m.* janitor; yardsman

уборщица ooBOHRshcheetsah *n.f.* cleaning lady

уважаемый oovahZHAHeemihy *adj.* respected

увлечённый oovleeCHOHnihy *adj.* enthusiastic

угол OOgahl *n.m.* corner; angle

угроза ooGROHzah *n.f.* threat

ударение oodahRYEHneeyeh *n.nt.* grammatical stress

удача ooDAHchah *n.f.* success

удивительный oodeeVEEteel'nihy *adj.* surprising

удобный ooDOHBnihy *adj.* comfortable

удобство ooDOHBSTvah *n.nt.* convenience; comfort

удовлетворение oodahvleetvahRYEHneeyeh *n.nt.* satisfaction

удовольствие oodahVOHL'stveeyeh *n.nt.* pleasure

удостоверение oodahstahveeRYEHneeyeh *n.nt.* identification

удочка OOdahchkah *n.f.* fishing pole

ужасный oozhAHSnihy *adj.* horrible

уже oozhEH *adv.* already

ужин OOZHeen *n.m.* supper

узкий OOSkeey *adj.* narrow

уклон ookLOHN *n.m.* bias; incline

укол ooKOHL *n.m.* injection

украсть ooKRAHST' *v.* to steal

украшение ookrahSHEHneeyeh *n.nt.* decoration; embellishment

улица OOLeetsah *n.f.* street

улыбка ooLIHPkah *n.f.* smile

уменьшение oomeen'SHEHneeyeh *n.nt.* decrease

умный OOMnihy *adj.* smart; intelligent; clever

универмаг ooneeveerMAHK *n.m.* department store

университет ooneeveerseeTYEHT *n.m.* university

упорный ooPOHRnihy *adj.* stubborn

упражнение ooprahzhNYEHneeyeh *n.nt.* exercise

уровень OOrahveen' *n.f.* level

урок ooROHK *n.m.* lesson

условие oosLOHveeyeh *n.nt.* condition

успех oosPYEHKH *n.m.* success

успокоительное средство oospahkahEE-teel'nahyeh SRYEHTstvah *n.nt.* sedative

устал(а) oosTAHL(ah) *adj.* tired

устный OOSnihy *adj.* oral; verbal

усы oosIH *n.pl.* mustache

утомление ootahmLYEHneeyeh *n.nt.* exhaustion

утренний OOTreeneey *adj.* morning

утро OOTrah *n.nt.* morning

утюг ooTYOOK *n.m.* iron

ухо OOKHah *n.nt.* ear

участие ooCHAHSTeeyeh *n.nt.* participation

учебник ooCHEHBneek *n.m.* textbook

учёный ooCHOHnihy *n.m.* scholar; scientist

учитель ooCHEEtyehl' *n.m.* teacher

учительница ooCHEEtyehl'neetsah *n.f.* teacher

учиться ooCHEET'sah *v.* to study

учреждение oochreezhDYEHneeyeh *n.nt.* institution

Ф

фальшивый fahl'SHEEvihy *adj.* fake; falsified
фамилия fahMEEleeyah *n.f.* last name; surname
фары FAHrih *n.pl.* headlights
фарфор fahrFOHR *n.f.* china
фарцовщик fahrTSOHFshcheek *n.m.*
  blackmarketeer
фасоль fahSOHL' *n.f.* beans
фен fyehn *n.m.* hairdryer
ферма FYEHRmah *n.f.* farm
фильм feel'm *n.m.* movie
флот floht *n.m.* navy
фойе fayYEH *n.nt.* lobby
фонтан fahnTAHN *n.m.* fountain
форель fahRYEHL' *n.f.* trout
фотоаппарат fohtahahpahRAHT *n.m.* camera
фотография fohtahGRAHfeeyah *n.f.* photograph
фраза FRAHzah *n.f.* phrase; sentence
фрукт frookt *n.m.* fruit
фунт foont *n.m.* pound
фут foot *n.m.* foot (measure)
футбол footBOHL *n.m.* soccer

X

халат khahLAHT *n.m.* robe
харчо kharCHOH *n.nt.* mutton soup
химчистка kheemCHEESTkah *n.f.* dry cleaning
хирург kheerOORK *n.m.* surgeon
хлеб khlyehp *n.m.* bread

хлебосольный khleebahSOHL'nihy *adj.* hospitable

хлопчатобумажный khlahpchahtahboo-MAHZHnihy *adj.* cotton (fabric)

хоккей khahkKEY *n.m.* hockey

холодец khalahDYEHTS *n.m.* aspic

холодный khahLOHDnihy *adj.* cold

хор khohr *n.m.* choir

хороший khahROHsheey *adj.* good

хотеть khahTYEHT' *v.* to want

хотя khahtYAH *conj.* although

храм khrahm *n.m.* cathedral; temple

хромой khrahMOY *adj.* lame

хрупкий KROOPkeey *adj.* fragile

художник khooDOHZHneek *n.m.* artist

худой khooDOY *adj.* thin

хуже KHOOzheh *comp.* worse

хулиган khooleeGAH *n.m.* hooligan

Ц

царь tsahr' *n.m.* tsar

цвет tsvyeht *n.m.* color

цветок tsveeTOHK *n.m.* flower

целый TSEHlihy *adj.*whole; entire

цель tsehl' *n.f.* goal; aim

цена tseeNAH *n.f.* price

ценный TSEHNnihy *adj.* valuable

центр tsehntr *n.m.* center

цепь tsehp' *n.f.* chain

церковь TSEHRkahf' *n.f.* church

цирк tseerk *n.m.* circus

цита́та tseeTAHtah *n.f.* quote
ци́фра TSEEfrah *n.f.* number; numeral
цыга́н/цыга́нка tsihGAHN/tsihGAHNkah *n.m./f.*
  gypsy

Ч

чаевы́е chahehVIHyeh *n.nt.* tip
чай chay *n.m.* tea
ча́йник CHAYneek *n.m.* tea kettle
ча́йница CHAYneetsah *n.f.* tea caddy
час chahs *n.m.* hour
ча́сто CHAHStah *adv.* often
частота́ chahstahTAH *n.f.* frequency
часть chahst' *n.f.* part
часы́ cheesih *n.pl.* watch; clock
ча́шка CHAHSHkah *n.f.* cup
чек chehk *n.m.* check
челове́к chehlahVYEHK *n.m.* person
чем chehm *conj.* than
чемода́н chehmahDAHN *n.m.* suitcase
чепуха́ chehpooKHAH *n.f.* nonsense
че́рез CHEHrees *prep.* through; within (time)
чере́шня chehRYEHSHnyah *n.pl.* sweet cherries
черни́ка chehrNEEkah *n.pl.* blueberries
черни́ла chehrNEElah *n.f.* ink
чёрный CHOHRnihy *adj.* black; dark
чёрный ры́нок CHOHRnihy RIHNahk *n.m.* black
  market.
чёрт chohrt *n.m.* devil
черта́ chehrTAH *n.f.* feature; trait; characteristic
чесно́к chehsNOHK *n.m.* garlic

честный CHEHSnihy *adj.* honest
четверть CHEHTveert' *n.f.* quarter
чёткий CHOHTkeey *adj.* clear; distinct
чиновник cheeNOHVneek *n.m.* official
число cheesLOH *n.nt.* number; date
чистый CHEEStihy *adj.* clean
читатель cheeTAHteel' *n.m.* reader
читать cheeTAHT' *v.* to read
чиханье cheeKHAHN'yeh *n.nt.* sneezing
член chlyehn *n.m.* member
что shtoh *inter.* what
что-бы SHTOHbih *conj.* in order to
что-нибудь SHTOHneeboot' *pron.* anything;
  something
чувство CHOOSTvah *n.nt.* feeling; sensitivity
чувствовать CHOOSTvahvaht' *v.* to feel
чудесный chooDYEHSnihy *adj.* wonderful;
  miraculous
чужой chooZHOY *adj.* not one's own; foreign
чулки choolKEE *n.pl.* stockings
чуть choot' *adv.* hardly; scarsely; barely
чучело CHOOchehlah *n.nt.* stuffed animal

Ш

шаг shahk *n.m.* step
шампанское shahmPAHNskahyeh *n.nt.*
  champagne
шампунь shahmPOON' *n.f.* shampoo
шапка SHAHPkah *n.f.* hat
шарф shahrf *n.m.* scarf
шахматы SHAHKHmahtih *n.pl.* chess

шашлык shahshLIHK *n.m.* shish kebob
швейцар shveyTSAHR *n.m.* doorman
шёпот SHOHpaht *n.m.* whisper
шерстяной shehrsteeNOY *adj.* woolen
шея SHEHyah *n.f.* neck
ширина sheereeNAH *n.f.* width
широкий sheeROHkeey *adj.* wide; broad
шкаф shkahf *n.m.* closet; cabinet
школа SHKOHlah *n.f.* school
шкура SHKOOrah *n.f.* skin; hide
шнурки SHNOORkee *n.pl.* shoe laces
шоколад shahkahLAHT *n.m.* chocolate
шорты SHOHRtihy *n.pl.* shorts
шоссе shahSEH *n.nt.* highway
штат shtaht *n.m.* state; staff
штатский SHTAHTskeey *adj.* civilian
штопор SHTOHpahr *n.m.* corkscrew
штраф shtrahf *n.m.* fine
шуба SHOObah *n.f.* fur coat
шум shoom *n.m.* noise
шумный SHOOMnihy *adj.* noisy
шутка SHOOTkah *n.f.* joke

Щ

щедрый SHCHEHDrihy *adj.* generous
щека shchehKAH *n.f.* cheek
щётка SHCHOHTkah *n.f.* brush
щи shchee *n.pl.* cabbage soup
щука SHCHOOkah *n.f.* pike

Э

экземпляр egzeemPLYAHR *n.m.* copy; edition
экскурсия ehksKOORseeyah *n.f.* tour; excursion
экскурсовод ehkskoorsahVOHT *n.m.* tour guide
экспресс ehksPRYEHS *n.m.* express
электрический ehleekTREEchehskeey *adj.*
  electrical
электричество ehleekTREEchehstvah *n.nt.*
  electricity
эмигрант ehmeeGRAHNT *n.m.* émigré
эмиграция ehmeeGRAHtseeyah *n.f.* emigration
эмоция ehMOHtseeyah *n.f.* emotion
эскалатор ehskahLAHtahr *n.m.* escalator
этаж ehTAHSH *n.m.* floor; story
этот EHtaht *pron.* that, this (one)

Ю

юбилей yoobeeLEY *n.m.* anniversary
юбка YOOPkah *n.f.* skirt
ювелирный yooveeLEERnihy *adj.* jewelry
юг yook *n.m.* south
южный YOOZHnihy *adj.* southern
юмор YOOmahr *n.m.* humor
юность YOOnahst' *n.f.* youth

Я

я yah *pron.* I
яблоко YAHBlahkah *n.nt.* apple
ягоды YAHgahdih *n.pl.* berries

яд yaht *n.m.* poison

язва YAHZvah *n.f.* ulcer

язык yeezIHK *n.m.* language; tongue

яичница yahEECHneetsah *n.f.* fried eggs

яичница-болтунья yahEECHneetsah-bahlTOOn'yah *n.f.* scrambled eggs

яйцо yayTSOH *n.nt.* egg

яркий YAHRkeey *adj.* bright

ярмарка YAHRmahrkah *n.f.* fair

ясно YAHSnah *adv.* clearly

ящик YAHshcheek *n.m.* box

English-Russian Dictionary

A

about *prep.* о/об, про oh/ohp, proh
above *prep.* наверку/над nahveerKHOO/naht
abscess *n.* нарыв *m.* nahRIHF
absence *n.* отсутствие *nt.* ahtSOOTSTveeyeh
absolutely *adv.* совершенно sahvehrSHEHNnah
absorbent cotton *n.* вата *m.* VAHtah
accent *n.* акцент *m.* ahkTSEHNT
accept *v.* принимать preeneeMAHT'
access *n.* доступ *m.* DOHstoop
accident *n.* несчастный случай *m.*
  neeSHCHAHSTnihy SLOOchay
accidentally *adv.* случайно slooCHAYnah
across *prep.* через CHEHRehz
acquaintance *n.* знакомство *nt.* znahKOHMstvah
acquainted *adj.* знакомый znahKOHmihy
act *n.* акт *m.* ahkt
act, take action *v.* действовать DEYSTvahvaht'
action *n.* действие *nt.* DEYSTveeyeh
actor *n.* актёр *m.* akhtTYOHR
actress *n.* актриса *f.* ahkTREEsah
address *n.* адрес *m.* AHdrees
admission *n.* впуск *m.* fpoosk
admission pass *n.* пропуск *m.* PROHpoosk
admit *v.* впускать fpoosKAHT'
adult *adj.* взрослый VZROHslih
advertising *n.* реклама *f.* reeKLAHmah
advice *n.* совет *m.* sahVYEHT
affectionate *adj.* ласковый LAHSkahvihy

after *prep.,/adv.* после POHSlee

afternoon *n.* после обеда POHSlee ahBYEHdah

afterwards *adv.* потом pahTOHM

again *adv.* опять/ещё раз ahpYAHT'/
yeeSHCHOH rahs

against *prep.* против PROHteef

age *n.* возраст *m.* VOHZrahst

agreement (in) *adj.* согласный sahGLAHSnihy

agreement *n.* согласие *nt.* sahGLAHSeeyeh

air *n.* воздух *m.* VOHZdookh

air conditioner *n.* кондиционер *m.* kandeetseeah-
NYEHR

airmail *n.* авиапочта *f.* ahveeahPOHCHtah

airplane *n.* самолёт *m.* sahmahLYOHT

airport *n.* аэропорт *m.* ahehrahPOHRT

alarm clock *n.* будильник *m.* booDEEL'neek

alcohol *n.* алкоголь *m.* ahlkahGOHL'

allergy *n.* аллергия *f.* ahleeehrGEEyah

almost *adv.* почти pahchTEE

alongside; next to *adv.* рядом RYAHdahm

aloud *adv.* вслух fslookh

alphabet *n.* азбука *f.* AHSbookah; алфавит
ahlfahVEET *m.*

already *adv.* уже ooZHEN

also; as well тоже *adv.* TOHzheh

always *adv.* всегда fseegDAH

ambulance *n.* скорая помощь *f.* SKOHrahyah
POHmahshch

American *adj.* американский
ahmeereeKAHNskeey

American *n.* американец/американка *m./f.*
ahmeereeKAHneets/ahmeereeKAHNkah

ancient *adj.* древний DREHVneey

and; also *conj.* и ee

anesthesia *n.* наркоз *m.* nahrKOHS

anger *n.* гнев *m.* gnyehf

angry *adj.* сердитый seerDEEtihy

animal *n.* животное *nt.* zheeVOHTnahyeh

ankle *n.* лодыжка *f.* lahDIHSHkah

anniversary *n.* юбилей *m.* yoobeeLEY

announcement *n.* объявление *nt.* ahb"yahv-
   LYEHneeyeh

answer *n.* ответ *m.* ahtVYEHT

antiobiotic *n.* антибиотик *m.* ahnteebeeOHteek

any *adj.* любой lyooBOY

anyone *pron.* кто-нибудь KTOHneeboot'

anything *pron.* что-нибудь *m.* SHTOHneeboot'

apartment *n.* квартира *f.* kvahrTEERah

appearance *n.* вид *m.* veet

appendicitis *n.* аппендицит *m.* apeendeeTSEET

appetizer *n.* закуска *f.* zahKOOSkah

applause *n.* аплодисменты *pl.*
   ahplahdeesMYEHNtih

apple *n.* яблоко *f.* YAHBlahkah

appointment; meeting; date *n.* свидание *nt.*
   sveeDAHneeyeh

approximately *adv.* около OHkahlah;
   приблизительно preebleeZEEtychl'nah

architect *n.* архитектор *m.* ahrkheeTYEHKtahr

architecture *n.* архитектура *f.* ahrkheeteekTOOrah

argument *n.* спор *m.* spohr

arm; hand *n.* рука *f.* rooKAH

armchair *n.* кресло *nt.* KRYEHSlah

arrival (plane) *n.* прилёт *m.* preeLYOHT

arrival (train) *n.* приезд *m.* preeYEHST;
прибытие *nt.* preeBIHteeyeh

art *n.* искусство *nt.* eesKOOSTvah

arthritis *n.* артрит *m.* ahrtREET

artificial *adj.* искусственный eesKOOSTveenihy

artist *n.* художник *m.* khooDOHZneek

ashtray *n.* пепельница *f.* PYEHpeel'neetsah

aspirin *n.* аспирин *m.* ahspeeREEN

assurance *n.* уверение *nt.* ooveeRYEHneeeyeh

asthma *n.* астма *f.* AHSTmah

as well; also *adv.* также TAHGzheh

at *prep.* у oo

at first *prep.* сначала snahCHAHlah

atheism *n.* безбожие *nt.* beesBOHzheeyeh; атеизм
m. ahtehEEZM

atheist *n.* безбожник *m.* beesBOHZHneek; атеист
m. ahtehEEST

athletic *adj.* атлетический ahtlyehTEEchehskeey

at least *adv.* по крайней мере pah KRAYnyeh
MYEHreh

ATM *n.* банкомат *m.* bahnkahMAHT

attention *n.* внимание *nt.* vneeMAHneeeyeh

audible *adj.* слышный SLIHSHnihy

aunt *n.* тётя *f.* TYOHtyah

author *n.* автор *m.* AHFtahr

autumn *n.* осень *f.* OHseen'

avenue *n.* проспект *m.* prahsPYEHKT

awkward *adj.* неловкий neeLOHFkeey

B

baby *n.* младенец *m.* mlahDYEHneets

back *n.* спина *f.* speeNAH
backpack *n.* рюкзак *m.* ryookZAHK
backwards *adv.* назад nahzAHT
bacon *n.* бекон *m.* beeKOHN
bad *adj.* плохой plahKHOY
badly *adv.* плохо PLOHkhah
bag *n.* сумка *f.* SOOMkah
baggage *n.* багаж *m.* bahGAHSH
baggage room *n.* камера хранения *f.* KAHmeerah
  khrahNYEHneeyah
bakery *n.* булочная *f.* BOOlahchnahyah
balalaika *n.* балалайка *f.* bahlahLAYkah
balcony *n.* балкон *m.* bahlKOHN
ball *n.* мяч *m.* myahch
ballet *n.* балет *m.* bahLYEHT
banana *n.* банан *m.* bahNAHN
bandage *n.* бинт *m.* beent
band-aid *n.* пластырь *m.* PLAHStihr'
bank *n.* банк *m.* bahnk
barber *n.* парикмахер *m.* pahreekMAHKHeer
basket *n.* корзина *f.* kahrZEEnah
bathing cap *n.* купальная шапочка *f.*
  kooPAHL'nahyah SHAHPahchakah
bathing suit *n.* купальник *m.* kooPAHL'neek
bathroom *n.* уборная/ванная *f.* ooBOHRnahyah/
  VAHNnahyah
bathtub *n.* ванна *f.* VAHNnah
battery *n.* батарея *f.* bahtahREEyah
bay; gulf *n.* залив *m.* zahLEEF
beach *n.* пляж *m.* plyahsh.
beans *n.* фасоль *f.* fahSOHL'
beard *n.* борода *f.* bahrahDAH

beat, strike *v.* бить beet'

beautiful *adj.* красивый krahSEEvihy

beauty *n.* красота *f.* krahsahTAH

because *conj.* потому что pahtahMOOshtah

because of *conj.* из-за eezzah

bed *n.* кровать *f.* krahVAHT'

bedbug *n.* клоп *m.* klohp

bedroom *n.* спальня *f.* SPAHL'nyah

bee *n.* пчела *f.* pchehLAH

beef *n.* говядина *f.* gahVYAHdeenah

beer *n.* пиво *nt.* PEEvah

beet *n.* свёкла *f.* SVYOHKlah

beet soup *n.* свекольник *m.* sveeKOHL'neek

before, formerly *adv.* прежде PRYEHZHdyeh

before, in front of *prep.* перед/до PYEHreet/doh

begin *v.* начать naCHAHT'

beginning *n.* начало *nt.* nahCHAHlah

behind; for; after *prep.* за zah

belief *n.* вера *f.* VYEHrah

believe *v.* верить VYEHreet'

bell *n.* колокол *m.* KOHlahkahl

belt; waist *n.* пояс *m.* POHees

bench *n.* скамейка *f.* skahMYEHYkah

berries *n.* ягоды *pl.* YEAHgahdih

better *comp.* лучше LOOCHscheh

between *prep.* между MYEHZHdoo

beware *adv.* осторожно ahstahROHZnah

Bible *n.* библия *f.* BEEbleeyah

bicycle *n.* велосипед *m.* veelahseePYEHT

big *adj.* большой bahl'SHOY

bill *n.* счёт *m.* shchoht

billion *n.* миллиард *m.* meeleeAHRT

birch *n.* берёза *f.* beerYOHzah

bird *n.* птица *f.* PTEEtsah

birth *n.* рождение *nt.* rahzhDYEHneeyeh

birthday *n.* день рождения *m.* dyehn' rahzhDYEHneeyah

bitter *adj.* горький GOHR'keey

black *adj.* чёрный CHOHRnihy

blackberries *n.* ежевика *pl.* yeezhehVEEkah

black market *n.* чёрный рынок *m.* CHOHRnihy RIHNahk

blackmarketeer *n.* фарцовщик *m.* fahrTSOHFshcheek

bladder *n.* мочевой пузырь *m.* mahcheeVOY poozIHR'

blanket *n.* одеяло *nt.* ahdeeYAHlah

bleed *v.* кровоточить krahvahtahCHEET'

blessing *n.* благословение *nt.* blahgahslahVYEHneeyeh

blonde *n.* блондин/блондинка *m./f.* blahnDEEN/ blahnDEENkah

blood *n.* кровь *f.* krohf'

blood pressure *n.* давление *nt.* dahvLYEHneeyeh

blouse *n.* блузка *f.* BLOOSkah

blue *adj.* синий SEEneey

blueberries *n.* черника *pl.* chehrNEEkah

boat *n.* пароход *m.* pahrahKHOT

body *n.* тело *nt.* TYEHlah

boiled *adj.* варёный vahRYOHnihy

bone *n.* кость *f.* kohst'

book *n.* книга *f.* KNEEgah

bookstore *n.* книжный магазин *m.* KNEEZHnihy mahgahZEEN

boots *n.* сапоги *pl.* sahpahGEE

border *n.* граница *f.* grahNEEtsah

boring *adj.* скучный SKOOCHnihy

both *pron.* оба OHbah

bottle *n.* бутылка *f.* booTIHLkah

boulevard *n.* вода *m.* bool'VAHR

bowl *n.* миска *f.* MEESkah

box *n.* коробка/ящик *f./m.* kahROHPkah/YAHshcheek

boy *n.* мальчик *m.* MAHL'cheek

bra *n.* бюстгальтер *m.* byoozGAHL'teer

brain *n.* мозг *m.* mohsk

brakes *n.* тормоза *f.* tahrmahZAH

brave *adj.* смелый SMYEHlihy

bread *n.* хлеб *m.* khlyehp

break *n.* перерыв *m.* peereeRIHF

break *v.* сломать slahMAHT'

breakdown (car) *n.* авария *f.* ahVAHreeyah

breakfast *n.* завтрак *m.* ZAHFtrahk

breakfast *v.* завтракать ZAHFtrahkaht'

breathe *v.* дышать dihSHAHT'

breathing *n.* дыхание *nt.* dihKHAHneeyeh

bribe *n.* взятка *f.* VZYAHTkah

bride *n.* невеста *f.* neeVYEHStah

bridge *n.* мост *m.* mohst

brief *adv.* недолго neeDOHLgah

briefcase *n.* портфель *m.* pahrtFYEHL'

bright *adj.* яркий YAHRkeey

British *adj.* английский ahngLEEYskeey

broadcast *n.* передача *f.* peereeDAHchah
brother *n.* брат *m.* braht
brother-in-law *n.* зять *m.* zyaht'
brown *adj.* коричневый kahREECHneevihy
bruise *n.* синяк *m.* seenYAHK
brunette *n.* брюнет/брюнетка *m./f.* bryooNYEHT/
  bryooNYEHTkah
brush *n.* щётка *f.* SHCHOHTkah
bucket *n.* ведро *nt.* veedROH
building *n.* здание *nt.* ZDAHneeyeh
burn *v.* жечь zhehch
bus *n.* автобус *m.* ahfTOHboos
bus stop *n.* остановка *f.* ahstahNOHFkah
business *adj.* деловой deelahVOY
business *n.* бизнес *m.* BEEZnes
businessman *n.* бизнесмен *m.* beeznehsMYEHN
business trip *n.* командировка *f.*
  kahmahndeeROHFkah
businesswoman *n.* бизнесменка *f.*
  beeznehsMYEHNkah
busy *adj.* занятый ZAHNyahtihy
but *conj.* но noh
butter *n.* масло *nt.* MAHSlah
button *n.* пуговица *f.* POOgahveetsah
buy *v.* купить kooPEET'
by; near *prep.* близко BLEESkah
by heart *adv.* наизусть naheeZOOST'

C

cabbage *n.* капуста *f.* kahPOOStah
cabbage soup *n.* щи *pl.* shchee

café *n.* кафе *nt.* kahFEH

cake *n.* торт *m.* tohrt

call *v.* позвонить pahzvahNEET'

call, name *v.* называть nahzihVAHT'

calm *adj.* спокойный spahKOYnihy

camel *n.* верблюд *m.* veerBLYOOT

camera *n.* фотоаппарат *m.* fohtahahpahRAHT

camp *n.* лагерь *m.* LAHgeer'

campfire *n.* костёр *m.* kahsTYOHR

camping *n.* кемпинг *m.* KYEHMpeeng

can *v.* мочь mohch'

Canadian *adj.* канадский kahNAHTskeey

Canadian *n.* канадец/канадка *m./f.*
kahNAHdeets/kahNAHTkah

candle *n.* свеча *f.* sveeCHAH

candy *n.* конфеты *pl.* kahnFYEHtih

canned goods *n.* консервы *pl.* kahnSYEHRvih

can opener *n.* консервный нож *m.*
kahnSYEHRVnihy nohsh

capital *n.* столица *f.* stahLEEtsah

car *n.* автомобиль/машина *m./f.*
ahftahmahBEEL'/mahSHEEnah

card *n.* карточка *f.* KAHRTahchkah

care *n.* забота *f.* zahBOHtah

careful *adv.* осторожно ahstahROHZHnah

careless *adj.* небрежный neeBRYEHZHnihy

carnation *n.* гвоздика *f.* gvahzDEEkah

carrot *n.* марковь *f.* mohrKOHF'

carry *v.* нести nehsTEE

cartoon *n.* мультфильм *m.* mool'tFEEL'M

cashier *n.* кассир *m.* kahSEER

cassette *n.* кассета *f.* kahSYEHtah

cast *n.* гипс *m.* geeps
cat *n.* кошка *f.* KOHSHkah
catch *v.* ловить lahVEET'
cathedral *n.* собор *m.* sahBOHR
caution *v.* берегись beereeGEES'
caviar *n.* икра *f.* eekRAH
cavity *n.* дупло *nt.* doopLOH
ceiling *n.* потолок *m.* pahtahLOHK
cemetery *n.* кладбище *nt.* KLAHTbeeshcheh
center *n.* центр *m.* tsehntr
century *n.* век *m.* vehk
certainly *adv.* безусловно beezoosLOHVnah
chain *n.* цепь *m.* tsehp'
chair *n.* стул *m.* stool
champagne *n.* шампанское *nt.*
  shahmPAHNskahyeh
change (coins) *n.* сдача *f.* ZDAHchah
check (monetary) *n.* счёт/чек *m.* shchoht/chehk
cheek *n.* щека *f.* shchehKAH
cheerful *adj.* бодрый BOHdrihy
cheese *n.* сыр *m.* sihr
cherries (sour) *n.* вишня *pl.* VEESHnyah
cherries (sweet) *n.* черешня *pl.* chehRYEIISHnyah
chess *n.* шахматы *pl.* SHAHKHmahtih
chest *n.* грудь *f.* groot'
chicken *n.* курица *f.* KOOreetsah
chief, boss *n.* начальник *m.* nahCHAHL'neek
child *n.* ребёнок *m.* reeBYOHnahk
children *n.* дети *pl.* DYEHTee
children's *adj.* детский DYEHTskeey
china *n.* фарфор *m.* fahrFOHR

---

chocolate *n.* шоколад *m.* shahkahLAHT
choice *n.* выбор *m.* VIHbahr
choir *n.* хор *m.* khohr
Christmas *n.* Рождество *nt.* rahzheestVOH
church *n.* церковь *f.* TSEHRkahf'
church service *n.* служба *f.* SLOOSHbah
cigar *n.* сигара *f.* seeGAHrah
cigarette *n.* сигарета *f.* seegahRYEHtah
cigarette lighter *n.* зажигалка *f.* zahzheeGAHLkah
circle *n.* круг *m.* krook
circus *n.* цирк *m.* tseerk
circular *adj.* круглый KROOGlihy
citizen *n.* гражданин/гражданка *m./f.*
   grahzhdahNEEN/grahzDAHNkah
citizenship *n.* гражданство *nt.* grahzhDAHNSTvah
city *n.* город *m.* GOHraht
civil *adj.* гражданский grahzhDAHNskeey
classical *adj.* классический klahSEECHehskeey
clean *adj.* чистый CHEEStihy
cleaning lady *n.* уборщица *f.* ooBOHRshcheetsah
clear, distinct *adj.* чёткий CHOHTkeey
clearly *adv.* ясно YAHSnah
clinic *n.* поликлиника *f.* pahleeKLEEneekah
clip-on earrings *n.* клипсы *pl.* KLEEPsih
cloakroom *n.* гардероб *m.* gahrdeeROHP
cloakroom attendant *n.* гардеробщик/
   гардеробщица *m./f.* gahrdeeROHPshcheek/
   gahrdeeROHPshcheetsah
close by *adv.* недалеко needahleeKOH
closed *adj.* закрытый zahKRIHtihy
closet *n.* шкаф *m.* shkahf

clothes *n.* одежда *f.* ahDYEHZHdah

coast *n.* берег *m.* BYEHreek

coat *n.* пальто *nt.* pahl'TOH

coat-check ticket *n.* номерок *m.* nahmeeROHK

cockroach *n.* таракан *m.* tahrahKAHN

cocoa *n.* какао *nt.* kahKAHoh

cod *n.* треска *f.* trehsKAII

coffee *n.* кофе *nt.* KOHfyeh

cognac *n.* коньяк *m.* kahn'YAHK

coin *n.* монета *f.* mahNYEHtah

cold *adj.* холодный khahLOHDnihy

cold (head) *n.* простуда *f.* prahsTOOdah

collection *n.* сбор *m.* zbohr

color *n.* цвет *m.* tsvyeht

colorless *adj.* бесцветный beesTSVEHTnihy

comb *n.* гребёнка *f.* grebYOHNkah

comedy *n.* комедия *f.* kahMYEHdeeyah

comfortable *adj.* удобный ooDOHBnihy

communal *adj.* коммунальный kahmoo-NAHL'nihy

compact disk *n.* компакт-диски *m.* kahm-PAHKT-deeskee

competition *n.* соревнование *nt.* sahreevnahVAHneeyeh

complaint *n.* жалоба *f.* ZHAHlahbah

completion, end *n.* окончание *nt.* ahkahnCHAHneeyeh

completely *adv.* совершенно sahveerSHEHNnah

complex, difficult *adj.* сложный SLOHZHnihy

complication *n.* осложнение *nt.* ahslahzhNYEHneey

composer *n.* композитор *m.* kahmpahZEEtahr

computer *n.* компьютер *m.* kahmp'YOOteer

comrade *n.* товарищ *m.* tahVAHReeshch

concert *n.* концерт *m.* kahnTSEHRT

conductor (music) *n.* дирижёр *m.* deereeZHOHR

confirmation *n.* подтверждение *nt.* pahttveerzh-DYEHneeyeh

congratulate *v.* поздравлять pahzdrahvLYAHT'

constant *adj.* постоянный pahstahYAHnihy

constipation *n.* запор *m.* zahPOHR

consulate *n.* консульство *nt.* KOHNsool'stvah

contact lens *n.* контактная линза *f.* kahnTAHKTnahyah LEENzah

contemporary *adj.* современный sahvreeMYEHNnihy

contraceptive *n.* презерватив *m.* preezeervahTEEF

contract *n.* договор *m.* dahgahVOHR

controversial *adj.* спорный SPOHRnihy

convenience *n.* удобство *nt.* ooDOHBSTvah

conversation *n.* разговор *m.* rahzgahVOHR

cook *n.* повар *m.* POHvahr

cook, boil *v.* варить vahREET'

cookie *n.* печенье *nt.* peeCHEHN'yeh

cool *adj.* прохладный prahkhLAHDnihy

corkskrew *n.* штопор *m.* SHTOHpahr

corner *n.* угол *m.* OOgahl

correct *adj.* правильный PRAHVeel'nihy

correction *n.* поправка *f.* pahPRAHFkah

correspondence *n.* переписка *f.* peereePEESkah

cottage *n.* дача *f.* DAHchah

cotton *adj.* хлопчатобумажный khlahpchahtahbooMAHZHnihy

cough *n.* кашель *f.* KAHshehl'

country *n.* страна *f.* strahNAH

countryside *n.* деревня *f.* deeRYEHVnyah

coupon *n.* талон *m.* tahLOHN

courage *n.* мужество *nt.* MOOZHehstvah

cousin *n* двоюродный брат/двоюродная сестра *m./f.* dvahYOOrahdnihy braht/dvaYOOrahdnahyah seestrah

cranberries *n.* клюква *pl.* KLYOOKvah

crazy, mad *adj.* сумасшедший soomahSHEHTsheey

cream (dairy) *n.* сливки *pl.* SLEEFkee

cream (lotion) *n.* крем *m.* kryehm

creative work *n.* творчество *nt.* TVOHRchehstvah

credit card *n.* кредитная карточка *f.* kreeDEETnahyah KAHRtahchkah

crime *n.* преступление *nt.* preestoopLYEHneeyeh

crisis *n.* кризис *m.* KREEzees

crooked *adj.* кривой kreeVOY

cross *n.* крест *m.* kryehst

crosswalk *n.* переход *m.* peereeKHOHT

crowd *n.* толпа *f.* tahlPAH

crowded *adj.* тесный TYEHSnihy

cruel *adj.* жестокий zhehsTOHkeey

cruise *n.* круиз *m.* krooEEZ

culture *n.* культура *f.* kool'TOOrah

cup *n.* чашка *f.* CHAHSHkah

curious *adj.* любопытный lyoobahPIHTnihy

current *adj.* актуальный ahktooAHL'nihy

curtain *n.* занавес *m.* ZAHnahvees

customer *n.* покупатель *m.* pahkooPAHteel'

customs, habits *n.* нравы *pl.* NRAHvih

customs charge, duty *n.* пошлина *f.* POHSHleenah

---

customs official *n.* таможеннник *m.*
tahMOHzheeneek

cut, sliced *adj.* резаный RYEHZahnihy

cute, sweet *adj.* миленький MEEleen'keey

D

daily *adj.* ежедневный yeezhehdNYEHVnihy

dairy *n.* молочная *f.* mahLOHCHnahyah

dance *n.* танец *m.* TAHneets

dangerous *adj.* опасный ahPAHSnihy

dark *adj.* тёмный TYOHMnihy

daughter *n.* дочь *f.* dohch'

daughter-in-law *n.* невестка *f.* neeVEYHSTkah

dawn; daybreak *n.* рассвет *m.* rahsSVYEHT

day *n.* день *m.* dyehn'

day after tomorrow *adv.* послезавтра
pahsleeZAHFtrah

day before yesterday *adv.* позавчера
pahzahfchehRAH

day off *n.* выходной день *m.* vihkhahdNOY dyehn'

daytime *adj.* дневной dneevNOY

dead *adj.* мёртвый MYOHRTvihy

deaf *adj.* глухой glooKHOY

death *n.* смерть *f.* smyehrt'

deception, fraud *n.* обман *m.* ahbMAHN

decision *n.* решение *nt.* reeSHEHneeyeh

decoration *n.* украшение *nt.* ookrahSHEHneeyeh

decrease *n.* уменьшение *nt.* oomeen'SHEHneeyeh

deep *adj.* глубокий glooBOHkeey

deficit *n.* дефицит *m.* deefeeTSEEt

definite *adj.* определёный ahpreedeeLYOHNnihy

delay, tardiness *n.* опоздание *nt.*
  ahpahzDAHneeyeh
deliberately *adv.* нарочно nahROHCHcnah
dentist *n.* зубной врач *m.* zoobNOY vrahch
denture *n.* протез *m.* prahTEHS
deodorant *n.* дезодоратор *m.* deezahdahRAHtahr
department *n.* отдел *m.* ahdDYEHL
department store *n.* универмаг *m.*
  ooneeveerMAHK
departure (plane) *n.* отлёт *m.* ahtLYOHT
departure (train) *n.* отход *m.* ahtKHOHT
description *n.* описание *nt.* ahpeeSAHneeyeh
dessert *n.* десерт *m.* deeSYEHRT
detail *n.* подробность *f.* pahdROHBnahst'
detour *n.* обход *m.* ahpKHOHT
development (film) *n.* проявление *nt.*
  praheevLYEH neeyeh
devil *n.* чёрт *m.* chohrt
diabetes *n.* диабет *m.* deeahBYEHT
diagnosis *n.* диагноз *m.* deeAHGnahs
diamond *n.* бриллиант *m.* breeleeAHNT
diaper *n.* подгузник *m.* pahdGOOZneek
diarrhea *n.* понос *m.* pahNOHS
dictionary *n.* словарь *m.* slahVAHR'
diet *n.* диета *f.* deeYEHtah
difference *n.* разница *f.* RAHSneetsah
different *adj.* разный RAHZnihy
differently *adv.* иначе eeNAHcheh
difficult *adj.* трудный TROODnihy
diner *n.* обед/ужин *m.* ahbYEHT/OOzheen
dining hall *n.* столовая *f.* stahLOHvahyah
director (manager) *n.* директор *m.* deeRYEHKtahr

director (theater) *n.* режиссёр *m.* reezhehSYOHR

dirt *n.* грязь *f.* gryahs'

dirty *adj.* грязный GRYAHZnihy

disability *n.* инвалидность *f.* eenvahLEEDnahst'

disabled person *n.* инвалид *m.* eenvahLEET

dish, food; course *n.* блюдо *f.* BLYOOdah

dishes *n.* посуда *f.* pahSOOdah

dishonest *adj.* несчестный neeCHEHSnihy

disinfect *v.* дезинфицировать
deezeenfeeTSEERahvaht'

dissatisfied *adj.* недовольный needahVOHL'nihy

distance *n.* расстояние *nt.* rahstahYAHneeyeh

diverse *adj.* многообразный
mnohgahahbRAHZnihy

do *v.* делать DYEHlaht'

dock *n.* пристань *f.* PREEstahn'

doctor *n.* врач *m.* vrahch

dog *n.* собака *f.* sahBAHkah

doll, puppet *n.* кукла *f.* KOOKlah

dollar *n.* доллар *m.* DOHlahr

door *n.* дверь *f.* dvyehr'

doorman *n.* швейцар *m.* shveyTSAHR

dormitory *n.* общежитие *nt.*
ahpshchehZHEEteeyeh

dosage *n.* дозировка *f.* dahzeeROHFkah

double occupancy *adj.* двуспальный
dvooSPAHL'nihy

doubt *n.* сомнение *nt.* sahmNYEHneeyeh

doughnut *n.* пончик *m.* POHNcheek

down (location) *adv.* внизу vneeZOO

dozen *n.* дюжина *f.* DYOOzheenah

drawing *n.* рисование *nt.* reesaVAHneeyeh

dress *n.* платье *nt.* PLAHT'yeh
drink *v.* пить peet'
drink *n.* напиток *m.* nahPEEtahk
drive *v.* ездить/ехать YEHZdeet'/YEHkhaht'
driver *n.* водитель *m.* vahDEEteel'
driver's license *n.* водительские права *pl.*
vahDEEteel'skeeyeh prahVAH
drugstore *n.* аптека *f.* ahpTYEHkah
drunk *adj.* пьяный P'YAHnihy
drunkard *n.* пьяница *f.* PYAHneetsah
dry *adj.* сухой sooKHOY
dry cleaning *n.* химчистка *f.* kheemCHEESTkah
duty (customs) *n.* пошлина *f.* POHSHleenah
duty-free *adj.* беспошлинный beesPOHSHleenihy
dye; hair coloring *n.* окраска *f.* ahKRAHSkah

E

ear *n.* ухо *nt.* OOkhah
earlier *adv.* раньше RAHN'sheh
early *adj.* ранний RAHNneey
earrings *n.* серьги *pl.* SYEHR'gee
easily *adv.* легко leekhKOH
east *n.* восток *m.* vahsTOHK
eastern *adj.* восточный vahsTOHCHnihy
Easter; Passover *n.* пасха *f.* PAHSkhah
easy *adj.* лёгкий LYOHKHkeey
eat *v.* есть yehst'
education *n.* образование *nt.* ahbrahzahVAHneeyeh
egg *n.* яйцо *nt.* yayTSOH
eggplant *n.* баклажан *m.* bahklahzhAHN
elbow *n.* локоть *m.* LOHkaht'

elderly *adj.* пожилой pahzheeLOY

elections *n.* выборы *pl.* VIHbahrih

electrical socket *n.* розетка *f.* rahZYEHTkah

electricity *n.* электричество *nt.*
ehleekTREEchehstvah

elevator *n.* лифт *m.* leeft

embassy *n.* посольство *nt.* pahSOHL'stvah

embroidered *adj.* вишитый VIHsheetihy

émigré *n.* эмигрант *m.* ehmeeGRANHT

emigration *n.* эмиграция *f.* ehmeeGRAHtseeyah

empty *adj.* пустой poosTOY

end *n.* конец *m.* kahNYEHTS

engineer *n.* инжинер *m.* eenzheeNYEHR

English, British *adj.* английский ahngLEEYskeey

English *n.* англичанин/англичанка *m./f.*
ahngleeCHAHneen/ angleeCHAHNkah

enjoy *v.* нравиться NRAHveetsah

enjoy oneself *v.* веселиться veeseeLEEtsah

enough *adv.* достаточно dahsTAHtahchnah

enter *v.* входить fkhahDEET'

entrance *n.* вход *m.* fkhoht

envelope *n.* конверт *m.* kahnVYEHRT

equal *adj.* равный RAHVnihy

escalator *n.* эскалатор *m.* ehskahLAHtahr

European *adj.* европейский yeevrahPEYskeey

evening *adj.* вечерний veeCHEHRneey

evening *n.* вечер *m.* VYEHchehr

every *adj.* каждый KAHZHdihy

everything *n.* всё *nt.* fsyoh

everywhere *adv.* везде veezDYEH

evil *adj.* злой zloy

exactly *adv.* точно TOHCHnah
examination, checkup *n.* осмотр *m.* ahsMOHTR
example *n.* пример *m.* preeMYEHR
except for *prep.* кроме KROHmyeh
exchange *n.* обмен *m.* ahbMYEHN
exchange *v.* обменять ahbmeeNYAHT'
excursion *n.* экскурсия *f.* ehksKOORseeyah
excuse, pardon *v.* извинять eezveeNYAHT'
exercise *n.* упражнение *nt.* ooprahzhNYEHneeyeh
exhaustion *n.* утомление *nt.* ootahmLYEHneeyeh
exhibition *n.* выставка *f.* VIHstahfkah
exit *n.* выход *m.* VIHkhaht
expenses *n.* расходы *pl.* rahsKHOHdih
expensive, valuable *adj.* дорогой dahrahGOY
experience *n.* опыт *m.* OHpiht
explanation *n.* объяснение *nt.*
  ahb"eesNYEHneeyeh
express *n.* экспресс *m.* ehksPRYEHS
eye *n.* глаз *m.* glahs
eyebrow *n.* бровь *f.* brohf'
eyelash *n.* ресница *f.* reesNEEtsah
eyesight *n.* зрение *nt.* ZRYEHneeyeh

F

fabric *n.* ткань *f.* tkahn'
face *n.* лицо *nt.* leeTSOH
fact *n.* факт *m.* fahkt
factory *n.* завод *m.* zahVOHT
failure *n.* неудача *f.* nyehooDACHah
fake *adj.* фальшивый fahl'SHEEvihy
fall, autumn *n.* осень *f.* OHseen'

fall *v.* падать PAHdaht'
false *adj.* ложный LOHZHnihy
family *n.* семья *f.* seem'YAH
famous *adj.* знаменитый znahmeeNEEtihy
fan *n.* веер/вентилятор *m.*
  VYEHeer/veenteeLYAHtahr
faraway *adv.* далеко dahleeKOH
farewell *n.* прощай *m.* prahSHCHAY
farm *n.* ферма *f.* FYEHRmah
farther *adv.* дальше DAHL'sheh
fashion *n.* мода *f.* MOHdah
fashionable *adj.* модный MOHDnihy
fast *adv.* быстро BIHStrah
fat *adj.* толстый TOHLstihy
fat *n.* жир *m.* zheer
fate *n.* судьба *f.* soot'BAH
father *n.* отец *m.* ahTYEHTS
fatherland *n.* отечество *nt.* ahTYEHcheshtvah
faucet *n.* кран *m.* krahn
fear, to be afraid *v.* бояться bahYAHTsah
fear *n.* страх *m.* strahkh
feature *n.* черта *f.* chehrTAH
feel *v.* чувствовать CHOOSTvahvaht'
feeling *n.* чувство *nt.* CHOOSTvah
feel sorry for *v.* жалеть zhahLYEHT'
feminine *adj.* женский ZHEHNskeey
fever *n.* жар *f.* zhahr
few *adv.* несколько NEEskahl'kah
fight *v.* биться BEETsah
fight *n.* борьба *f.* bahr'BAH
filling (tooth) *n.* пломба *f.* PLOHMbah

film *n.* плёнка *f.* PLYOHNkah

finally *n.* наконец *m.* nahkahnYEHTS

find *v.* найти nayTEE

fine *n.* штраф *f.* shtrahf

finger *n.* палец *m.* PAHleets

fire *n.* пожар *m.* pahZHAHR

first-aid kit *n.* аптечка *f.* ahpTYEHCHkah

fish *n.* рыба *f.* RIHBah

fishing pole *n.* удочка *f.* OOdahchkah

flashlight *n.* карманный фонарь *m.* kahrMAHnihy fahNAHR'

flight *n.* полёт *m.* pahLYOHT

flood *n.* наводнение *nt.* nahvahdNYEHneeyeh

floor, story *n.* этаж *m.* ehTAHSH

flounder *n.* камбала *f.* KAHMbahlah

flour *n.* мука *f.* mooKAH

flower *n.* цветок *m.* tsveeTOHK

flu *n.* грипп *m.* greep

fly *n.* муха *f.* MOOKhah

fog *n.* туман *m.* tooMAHN

food *n.* еда *f.* yeeDAH

fool *n.* дурак/дура *m./f.* dooRAHK/DOOrah

foot (on) *adv.* пешком peeshKOHM

foot, leg *n.* нога *f.* nahGAH

for *prep.* для dlyah

for example *adv.* например nahprecMYEHR

for some reason *conj.* почему-то pahcheeMOOtah

for the first time *adv.* впервые fpeerVIHyeh

forbid *v.* запрещать zahpreeSHCHAHT'

forbidden *adj.* воспрещён vahspreeSHCHYOHN

foreign *adj.* иностранный eenahsTRAHnihy

foreigner *n.* иностранец/иностранка *m./f.*
eenahsTRAHneets/ eenahsTRAHNkah

forest *n.* лес *m.* lyehs

forever *adv.* навсегда nahfseegDAH

forget *v.* забывать zahbihVAHT'

forgotten *adj.* забытый zahBIHTihy

fork *n.* вилка *f.* VEELkah

form, blank; survey *n.* анкета *f.* ahnKYEHtah

former *adj.* прежний/бывший PRYEHZHneey
/BIHFsheey

forward, ahead *adv.* вперёд fpeeRYOHT

found, to be located *v.* находиться
nahkhahDEETsah

fragile ; brittle *adj.* хрупкий KHROOPkeey

free, vacant *adj.* свободный svahBOHDnihy

freedom *n.* свобода *f.* svahBOHdah

free of charge *adj.* бесплатный beesPLAHTnihy

fresh *adj.* свежий SVYEHzheey

fried eggs *n.* яичница *f.* yahEECHneetsah

friend *n.* друг/подруга *m./f.* drook/pahDROOgah

friendship *n.* дружба *f.* DROOSHbah

from *prep.* от oht

front *adj.* передний peeRYEHDneey

frost *n.* мороз *m.* mahROHS

frozen *adj.* замороженный zahmahROHzhehnihy

fruit *n.* фрукт *m.* frookt

fry *v.* жарить ZHAHreet'

full, complete *adj.* полный POHLnihy

full, satiated *adj.* сытый SIHtihy

funny *adj.* смешной smeeshNOY

fur *adj.* меховой meekhahVOY

fur *n.* мех *m.* myehkh

fur coat *n.* шуба *f.* SHOObah

fur hat *n.* меховая шапка *f.* meekhahVAHyah
SHAHPkah

furniture *n.* мебель *f.* MYEHbeel'

future *adj.* будущий BOOdooshcheeyeh

G

game *n.* игра *f.* eegRAH

garage *n.* гараж *m.* gahRAHSH

garden *n.* сад *m.* saht

garlic *n.* чеснок *m.* chehsNOHK

garnet *n.* гранат *m.* grahNAHT

gas *n.* бензин *f.* beenZEEN

gastritis *n.* гастрит *m.* gahsTREET

gate *n.* ворота *f.* vahROHtah

generous *adj.* щедрый SHCHEHDrihy

genitals *n.* половые органы *pl.* pahlahVIHyeh
OHRgahnih

German *adj.* немецкий nyeMYEHTSkeey

German *n.* немец/немка *m./f.*
NYEHmets/NYEHMkah

get up *v.* вставать fstahVAHT'

gift *n.* подарок *m.* pahDAHrahk

girl *n.* девочка *f.* DYEHvahchkah

give *v.* давать dahVAHT'

glad, pleased *adj.* рад raht

glass (drinking) *n.* стакан *m.* stahKAHN

glass *n.* стекло *nt.* steekLOH

glasses *n.* очки *pl.* ahchKEE

gloves *n.* перчатки *pl.* peerCHAHTkee

go, walk *v.* ходить/идти khahDEET'/EETtee

God *n.* бог *m.* bohkh

gold *adj.* золотой zahlahTOY

gold *n.* золото *nt.* ZOHlahtah

good *adj.* хороший khahROHsheey

good-bye *interj.* до свидания dahsveeDAHneeyah

government *n.* правительство *nt.* prahVEEteel'stvah

graduate student *n.* аспирант/аспирантка *m./f.* ahspeeRAHNT/ ahspeeRAHNTkah

grammar *n.* грамматика *f.* grahmAHteekah

granddaughter *n.* внучка *f.* VNOOCHkah

grandfather *n.* дедушка *f.* DYEHdooshkah

grandmother *n.* бабушка *f.* BAHbooshkah

grandson *n.* внук *m.* vnook

grapes *n.* виноград *pl.* veenahGRAHT

grapefruit *n.* грейпфрут *m.* GREYPfroot

grass *n.* трава *f.* trahVAH

grave *n.* могила *f.* mahGEElah

gray *adj.* серый SYEHrihy

greasy *adj.* жирный ZHEERnihy

great *adj.* великий veeLEEkeey

greedy *adj.* жадный ZHAHDniy

grief *n.* горе *nt.* GOHRyeh

grocery store *n.* гастроном *m.* gahstrahNOHM

ground, earth *n.* земля *f.* zeemLYAH

group *n.* группа *f.* GROOPah

guard *n.* караул *m.* kahrahOOL

guest *n.* гость *f.* gohst'

guide *n.* гид *m.* geet

guidebook *n.* путеводитель *f.* pooteevahDEEteel'

guilt *n.* вина *f.* veeNAH

guilty *adj.* виноватый veenahVAHtihy

guitar *n.* гитара *f.* geeTAHrah

gynecologist *n.* гинеколог *m.* geeneeKOHlahk

gypsy *n.* цыган/цыганка *m./f.*
tsihGAHN/tsihGAHNkah

H

hair *n.* волосы *pl.* VOHlahsih

haircut *n.* стрижка *f.* STREESHkah

hairdo *n.* причёска *f.* preeCHOHSkah

hairdresser/barber *n.* парикмахер *m.*
pahreekMAHKHeer

hairdryer *n.* фен *m.* fyehn

half *n.* половина *f.* pahlahVEEnah

half hour *n.* полчаса *f.* pohlcheeSAH

ham *n.* ветчина *f.* veecheeNAH

hand, arm *n.* рука *f.* rooKAH

handshake *n.* пожатие *n.* pahZHAHteeyeh

hanger *n.* вешалка *f.* VYEHshahlkah

happy, lucky *adj.* счастливый shahsLEEvihy

hard *adj.* твёрдый TVYOHRdiy

hard currency *n.* валюта *f.* vahLYOOtah

harmful *adj.* вредный VRYEHDnihy

hat *n.* шапка *f.* SHAHPkah

he *pron.* он ohn

head *n.* голова *f.* gahlahVAH

headache *n.* головная боль *f.* gahlahvNAHyah
bohl'

head cold *n.* насморк *m.* NAHsmahrk

health *n.* здоровье *nt.* zdahROHV'yeh

healthy *adj.* здоровый zdahROHvihy

heart *n.* сердце *nt.* SYEHRtseh
heart attack *n.* сердечный припадок *m.*
　seerDYEHCHnihy preePAHdahk
heavy *adj.* тяжёлый teeZHOHLihy
headgehog *n.* ёж *m.* yohsh
hello *interj.* здравствуйте ZDRAHSTvooytyeh
hello (on the phone) *interj.* алло ahLOH
help *n.* помощь *f.* POHmahshch'
hemorrhoids *n.* геморрой *m.* geemahROY
her *pro.* её yeeYOH
here *adv.* тут/здесь toot/zdyehs'
here is *part.* вот voht
hernia *n.* грыжа *f.* GRIHzhah
hero *n.* герой *m.* geeROY
herring *n.* сельдь *f.* syehl't'
hi *interj.* привет preeVYEHT
hidden *adj.* скрытый SKRIHtihy
hide *v.* скрыть skriht'
high blood pressure *n.* гипертония *f.*
　geepeertahNEEyah
high, tall *adj.* высокий vihSOHkeey
highway *n.* шоссе *nt.* shahSEH
hip *n.* бедро *nt.* beedROH
his *pro.* его yeeVOH
history, story *n.* история *f.* eesTOHreeyah
hockey *n.* хоккей *m.* khahKEY
hold, keep *v.* держать deerZHAHT'
hole *n.* дыра *f.* dihRAH
holiday *n.* праздник *m.* PRAHSDneek
holy, sacred *adj.* святой sveeTOY
homeland *n.* родина *f.* ROHdeenah

homosexuality *n.* гомосексуализм *m.* gohmahseeksooahLEEZM

honest *adj.* чистый CHESnihy

honey *n.* мёд *m.* myoht

hope *n.* надежда *f.* nahDYEHZHdah

horrible *adj.* ужасный ooZHAHSnihy

horse *n.* лошадь *f.* LOHshaht'

horseradish *n.* крем *m.* khryehn

hospital *n.* больница *f.* bahl'NEEtsah

hot, intense *adj.* горячий gahRYAHcheey

hot (weather) *adj.* жаркая (погода) ZHAHRkahyah (pahGOHdah)

hotel *n.* гостиница *f.* gahsTEEneetsah

hotel room *n.* номер *m.* NOHmeer

hour *n.* час *m.* chahs

house *n.* дом *m.* dohm

housewife *n.* домохозяйка *f.* dohmahkahZYAYkah

how *adv.* как kahk

however, but *conj.* однако ahdNAHkah

how far *adv.* как далеко kahk dahleeKOH

how long *adv.* как долго kahk DOHLgah

how much *adv.* сколько SKOHL'kah

humid *adj.* влажный VLAHZHnihy

humor *n.* юмор *m.* YOOmahr

hundred *num.* сто stoh

hundredth *num.* сотный SOHTihy

hunger *n.* голод *m.* GOHlaht

hungry *adj.* голодный gahLOHDnihy

husband *n.* муж *m.* moosh

I

I *pro.* я yah

ice *n.* лёд *m.* lyoht

ice cream *n.* мороженое *nt.* mahROHzhehnahyeh

icon *n.* икона *f.* eeKOHnah

iconostasis *n.* иконостас *m.* eekohnnahSTAHS

idea *n.* идея *f.* eeDYEHyah

identical *adj.* одинаковый ahdeeNAHkahvihy

identification *n.* удостоверение *nt.*
  oodahstahveeRYEHneeyeh

if, when *conj.* если YEHSlee

if, whether *conj.* ли lee

ill (fall) *v.* заболеть zahbahLYEHT'

illegal *adj.* незаконый neezahKOHNnihy

illness *n.* болезнь *f.* bahLYEHZN'

impatience *n.* нетерпение *nt.* neeteerPYEHneeyeh

important *adj.* важный VAHZHnihy

impossible *adj.* невозможно neevahzMOZHnah

improper *adj.* неприличный neepreeLEECHnihy

in, at, for, to *prep.* в v

in advance *adv.* заранее zahRAHnehyeh

in front, ahead *adv.* впереди fpeereeDEE

in order to *conj.* чтобы SHTOHbih

in the distance *adv.* вдали vdahLEE

in vain *adv.* напрасно nahPRAHSnah

inaudible *adj.* неслышный neeSLIHSHnihy

incident *n.* случай *m.* SLOOchay

income *n.* доход *m.* dahKHOHT

increase *n.* увеличение *nt.* ooveeleeCHEHneeyeh

independent *adj.* самостоятельный
  sahmahstahYAHteel'nihy

indifferent *adj.* равнодушный rahvnahDOOSHnihy

indigestion *n.* расстройство желудка *nt.* rahSTROYstva zhehLOOTkah

inexpensive *adj.* дешёвый deeSHOHvihy

infection *n.* заражение *nt.* zahrahZHEHneeyeh

influential *adj.* влиятельный vleeYAHteel'nihy

injection *n.* укол *m.* ooKOHL

inscription *n.* надпись *m.* NAHTpees'

insect *n.* насекомое *nt.* nahseeKOHmahyeh

insect repellent *n.* средство от комаров *nt.* SRYEHTstvah aht kahmahROHF

inside *adv.* внутри vnooTREE

instead of *prep.* вместо VMYEHstah

instructions *n.* инструкция *f.* eenSTROOKtseeyah

interesting *adj.* интересный eenteeRYEHSnihy

intermission *n.* антракт *m.* ahnTRAHKT

internal *adj.* внутренний VNOOtreeneey

international *adj.* международный meezhdoonahROHDnihy

interpreter *n.* переводчик *m.* peereeVOHTcheek

invitation *n.* приглашение *nt.* preeglahSHEHneeyeh

iodine *n.* йод *m.* yoht

iron *n.* утюг *m.* ooTYOOK

iron *v.* гладить GLAHdeet'

island *n.* остров *m.* OHStrahf

issue, edition *n.* выпуск *m.* VIHpoosk

J

jam *n.* варенье *nt.* vahRYEHN'yeh

jar, can *n.* банка *f.* BAHNkah
jeans *n.* джинсы *pl.* DZHEENsih
Jew *n.* еврей/еврейка *m./f.* yeevREY/yeevREYkah
jewel *n.* драгоценность *f.* drahgahTSEHnahst'
jewelry *adj.* ювелирный yooveeLEERnihy
Jewish *adj.* еврейский yeevREYskeey
joke *n.* шутка *f.* SHOOTkah
journalist *n.* журналист *m.* zhoornahLEEST
juice *n.* сок *m.* sohk

K

kerchief *n.* платок *m.* plahTOHK
key *n.* ключ *m.* klyooch
kilogram *n.* килограмм *m.* keelahGRAHM
kind, good *adj.* добрый DOHBrihy
kiss *n.* поцелуй pahtsyehlOOY
kiss *v.* целовать tsyehlahVAHT'
knee *n.* колено *nt.* kahLYEHnah
knife *n.* нож *m.* nohsh
know *v.* знать znaht'
known (well) *adj.* известный eezVYEHSTnihy
kopeck *n.* копейка *f.* kahPEYkah
kosher *adj.* кошерный kahSHEHRnihy

L

ladies' *adj.* дамский DAHMskeey
lake *n.* озеро *nt.* OHzeerah
lamp *n.* лампа *f.* LAHMpah
language *n.* язык *m.* yeeZIHK
large *adj.* большой bahl'SHOY

larger, bigger *comp.* больше BOHL'sheh
last, latest *adj.* последний pahsLYEHDneey
last (sur)name *n.* фамилия *f.* fahMEEleeyah
late *adj.* поздний POHZneey
late *v.* опоздать ahpahzDAHT'
later *comp.* позже POHZHzheh
laundry, linen *n.* бельё *nt.* beel'YOH
law *n.* закон *m.* zahKOHN
lawyer *n.* адвокат *m.* ahdvahKAHT
laxative *n.* слабительное *nt.* slahBEEteel'nahyeh
leather *adj.* кожаный KOHzhahnihy
leave, go out, exit *v.* выходить vikhkhahDEET'
left *adv.* левый LYEHvihy
leg, foot *n.* нога *f.* nahGAH
legal *adj.* законный zahKOHnihy
lemon *n.* лимон *m.* leeMOHN
less *comp.* меньше MYEHN'sheh
let's *v./part.* давай dahVAY
letter *n.* письмо *nt.* pees'MOH
library *n.* библиотека *f.* beebleeahTYEHkah
life *n.* жизнь *f.* zheezn'
light *n.* свет *m.* svyeht
light bulb *n.* лампочка *f.* LAHMpahchkah
lilac *n.* сирень *f.* seeRYEHN'
line *n.* очередь *f.* OHCHehreet'
lip *n.* губа *f.* gooBAH
literature *n.* литература *f.* leeteerahTOOrah
little *adj.* маленький MAHlyehnkeey
little, not enough *adv.* мало MAHlah
live *v.* жить zheet'
local *adj.* местный MYEHSnihy

lock *n.* замок *m.* zahMOHK
long (measure) *adj.* длинный DLEEnihy
long (time) *adj.* долгий DOHLgeey
long ago *adv.* давно dahvNOH
look *v.* смотреть smahtRYEHT'
lose *v.* потерять pahteerYAHT'
loud *adj.* громкий GROHMkeey
love *v.* любить lyooBEET'
love *n.* любовь *f.* lyooBOHF'
luggage *n.* багаж *m.* bahGAHSH
lunch *n.* обед *m.* ahBYEHT
lunch *v.* обедать ahBYEHdaht'
lungs *n.* лёгкие *pl.* LYOHKHkeeyeh
luxurious *adj.* роскошный rahsKOHSHnihy

M

magazine *n.* журнал *m.* zhoorNAHL
maid *n.* горничная *f.* GOHRneechnahyah
mail, post office *n.* почта *f.* POHCHtah
mailbox *n.* почтовый ящик *m.* pahchTOHvihy
　　YAHshcheek
makeup *n.* косметика *f.* kahsMYEHteekah
man *n.* мужчина *f.* mooshCHEEnah
manager *n.* заведующий *m.*
　　zahVYEHdooyooshcheey
map *n.* карта *f.* KAHRtah
market *n.* рынок *m.* RIHnahk
married (for men) *adj.* женат zhehNAHT
married (for women) *adj.* замужем
　　ZAHmoozhehm
match *n.* спичка *f.* SPEECHkah

---

may, can *pred.* можно MOHZHnah

meat *n.* мясо *nt.* MYAHsah

meatballs *n.* тефтели *pl.* TYEHFteelee

meat loaf *n.* рулет *m.* rooLYEHT

medicine *n.* лекарство *nt.* leeKAHRstvah

meet *v.* встречать fstreeCHANT'

meeting *n.* собрание *nt.* sahBRAHneeyeh

men's *adj.* мужской mooshSKOY

menstruation *n.* менструация *f.*
  meenstrooAHtseeyah

menu *n.* меню *nt.* meenYOO

middle *adj.* средний SRYEHDneey

midnight *n.* полночь *f.* POHLnahch'

military *adj.* военный vahYEHnihy

milk *n.* молоко *nt.* mahlahKOH

million *num.* миллион meeleeOHN

minute *n.* минута *f.* meeNOOTah

mirror *n.* зеркало *nt.* ZYEHRkahlah

misfortune *n.* беда *f.* beeDAH

mistake *n.* ошибка *f.* ahSHEEPkah

mitten *n.* рукавица *f.* rookahVEEtsah

modest *adj.* скромный SKROHMnihy

monastery *n.* монастырь/лавра *f.*
  mahnnahsTIHR'/LAHVrah

money *n.* деньги *pl.* DYEHN'gee

money order *n.* денежный перевод *m.*
  DYEHneezhnihy peereeVOHT

month *n.* месяц *m.* MYEHSeets

monument *n.* памятник *m.* PAHMeetneek

moon *n.* луна *f.* looNAH

more *comp.* более/больше BOHleeyeh/BOHL'sheh

morning *adj.* утрений OOTreeneey

---

morning *n.* утро *nt.* OOTrah
Moscow *adj.* московский mahsKOHFskeey
mosquito *n.* комар *m.* kahMAHR
mother *n.* мать *f.* maht'
motorcycle *n.* мотоцикл *m.* mahtahTSEEKL
mountain *n.* гора *f.* gahRAH
mouse *n.* мышь *m.* mihsh'
mouth *n.* рот *m.* roht
movement *n.* движение *nt.* dveeZHEHneeyeh
movie *n.* фильм/кино *m.* feel'm/keeNOH
movie theater *n.* кинотеатр *m.* keenahteeAHTR
Mr. *n.* господин *m.* gahspahDEEn
Mrs. *n.* госпожа *f.* gahspahZHAH
much, a lot *adv.* много MNOHgah
muscle *n.* мускул *m.* MOOSkool
museum *n.* музей *m.* mooZEY
mushrooms *n.* грибы *pl.* greeBIH
music *n.* музыка *f.* MOOzihkah
must *v.* надо NAHdah
mustache *n.* усы *pl.* ooSIH
mustard *n.* горчица *f.* gahrCHEEtsah
mutton *n.* баранина *f.* bahRAHneenah
mystery novel *n.* детектив *m.* dehtehkTEEF

N

naked *adj.* голый GOHlihy
name (first) *n.* имя *nt.* EEMyah
name (last) *n.* фамилия *f.* fahMEEleeyah
name, title *n.* название *nt.* nahzVAHneeyeh
napkin *n.* салфетка *f.* sahlFYEHTkah

narrow *adj.* узкий OOSkeey

national, folk *adj.* народный nahROHDnihy

nationality *n.* национальность *f.*
nahtseeahNAHL'nahst'/гражданство *nt.*
GRAHZHdahnstvah

native *adj.* родной rahdNOY

nature *n.* природа *f.* preeROHdah

nausea *n.* тошнота *f.* tashnahTAH

near *adj.* близкий BLEESkeey

necessary *adj.* необходимый neeahpkhahDEEmihy

neck *n.* шея *f.* SHEHyah

necklace *n.* ожерелье *nt.* ahzheeRYEHL'yeh

needle *n.* иголка *f.* eeGOHLkah

negotiations *n.* переговоры *pl.* peereegahVOHrih

neighbor *n.* сосед/соседка *m./f.*
sahSYEHT/sahSYEHTkah

nephew *n.* племянник *m.* plehmYAHNneek

nerve *n.* нерв *m.* nyehrf

nervous, irritable *adj.* нервный NYEHRVnihy

neutral *adj.* нейтральный nyetRAHL'nihy

never *adv.* никогда neekahgDAH

new *adj.* новый NOHvihy

news *n.* известие *f.* eezVYEHSteeyeh

newspaper *n.* газета *f.* gahZYEHtah

New Year *n.* новый год *m.* NOHvihy goht

next *adj.* следующий SLYEHdooyooshcheey

nice, sweet, dear *adj.* милый MEElihy

niece *n.* племянница *f.* pleemYAHNeetsah

night *n.* ночь *f.* nohch'

no *part.* нет nyeht

noise *n.* шум *m.* shoom

noisy *adj.* шумный SHOOMnihy

nonalcoholic *adj.* безалкогольный
    beezahlkahGOHL'nihy

nonstop (of a flight) *adj.* беспосадочный
    beespahSAHdahchnihy

noon *n.* полдень *m.* POHLdyen'

no one *pron.* никто neeKTOH

normal *adj.* нормальный nahrMAHL'nihy

north *n.* север *m.* SYEHveer

northern *adj.* северный SYEHveernihy

nose *n.* нос *m.* nohs

not *part.* не nyeh

nothing *n.* ничего *nt.* neecheeVOH

notify *v.* сообщать sahahpSHCHAHT'

novel *n.* роман *m.* rahMAHN

now *adv.* сейчас sehCHAHS

no way *adv.* никак neeKAHK

number *n.* число *nt.* cheesLOH

nurse *n.* медсестра *f.* myehdseesTRAH

O

oatmeal *n.* овсянка *f.* ahfSYAHNkah

obligatory *adj.* обязательный ahbeeZAHteel'nihy

obstetrician *n.* акушёр *m.* ahkooSHOHR

of course *adv.* конечно kahnYEHSHnah

offense, insult *n.* обида *f.* ahBEEdah

offer, proposal *n.* предложение *nt.*
    preedlahZHEHneeyeh

official *n.* чиновник *m.* cheeNOHVneek

often *adv.* часто CHAHStah

ok *adv.* ладно LAHDnah

old *adj.* старый STAHrihy

olive *n.* маслина *f.* mahsLEEnah

on, in *prep.* на nah

once, one day *adv.* однажды ahdNAHZHdih

one and a half *num.* полтора pahltahRAH

one-way (ticket) *adj.* в один конец vahDEEn kahNYEHTS

onion *n.* лук *m.* look

only *adv.* только TOHL'kah

on the contrary *adv.* наоборот nahahbahROHT

on the right *adv.* направо nahPRAHvah

on time *adv.* вовремя VOHvreemyah

open *adj.* открытый ahtKRIHtihy

opera *n.* опера *f.* OHperrah

opera glasses *n.* бинокль *f.* beeNOHKL'

operator *n.* телефонистка *f.* teeleefahNEESTkah

opinion *n.* мнение *nt.* MNYEHneeyeh

opportunity *n.* возможность *f.* vahzMOHZHnahst'

opposite, facing *adv.* напротив nahPROHteef

optician *n.* оптик *m.* OPteek

or *conj.* или EElee

orange *adj.* оранжевый ahRAHNzhevihy

orange *n.* апельсин *m.* ahpeel'SEEN

orchestra *n.* оркестр *f.* ahrKYEHSTR

order *v.* заказать zahkahzAHT'

orthodox *adj.* православный pravahSLAHVnihy

other *adj.* другой drooGOY

overcast *adj.* пасмурный PAHSmoornihy

oxygen *n.* кислород *m.* keeslahROHT

P

pacifier *n.* соска *f.* SOHSkah
package *n.* посылка *f.* pahSIHLkah
page *n.* страница *f.* strahNEEtsah
pain *n.* боль *f.* bohl'
painting *n.* живопись *f.* ZHEEvahpees'
pair *n.* пара *f.* PAHrah
palace *n.* дворец *m.* dvahRYEHTS
pale *adj.* бледный BLYEHDnihy
pancake *n.* блин *m.* bleen
pants *n.* брюки *pl.* BRYOOkee
paper *n.* бумага *f.* booMAHgah
parents *n.* родители *pl.* rahDEEteelee
park *n.* парк *m.* pahrk
park *v.* парковать pahrkOHvaht'
parking lot *n.* автостоянка *f.* ahvtahstahYAHNkah
part *n.* часть *f.* chahst'
passenger *n.* пассажир *m.* pahsahZHEER
passionate *adj.* страстный STRAHSnihy
passport *n.* паспорт *m.* PAHSpahrt
past *adj.* прошлый PROHSHlihy
patient *adj.* терпеливый teerpeeLEEvihy
patient *n.* пациент *m.* pahtseeEHNT
patryonymic *n.* отчество *nt.* OHTchehstvah
pay *v.* платить plahTEET'
pay phone *n.* телефон-автомат *m.* teeleeFOHN-ahftahMAHNT
peace *n.* мир *m.* meer
peach *n.* персик *m.* PYEHRseek
pear *n.* груша *f.* GROOshah

pearl *n.* жемчуг *m.* ZHEHMchook
peas *n.* горох *pl.* gahROHKH
pediatrician *n.* педиатр *m.* peedeeAHTR
pen *m.* ручка *f.* ROOCHkah
pencil *n.* карандаш *m.* kahrahnDAHSH
penicillin *n.* пенициллин *m.* peeneetseelLEEN
people (a) *n.* народ *m.* nahROHT
people *n.* люди *pl.* LYOOdee
pepper *n.* перец *m.* PYEHryehts
pepper brandy *n.* перцовка *f.* peerTSOHFkah
performance, play *n.* спектакль *m.* speekTAHKL'
performer *n.* артист *m.* ahrTEEST
perfume *n.* духи *pl.* dooKHEE
perhaps *conj.* может быть MOHzheht biht'
permission, permit *n.* разрешение *nt.*
    rahzreeSHEHneeyeh
person *n.* человек *m.* chehlahVYEHK
personal *adj.* личный LEECHnihy
photograph *n.* фотография *f.* fahtahGRAHfeeyah
phrasebook *n.* разговорник *m.* rahzgahVOHRneek
picture *n.* картина *f.* kahrTEEnah
pie *n.* пирог *m.* peeROHK
piece *n.* кусок *m.* kooSOHK
pill, tablet *n.* таблетка *f.* tahbLYEHTkah
pillow *n.* подушка *f.* pahDOOSHkah
pillowcase *n.* наволочка *f.* NAHvahlahchkah
pin *n.* булавка *f.* booLAHFkah
pipe *n.* трубка *f.* TROOPkah
pity *n.* жаль *f.* zhahl'
place, seat, site *n.* место *nt.* MYEHStah
plant *n.* растение *nt.* rahsTYEHneeyeh

plate *n.* тарелка *f.* tahRYEHLkah

play *v.* играть eegRAHT'

playwright *n.* драматург *m.* drahmahTOORK

pleasant *adj.* приятный preeYAHTnihy

please *interj.* пожалуйста pahZHAHLstah

pleasure *n.* удовольствие *nt.* oodahVOHL'stveeyeh

plum *n.* слива *f.* SLEEvah

pneumonia *n.* воспаление лёгких *nt.*
    vahspahLYEHneeyeh LYOHKHkeekh

pocket *n.* карман *m.* kahrMAHN

poet *n.* поэт *m.* pahEHT

poetry *n.* поэзия *f.* pahEHzeeyah

poison *n.* отрава *f.* ahtRAHvah/яд *m.* yaht

police *n.* милиция *f.* meeLEEtseeyah

policeman *n.* милиционер *m.* meeleetseeahNYEHR

polite *adj.* вежливый VYEHZHleevihy

politics *n.* политика *f.* pahLEEteekah

pond *n.* пруд *m.* proot

pool *n.* бассейн *m.* bahSEYN

poor *adj.* бедный BYEHDnihy

poppy *n.* мак *m.* mahk

pork *n.* свинина *f.* sveeNEEnah

portable *adj.* переносный peereeNOHSnihy

porter *n.* носильщик *m.* nahSEEL'shcheek

postcard *n.* открытка *f.* ahtKRIHTkah

poster *n.* плакат *m.* plahKAHT

poster, playbill *n.* афиша *f.* ahFEEshah

post office (main branch) *n.* главпочтамт *m.*
    glahfPOHCHtahmt

post office *n.* почта *f.* POHCHtah

pot, saucepan *n.* кастрюля *f.* kahstRYOOlyah

potato *n.* картофель *f.* kahrTOHfeel'
prayer *n.* молитва *f.* mahLEETvah
pregnant *adj.* беременная beeRYEHmeenahyah
prepare *v.* готовить gahTOHVeet'
prescription *n.* рецепт *m.* reeTSEHPT
present *n.* подарок *m.* pahDAHrahk
pressure *n.* давление *nt.* davLYEHneeyeh
pretty *adj.* красивый krahsEEVihy
price *n.* цена *f.* tseeNAH
priest *n.* священник *m.* sveeshCHEHneek
probably *adv.* наверно nahVYEHRnah
problem *n.* проблема *f.* prahbLYEHmah
processing *n.* оформление *nt.* ahfahrmLYEHneeyeh
profession *n.* профессия *f.* prahFYEHseeyah
professor *n.* профессор *m.* prahFYEHsahr
profitable *adj.* выгодный VIHgahdnihy
prognosis *n.* прогноз *m.* prahgNOHS
promise *n.* обещание *nt.* ahbeeSHCHAHneeyeh
pronunciation *n.* произношение *nt.*
　　praheeznahSHEHneeyeh
proper *adj.* приличный preeLEESHnihy
proverb *n.* пословица *f.* pahSLOHveetsah
public *n.* публика *f.* POOBleekah
public *adj.* общественный ahpSHEHSTvyehnih
public bath *n.* баня *f.* BAHnyah
purchase *n.* покупка *f.* pahKOOPkah

Q

quality *n.* качество *nt.* KAHchehstvah
quantity *n.* количество *nt.* kahLEECHehstvah
quarter *n.* четверть *f.* CHEHTveert'

question *n.* вопрос *m.* vahPROHS
quick *adj.* скорый SKOHrihy
quickly *adv.* скоро SKOHrah
quiet *adj.* тихий TEEkheey
quote *n.* цитата *f.* tseeTAHtah

R

rabbi *n.* раввин *m.* rahvVEEN
rabbit *n.* кролик *m.* KROHleek
radio *n.* радио *nt.* RAHdeeoh
radio station *n.* радиостанция *f.*
    rahdeeahSTAHNtseeyah
radish *n.* редиска *f.* reeDEESkah
rail, track *n.* рельс *m.* ryehl's
railroad car *n.* вагон *m.* vahGOHN
rain *n.* дождь *f.* dohsht'
raincoat *n.* плащ *m.* plahschch
raisins *n.* изюм *m.* eeZYOOM
rare, infrequent *adj.* редкий RYEHTkeey
rarely *adv.* редко RYEHTkah
raspberries *n.* малина *f.* mahLEEnah
rate of exchange *n.* валютный курс *m.*
    vahLYOOtnihy koors
raw *adj.* сырой sihROY
razor *n.* бритва *f.* BREETvah
razor blades *n.* лезвия *f.* LYEHZveeyah
read *v.* читать cheeTAHT'
ready *adj.* готовый gahTOHvihy
real *adj.* действительный deystVEEteel'nihy
really *adv.* разве RAHZveh
rear *adj.* задний ZAHDneey

reason *n.* причина *f.* preeCHEEnah
reception *n.* приём *m.* preeYOHM
recommend *v.* посоветовать pahsahVYEHtahvaht'
record *n.* грампластинка *f.* grahmplahsTEENkah
recording *n.* запись *f.* ZAHpees'
red *adj.* красный KRAHSnihy
reference, information *n.* справка *f.* SPRAHFkah
refrigerator *n.* холодильник *m.* khahlahDEEL'neek
refusal *n.* отказ *m.* ahtKAHS
registration *n.* регистрация *f.*
    reegeesTRAHtseeyah
relationship *n.* отношение *nt.* ahtnahSHEHneeyeh
relatives *n.* родственники *pl.* ROHTSTveeneekee
reluctantly *adv.* неохотно neeahKHOHTnah
remainder *n.* остаток *m.* ahsTAHtahk
rent *v.* взять напрокат vzyaht' nahprahKAHT
repair *n.* ремонт *m.* reeMOHNT
repeat *v.* повторить pahftahREET'
request *n.* просьба *f.* PROZ'bah
resident *n.* житель *m.* ZHEEteel'
resort *n.* курорт *m.* kooROHRT
respected *adj.* уважаемый oovahZHAHeemihy
rest *n.* отдых *m.* OHDdihkh
restaurant *n.* ресторан *m.* reestahRAHN
return *v.* возвращать vahzvrahSHCHAHT'
reward *n.* награда *f.* nahGRAHdah
rib *n.* ребро *nt.* reebROH
rice *n.* рис *m.* rees
rich *adj.* богатый bahGAHtihy
right *adj.* правый PRAHvihiy
right, correct *adj.* правильный PRAHveel'nihy

ripe, mature *adj.* зрелый ZRYEHlihy

river *n.* река *f.* reeKAH

road *n.* дорога *f.* dahROHgah

roast beef *n.* ростбиф *m.* ROHSTbeef

robe *n.* халат *m.* khahLAHT

rock *n.* камень *f.* KAHmeen'

roll *n.* булка *f.* BOOLkah

roof *n.* крыша *f.* KRIHshah

room *n.* комната *f.* KOHMnahtah

rope, string *n.* верёвка *f.* veeRYOHFkah

rose *n.* роза *f.* ROHzah

roundtrip (ticket) *adv.* туда и обратно tooDAH ee ahbRAHTnah

ruble *n.* рубль *m.* roobl'

rude *adj.* грубый GROObihy

rule *n.* правило *nt.* PRAHveelah

run *v.* бегать BYEHgaht'

Russian *adj.* русский ROOSkeey

Russian *n.* русский/русская *m./f.* ROOSkeey/ROOSkahyah

S

sad *adj.* грустный GROOSnihy

safe (bank) *n.* сейф *m.* seyf; несгораемый шкаф *m.* neezgahRAHeemihy shkahf

safe *adj.* безопасный beezahPAHSnihy

safely *adv.* благополучно blahgahpahLOOCHnah

salad *n.* салат *m.* sahLAHT

sale *n.* продажа/скидка *f.* prahDAHzhah/SKEET-kah

salesman *n.* продавец *m.* prahdahVYEHTS

salmon *n.* лососина *f.* lahsahSEEnah

salt *n.* соль *m.* sohl'

salty *adj.* солёный sahLYOHnihy

sand *n.* песок *m.* peeSOHK

sandals *n.* сандалии *pl.* sahnDAHlee

sandwich *n.* бутерброд *m.* bootehrBROHT

satire *n.* сатира *f.* sahTEErah

satisfaction *n.* удовлетворение *nt.* oodohvleetvah-RYEHneeyeh

sauce *n.* соус *m.* SOHoos

sausage *n.* колбаса *f.* kahlbahSAH

scarf *n.* шарф *m.* shahrf

schedule *n.* расписание *nt.* rahspeeSAHneeyeh

scholar, scientist *n.* учёный *m.* ooCHOHnihy

school *n.* школа *f.* SHKOHlah

school vacation *n.* каникулы *pl.* kahNEEkoolih

scissors *n.* ножницы *pl.* NOHZHneetsih

scrambled eggs *n.* яичница-болтунья *f.* yahEECHneetsah-bahlTOOn'yah

screen *n.* экран *m.* ehkRAHN

sculpture *n.* скульптура *f.* skool'pTOOrah

sea *n.* море *nt.* MOHryeh

seat *n.* место *nt.* MYEHStah

section *n.* секция *f.* SYEHKtseeyah

see *v.* видеть VEEdeet'

self-service *n.* самообслуживание *nt.* sahmahahpSLOOzheevahneeyeh

sell *v.* продать prahDAHT'

send *v.* послать pahSLAHT'

separately *adv.* отдельно ahdDYEHL'nah

serious *adj.* серьёзный seer'YOHZnihy

set *n.* комплект *m.* kahmPLYEHKT

shame *n.* стыд *m.* stiht
shampoo *n.* шампунь *m.* shahmPOON'
share *n.* доля *f.* DOHLyah
share, divide *v.* делить deeLEET'
sharp, pungent *adj.* острый OHStrihy
shave *v.* бриться BREETsah
she *pron.* она ahNAH
sheet *n.* простыня *f.* prahstihNYAH
shirt *n.* рубашка *f.* rooBAHSHkah
shoe laces *n.* шнурки *pl.* shnoorKEE
shoes *n.* туфли *pl.* TOOFlee
short *adj.* короткий kahROHTkeey
shortage *n.* недостаток *m.* needahsTAHtahk
shorts *n.* шорты *pl.* SHOHRtihy
should, must *pred.* должен DOHLzhehn
shoulder *n.* плечо *nt.* plyeeCHOH
show *v.* показать pahkahZAHT'
shower *n.* душ *m.* doosh
sick *adj.* больной bahl'NOY
side street *n.* переулок *m.* peereeOOlahk
sidewalk *n.* тротурар *m.* trahtooAHR
sign *v.* подписать pahtpeeSAHT'
sign *n.* знак *m.* znahk
signature *n.* подпись *m.* POHTpees'
sign up *v.* записаться zahpeeSAHTsah
silence *n.* молчание *nt.* mahlCHAHneeyeh
silver *adj.* серебряный seeRYEHBreenihy
similar *adj.* похожий pahKHOHzheey
simple, easy *adj.* простой prahsTOY
since *prep.* с s

singer *n.* певец/певица *m./f.* peevYEHTS/peeVEEtsah

sister *n.* сестра *f.* seesTRAH

sister-in-law *n.* невестка *f.* neeVYEHSTkah

size *n.* размер *m.* rahzMYEHR

skate (ice) *v.* кататься на коньках kahTAHTsyah nah kahn'KAHK

skates *n.* коньки *pl.* kahn'KEE

skating rink *n.* каток *m.* kahTOHK

skis *n.* лыжи *pl.* LIHzhee

skin *n.* шкура *f.* SHKOOrah

skirt *n.* юбка *f.* YOOPkah

skullcap *n.* ермолка *f.* yeerMOHLkah

sky *n.* небо *nt.* NYEHbah

sleep *v.* спать spaht'

sleeve *n.* рукав *m.* rooKAHF

slippers *n.* тапочки *pl.* TAHpahchkee

slippery *adj.* скользкий SKOHL'skeey

slow *adj.* медленный MYEHDleenihy

small *adj.* маленький MAHleen'keey

small change *n.* мелочь *f.* MYEHlach

smart *adj.* умный OOMnihy

smell *v.* пахнуть PAHKHnoot'

smell *n.* запах *m.* ZAHpahkh

smile *n.* улыбка *f.* ooLIHPkah

smoke *v.* курить kooREET'

smoke *n.* дым *m.* dihm

smooth *adj.* гладкий GLAHTkeey

snack, appetizer *n.* закуска *f.* zahKOOSkah

snack bar *n.* буфет *m.* booFYEHT

sneakers *n.* кеды *pl.* KYEHdih

sneezing *n.* чиханье *nt.* cheeKHAHN'yeh

snow *n.* снег *m.* snyehk

snow *v.* идёт снег eeDYOHT snyehk

soap *n.* мыло *f.* MIHlah

soccer *n.* футбол *m.* footBOHL

socks *n.* носки *pl.* nahsKEE

soft *adj.* мягкий MYAHKHkeey

sold out *adv.* распродано rahsPROHdahnah

somehow *adv.* как-то KAHKtah

someone *pron.* кто-нибудь KTOHneeboot'

something *pron.* что-нибудь SHTOHneeboot'

sometimes *adv.* иногда eenahgDAH

somewhere *adv.* где-нибудь GDYEHneeboot'

son *n.* сын *m.* sihn

song *n.* песня *f.* PYEHSnyah

son-in-law *n.* зять *m.* zyaht'

sorry *interj.* простите/извините prahsTEEtyeh/
    eezveeNEEtyeh

sound, noise *n.* звук *m.* zvook

soup *n.* суп *m.* soop

sour *adj.* кислый KEESlihy

sour cream *n.* сметана *f.* smeeTAHnah

south *n.* юг *m.* yook

southern *adj.* южный YOOZHnihy

souvenir *n.* сувенир *m.* sooveeNEER

spare, extra *adj.* лишний LEESHneey

speak *v.* говорить gahvahrEET'

spectator *n.* зритель *m.* ZREEteel'

speed *n.* скорость *f.* SKOHrahst'

spider *n.* паук *m.* pahOOK

spoiled, rotten *adj.* испорченный
   eesPOHRchehnnihy
spoon *n.* ложка *f.* LOHSHkah
sports fan *n.* болельщик *m.* bahLYEHL'schcheek
sports match *n.* матч *m.* mahtch
sports team *n.* команда *f.* kahMAHNdah
spot, stain *n.* пятно *m.* peetNOH
spring *n.* весна *f.* veesNAH
square *n.* площадь *f.* PLOshaht'
square *adj.* квадратный kvahdRAHTnihy
stadium *n.* стадион *m.* stahdeeOHN
stairs *n.* лестница *f.* LYEHSneetsah
stamp *n.* марка *f.* MAHRkah
state (government) *n.* государство *nt.*
   gahsooDAHRstvah
state (governmental) *adj.* государственный
   gahsooDAHRSTveenihy
station *n.* станция *f.* STAHNtseeyah
station (train) *n.* вокзал *m.* vahkZAHL
stay *n.* пребывание *nt.* preebihVAHneeyeh
steak *n.* бифштекс *m.* beefSHTEHKS
steal *v.* украсть ooKRAHST'
steam room *n.* парильня *f.* pahREEL'nyeh
stepmother *n.* мачеха *f.* MAHchehkhah
stepfather *n.* отчим *m.* OHTcheem
stewardess *n.* стюардесса *f.* styooahrDYEHsah
sticky *adj.* липкий LEEPkeey
stockings *n.* чулки *pl.* choolKEE
stomach *n.* живот *m.* zheeVOHT
stop *n.* стоп *m.* stohp
store *n.* магазин *m.* mahgahZEEN
storm *n.* буря *f.* BOOryah

stormy, violent *adj.* бурный BOORnihy

story, floor *n.* этаж *m.* ehTAHSH

story, tale *n.* рассказ *m.* rahsKAHS

stove *n.* печь *f.* pyehch'

straight *adj.* прямой preeMOY

strange *adj.* странный STRAHNnihy

stranger *n.* незнакомец *m.* neeznahKOHmeets

strawberries *n.* земляника *pl.* zeemleeNEEkah

street *n.* улица *f.* OOleetsah

street car *n.* трамвай *m.* trahmVAY

strength *n.* сила *f.* SEElah

strict, harsh *adj.* строгий STROHgeey

strong *adj.* сильный SEEL'nihy

stubborn *adj.* упорный ooPOHRnihy

student *n.* студент/студентка *m./f.* stooDYEHNT/
stooDYEHNTkah

study *v.* учиться ooCHEETsah

stuffed cabbage *n.* голубцы *pl.* gahloopTSIH

stuffy *adj.* душный DOOSHnih

stupid, silly *adj.* глупый GLOOpihy

substitution *n.* замена *f.* zahMYEHnah

suburb *n.* пригород *m.* PREEgahraht

subway *n.* метро *nt.* meeTROH

success *n.* успех *m.* oosPYEHKH

suddenly *adv.* вдруг vdrook

sugar *n.* сахар *m.* SAHkhahr

suit *n.* костюм *m.* kahsTYOOM

suitcase *n.* чемодан *m.* chehmahDAHN

summer *n.* лето *nt.* LYEHtah

sun *n.* солнце *nt.* SOHNtseh

sunburn *n.* загар *m.* zahGAHR

sunglasses *n.* тёмные очки *pl.* TYOMnihyeh
 ahchKEE

supper *n.* ужин *m.* OOzheen

supper *v.* ужинать OOzheenaht'

surprising *adj.* удивительный oodeeVEEteel'nihy

swallow *v.* глотать glahTAHT'

sweater *n.* пуловер *m.* poolOHveer

sweet *adj.* сладкий SLAHTkeey

swim *v.* плавать PLAHvaht'

swollen *adj.* раздутый/опухший
 rahzDOOtihy/ohPOOKHshihy

sympathy *n.* сочувствие *nt.* sahCHOOSTveeyeh

synagogue *n.* синагога *f.* seenahGOHgah

T

T-shirt *n.* майка *f.* MAYkah

table *n.* стол *m.* stohl

take, seize *v.* брать braht'

takeoff (airplane) *n.* взлёт *m.* vzlyoht

talk, chat *v.* беседовать beeSYEHdahvaht'

tampon *n.* тампон *m.* tahmPOHN

tangerine *n.* мандарин *m.* mahndahREEN

tape recorder *n.* магнитофон *m.* mahgneetahFOHN

tasteless *adj.* безвкусный beesVKOOSnihy

tax *n.* налог *m.* nahLOHK

taxi *n.* такси *pl.* tahkSEE

taxi stop *n.* стоянка *f.* stahYAHNkah

tea *n.* чай *m.* chay

teacher *n.* преподаватель/преподавательница *m./f.* preepahdahVAHteel'/preepahdahVAHteel'-neetsah

teddy bear *n.* мишка *m.* MEESHkah

telegram *n.* телеграмма *f.* teelee GRAHmah

telephone *n.* телефон *m.* teeleeFOHN

telephone booth *n.* телефон-автомат *m.* teeleeFOHNahftahMAHT

television *n.* телевизор *m.* teeleeVEEzahr

temperature *n.* температура *f.* teempeerahTOOrah

temporarily *adv.* временно VRYEHmeennah

tension, stress *n.* напряжение *nt.* nahpreeZHEHneeyeh

tent *n.* палатка *f.* pahLAHTkah

thank *v.* благодарить blahgahdahREET'

thank you *interj.* спасибо spahSEEbah

thank you very much *interj.* большое спасибо bahl'SHOHyeh spahSEEbah

that way *adv.* туда tooDAH

theater *n.* театр *m.* teeAHTR

then, next; afterwards *adv.* потом pahTOHM

there *adv.* там tahm

therefore *conj.* поэтому pahEHtahmoo

they *pro.* они ahNEE

thick *adj.* толстый TOHLstihy

thick, dense *adj.* густой goosTOY

thin *adj.* тонкий TOHNkeey

thirst *n.* жажда *f.* ZHAHZHdah

this (one) *pro.* этот EHtaht

thousand *n.* тысяча *f.* TIHseechah

thread *n.* нитка *f.* NEETkah

threat *n.* угоза *f.* ooGROHzah
throat *n.* горло *f.* GOHRlah
through *prep.* сквозь skvohs'
thunderstorm *n.* гроза *f.* grahZAH
ticket *n.* билет *m.* beeLYEHT
ticket office *n.* касса *f.* KAHsah
tie *n.* галстук *m.* GAHLstook
time *n.* время *nt.* VRYEHmyah
time (it's) *pred.* пора pahRAH
timetable *n.* расписание *nt.* rahspeeSAHneeyeh
timid *adj.* робкий ROHPkeey
tip *n.* чаевые *nt.* chahyehVIHyeh
tired *adj. m./f.* устал/(а) oosTAHL(ah)
to, toward *prep.* к k
to, up to, before *prep.* до doh
tobacco *n.* табак *m.* tahBAHK
today *adv.* сегодня seeVOHdnyah
today's *adj.* сегодняшний seeVOHdnyahshneey
together *adv.* вместе VMYEHstyeh
toilet *n.* туалет *m.* tooahLYEHT
toilet paper *n.* туалетная бумага *f.*
    tooahLYEHTnahyah booMAHgah
tomato *n.* помидор *m.* pahmeeDOHR
tombstone *n.* надгробный камень *f.*
    nahdGROHBnihy KAHmeen'
tomorrow *adv.* завтра ZAHFtrah
tomorrow's *adj.* завтрашний ZAHFtrahshneey
tongue, language *n.* язык *m.* yeezIHK
too (much) *adv.* слишком SLEESHkahm
tooth *n.* зуб *m.* zoop
toothache *n.* зубная боль *f.* zoobNAHyah bohl'

---

toothbrush *n.* зубная щётка *f.* zoobNAHyah SHCHOHTkah

toothpaste *n.* зубная паста *f.* zoobNAHyah PAHStah

top *adv.* верх vyehrkh

torn, ripped *adj.* рваный RVAHnihy

touch *v.* трогать TROHgaht'

tour *n.* экскурсия *f.* ehksKOORseeyah

tour guide *n.* экскурсовод *m.* ehskoorsahVOHT

tourist *n.* турист *m.* tooREEST

towel *n.* полотенце *nt.* pahlahTYEHNtseh

tower *n.* башня *f.* BAHSHnyah

toy *n.* игрушка *f.* eegROOSHkah

traffice light *n.* светофор *m.* sveetahFOHR

tragedy *n.* трагедия *f.* trahGYEHdeeyah

train *n.* поезд *m.* POHeest

train compartment *n.* купе *nt.* koopEH

transfer *n.* пересадка *f.* peereeSAHTkah

translate *v.* перевести peereeveesTEE

translation *n.* перевод *m.* peereeVOHT

translator *n.* переводчик *m.* peereeVOHTcheek

trash *n.* мусор *m.* MOOsahr

traveler *n.* путешественник *m.* pooteeshEHSTveeneek

travel, trip *n.* путешествие *f.* pooteeshEHSTveeyeh

tree *n.* дерево *nt.* DYEHreevah

trip, flight *n.* рейс *m.* reys

trolley bus *n.* троллейбус *m.* trahLEYboos

truck *n.* грузовик *m.* groozahVEEK

true, faithful *adj.* верный VYEHRnihy

truth *n.* правда *f.* PRAHVdah

tuna *n.* тунец *m.* tooNYEHTS
turkey *n.* индейка *f.* eenDEYkah
turn off *v.* выключать vihklyooCHAHT'
turn on *v.* включать fklyooCHAT'
turnip *n.* репа *f.* RYEHpah

U

ugly *adj.* некрасивый neekrhaSEEvihy
umbrella *n.* зонтик *m.* ZOHNteek
uncle *n.* дядя *f.* DYAHdyah
unclean *adj.* нечистный neeCHEEStihy
unclear *adj.* неясный neeYAHSnihy
uncomfortable *adj.* неудобный neeooDOHBnihy
unconscious *adj.* бессознательный
    beessahZNAHteelnihy
under, beneath *prep.* под poht
underpants *n.* трусы *pl.* trooSIH
undershirt *n.* майка *f.* MAYkah
understand *v.* понимать pahneeMAHT'
understandable *adj.* понятный pahnYAHTnihy
underwear *n.* нижнее бельё *nt.* NEEZHneeyeh
    beel'YOH
unfair *adj.* несправедливый neesprahveedLEE-
    vihy
unfamiliar *adj.* незнакомый neeznahKOHmihy
unfortunate *adj.* неблагополучный neeblahgah-
    pahLOOCHnihy
unhappy *adj.* несчастный neeSHAHSnihy
unimportant *adj.* неважный neeVAHZHnihy
unintentional *adj.* невольный neeVOHL'nihy
universal *adj.* всеобщий fseeOHPshcheey

university *n.* университет *m.* ooneeveerseeTYEHT
unknown *adj.* неизвестный neeeezVYEHSnihy
unnatural *adj.* неестественный neeyehstEHST-veenihy
unnoticable *adv.* незаметно neezahMYEHTnah
unpleasant *adj.* неприятный neepreeYAHTnihy
unprofitable *adj.* невыгодный neeVIHgahdnihy
unripe *adj.* незрелый neeZRYEHlihy
unsuccessful *adj.* безуспешный beezoosPHYEHSHnihy
until *prep.* до doh
untruth *n.* неправда *f.* neePRAHVdah
unusual *adj.* необыкновенный neeahbihknahVYEHnihy
up, upwards (destination) *adv.* вверх vvyehrkh
up, upwards (location) *adv.* наверху nahvyehrKHOO
upper, top *adj.* верхний VYEHRKHneey
urgent *adj.* срочный SROHCHnihy
urine *n.* моча *f.* mahCHAH
use *n.* польза *f.* POHL'zah
useful *adj.* полезный pahLYEHZnihy
useless *adj.* бесполезный beespahLYEHZnihy
usually *adv.* обычно ahBIHCHnah

V

vacancy *n.* вакансия *f.* vahKAHNseeyah
vacation *n.* отпуск *m.* OHTpoosk
vague *adj.* неопределённый neeahpreedeeLYOHnihy
valid *adj.* действительный dehstVEEtyehl'nihy

valley *n.* долина *f.* dahLEEnah

valuable *adj.* ценный TSEHnihy

value, worth *n.* достоинство *nt.* dahsTOHeenstvah

veal *n.* телятина *f.* teeLYAHteenah

vegetables *n.* овощи *pl.* OHvahshchee

vegetarian *n.* вегетарианец/вегетарианка *m./f.*
  veegeetahreeAHneets/veegeetahreeAHNkah

vending machine *n.* автомат *m.* ahftahMAHT

venison *n.* оленина *f.* ahLYEHneenah

verb *n.* глагол *m.* glahGOHL

very *adv.* очень OHcheen'

victory *n.* победа *f.* pahBYEHdah

village *n.* село *nt.* seeLOH

violence *n.* насилие *nt.* nahSEEleeyeh

virus *n.* вирус *m.* VEEroos

visa *n.* виза *f.* VEEzah

visible *adv.* видно VEEDnah

vitamins *n.* витамины *pl.* veetahMEEnih

vodka *n.* водка *f.* VOHTkah

voice *n.* голос *m.* GOHlahs

voltage *n.* вольтаж *m.* vahl'TAHSH

vote *v.* голосовать gahlahsahVAHT'

W

waist *n.* талия *f.* TAHleeyah

wait *v.* ждать zhdaht'

waiter *n.* официант/официантка *m./f.*
  ahfeetseeAHNT/ ahfeetseeAHNTkah

wall *n.* стена *f.* steeNAH

wallet *n.* бумажник *m.* booMAHZHneek

want *v.* хотеть khahTYEHT'

war *n.* война *f.* voyNAH

warm *adj.* тёплый TYOHPlihy

warning *n.* предупреждение *nt.*
  preedoopreezhDYEHneeyeh

wasp *n.* оса *f.* ahSAH

watch *n.* часы *pl.* cheeSIH

water *n.* вода *f.* vahDAH

watermelon *n.* арбуз *m.* ahrBOOS

wave *n.* волна *f.* vahlNAH

we *pro.* мы mih

weak *adj.* слабый SLAHbihy

weather *n.* погода *f.* pahGOHdah

wedding *n.* свадьба *f.* SVAHT'bah

week *n.* неделя *f.* neeDYEHlyah

weekday *n.* будний день *m.* BOODneey dyehn'

weight *n.* вес *m.* vyehs

well, healthy *adj.* здоровый zdahROHvihy

west *n.* запад *m.* ZAHpaht

western *adj.* западный ZAHpadnihy

wet *adj.* мокрый MOHKrihy

what *inter.* что shtoh

wheat *n.* пшеница *f.* pshehNEEtsah

wheel *n.* колесо *nt.* kahleeSOH

when *inter.* когда kahgDAH

where *inter.* где gdyeh

where to *inter.* куда kooDAH

which *inter.* какой kahKOY

white *adj.* белый BYEHlihy

who *inter.* кто ktoh

whole *adj.* целый TSEHlihy

why *inter.* почему pahcheeMOO

wide, broad *adj.* широкий sheeROHkeey
widow *n.* вдова *f.* vdahVAH
widower *n.* вдовец *m.* vdahVYEHTS
width *n.* ширина *f.* sheereeNAH
wife *n.* жена *f.* zhehNAH
wild *adj.* дикий DEEkey
wild game *n.* дичь *m.* deech'
wind *n.* ветер *m.* VYEHteer
window *n.* окно *nt.* ahkNOH
windy *adj.* ветреный VYEHTreenihy
wine *n.* вино *nt* veeNOH
winter *n.* зима *f.* zeeMAH
winter *adj.* зимний ZEEmneey
wish, desire *n.* желание *nt.* zheeLAHneeyeh
with, off, since *prep.* с s
without *prep.* без byehs
woman *n.* женщина *f.* ZHEHNshcheenah
wonderful *adj.* чудесный chooDYEHSnihy
wooden *adj.* деревянный deereeevYAHnihy
woolen *adj.* шерстяной shehrsteeNOY
word *n.* слово *nt.* SLOHvah
work *n.* работа *f.* rahBOHtah
work *v.* работать rahBOHtaht'
worker *n.* рабочий *m.* rahBOHcheey
world *n.* мир *m.* meer
worry, trouble, disturb *v.* беспокоить
    beespahKOHeet'
worship service *n.* богослужение *f.*
    bohgahslooZHEHneeyeh
wounded *adj.* раненый RAHneenihy
write *v.* писать peeSAHT'

writer *n.* писатель *m.* peeSAHteel'
writing (in) *adv.* письменно PEES'meenah
wrong, incorrect *adj.* неправильный
neePRAHveel'nihy

X

x-ray *n.* рентген *m.* reenGYEHN

Y

year *n.* год *m.* goht
yearly *adj.* ежегодный yeezhehGOHDnihy
yellow *adj.* жёлтый ZHOHLtihy
yes *part.* да dah
yesterday *n.* вчера *f.* fcheeRAH
yesterday's *adj.* вчерашний fcheeRAHSHneey
young *adj.* молодой mahlahDOY
young lady *n.* девушка *f.* DYEHvooshkah
young people *n.* молодёжь *m.* mahlahDYOHSH
younger *adj.* младший MLAHTsheey
youth *n.* юность *m.* YOOnahst'

Z

zero *num.* ноль *f.* nohl'
zipper *n.* молния *f.* MOHLneeyah
zoo *n.* зоопарк *m.* zahahPAHRK

PHRASEBOOK CONTENTS

ESSENTIAL EXPRESSIONS

The Basics

After да *(dah)* and нет *(nyeht),* the two most useful
Russian words for the foreign traveler are *извините
(eezveeNEEtyeh)* and *пожалуйста (pahZAHLstah).*
Извините can be used to approach a stranger for
help or information, to apologize for a mistake or to
get around someone in a crowded place.
Пожалуйста can mean please, thank you or be used
as an invitation to the table.

Yes./No.
Да./Нет.
dah/nyeht
Maybe.
Может быть.
MOHzheht biht'
Please.
Пожалуйста.
pahZHAHLstah
Thank you.
Спасибо.
spahSEEbah
Thank you very much.
Большое спасибо.
bahl'SHOHyeh spahSEEbah
Thank you for the help/information.
Спасибо за помощь/за информацию.
*spahSEEbah zah POHmahshch/zah
eenfahrMAHtseeyoo*

You're welcome.

Не за что./Пожалуйста.
NYEHzahshtah/pahZHAHLstah

Ok.

Ладно.
LAHDnah

I beg your pardon.

Простите.
prahsTEEtyeh

Excuse me.

Извините.
eezveeNEEtyeh

Why?

Почему?
pahcheeMOO

Because.

Потому что.
pahtahMOOshtah

That's the way it is.

Просто так.
PROHStah tahk

Good.

Хорошо.
khahrahSHOH

Bad.

Плохо.
PLOHkhah

Can you tell me, please…

Скажите, пожалуйста…
skahZHEEtyeh pahZHAHLstah

Help me.

Помогите мне.
pahmahGEEtyeh mnyeh

Is that right?

Правильно?
PRAHveel'nah

Be so kind...

Будьте добры...
BOOT'tyeh dahbRIH

What?/What's that?

Что?/Что это?
shtoh/shtoh EHtah

What does that mean?

Что это значит?
shtoh EHtah ZNAHcheet

Where?

Где?
gdyeh

Where to?

Куда?
kooDAH

How?

Как?
kahk

How far?

Как далеко?
kahk dahleeKOH

How long?

Как долго?
kahk DOHLgah

When?

Когда?
kahgDAH

Who?

Кто?
ktoh

Who is that?

Кто это?
ktoh EHtah

I can't.

Я не могу.
yah nee mahGOO

I want to rest/eat/drink/sleep.

Я хочу отдохнуть/есть/пить/спать.
yah khahCHOO ahddahkhNOOT'/yehst'/peet'/spaht'

Greetings

Like French, German and Spanish, Russian has both
formal *(вы)* and informal *(ты)* forms of address.
Unless told otherwise by the person with whom you
are speaking, you should stick to the formal form,
except when addressing children.

Hello.

Здравствуйте.
ZDRAHSTvooytyeh

Hi. *(coll.)*

Привет.
preeVYEHT

Good morning.

Доброе утро.
DOHBrahyeh OOtrah

Good afternoon.

Добрый день.
DOHBrihy dyehn'

Good evening.

Добрый вечер.
DOHBrihy VYEHchehr
Good night.

Спокойной ночи.
spahKOYnoy NOHchee
Goodbye.

До свидания.
dahsveeDAHneeyah
Bye. *(coll.)*

До скорого./Пока.
dahSKOHrahvah/pahKAH
All the best!

Всего доброго!
vseeVOH DOHbrahvah

Introductions

In Russia, people usually address one another by
their first name and patronymic. To form the
patronymic they add a suffix—usually "-ovich"
for men and "-ovna" for women—to their father's
first name. For example, if Ivan's father's name
is Boris, he would be called "Ivan Borisovich."
Likewise, if Anna's father's name is Mikhail, her
patronymic would be "Anna Mikhailovna." If
they know one another well or if they are talking
to a child, Russians may use a diminutive form
like Vanya and Anya.

When their first names and patronymics are
unknown or when addressing non-Russians, you

may hear men addressed as *господин*
(gahspahDEEN) and women as *госпожа*
(gahspahZHAH). These are roughly equivalent to
"Mr." and "Mrs."

Upon being introduced, Russians typically shake
hands, but they may also be seen kissing one
another up to three times on the cheeks,
especially when they have not seen one another
for a long time. Russians believe it is bad luck to
shake or embrace across a threshold, so be sure
to go through the doorway before attempting a
greeting.

What's your name?
Как вас зовут?
kahk vahz zahVOOT
My name is...

Меня зовут...
meeNYAH zahVOOT
Pleased to meet you.

Очень приятно.
OHcheen' preeYAHTnah
It's a pleasure to meet you.

Очень рад с вами познакомиться.
OHcheen' raht SVAHmee pahznahKOHmeetsah
May I introduce you to...

Разрешите познакомить вас...
rahzreeSHEEtyeh pahznahKOHmeet' vahs
...my husband.

...с моим мужем.
smahEEM MOOzhehm
...my wife.

...с моей женой.
smahEY zhehNOY

ESSENTIAL EXPRESSIONS

How are you?

Как вы поживаете?
kahk vih pahzhehVAHeetyeh
I'm fine, thanks.

Прекрасно, спасибо.
preeKRAHSnah spahSEEbah
And you?

А вы?
ah VIH
I'm ok.

Так себе./Ничего.
tahk seeBYEH/neecheeVOH
I'm not well.

Мне плохо.
mnyeh PLOHkhah
How're things?

Как дела? *(coll.)*
kahk deeLAH

Personal Information

Upon first meeting, Russians may seem reserved or
downright chilly, but once they accept you into their
circle of friends and acquaintances, they will make
you feel like royalty.

Where are you from?

Откуда вы?
ahtKOOdah vih
I am from... America./Canada./England.

Я из...Америки./Канады./Англии.
yah ees ahMYEHreekee/kahNAHdih/AHNgleeee

ESSENTIAL EXPRESSIONS

What's your nationality?

Кто вы по национальности?
ktoh vih pah nahtseeahNAHL'nahstee

I am...

Я...
yah

...American. *(m./f.)*

...американец/американка.
ahmeereeKAHneets/ahmeereeKAHNkah

...Canadian. *(m./f.)*

...канадец/канадка.
kahNAHdeets/kahNAHTkah

...British. *(m./f.)*

...англичанин/англичанка.
ahngleeCHAHneen/ahngleeCHAHNkah

What are you doing here?

Что вы здесь делаете?
shtoh vih zdyehs' DYEHlaheetyeh

I am a tourist. */(f.)*

Я турист/туристка.
yah tooREEST tooREESTkah

I'm studying.

Я учусь.
yah oochOOS'

I'm here on business.

Я здесь по делам.
yah zdyehs' pah deeLAHM

What's your profession?

Кто вы по профессии?
ktoh vih pahprahFYEHseeee

I am a(n)...

Я...
yah

…student. *(m./f.)*

…студент/студентка.
stooDYEHNT/stooDYEHNTkah

…teacher. *(m./f.)*

…учитель/учительница.
ooCHEEtyehl'/ooCHEEtyehl'neetsah

…professor.

…профессор.
prahfYEHsahr

…businessman.

…бизнесмен.
beeznehsMYEHN

…journalist. *(m./f.)*

…журналист/журналистка.
zhoornahLEEST/zhoornahLEESTkah

…nurse.

…медсестра.
meedseesTRAH

…housewife.

…домохозяйка.
dohmahkhahZYAYkah

…doctor.

…врач.
vrahch

…lawyer.

…адвокат.
ahdvahKAHT

…engineer.

…инженер.
eenzhehNYEHR

…chemist.

…химик.
KHEEmeek

ESSENTIAL EXPRESSIONS

How long have you been here already?

Сколько времени вы ужё здесь?
SKOHL'kah VRYEHmeenee vih ooZHEH zdyehs'

I have been here...

Я уже здесь...
yah oozhEH zdyehs'

...a day.

...день.
dyehn'

...a week.

...неделю.
neeDYEHlyoo

...a month.

...месяц.
MYEHseets

Do you like it here?

Вам тут нравится?
vahm toot NRAHveetsah

Yes, very much.

Да, мне очень нравится.
dah mnyeh OHcheen' NRAHveetsah

No, not at all.

Нет, мне совсем не нравится.
nyeht, mnyeh sahfSYEHM nee NRAHveetsah

We're having a good time.

Мы хорошо проводим время.
mih kharahSHOH prahVOHdeem VRYEHmyah

I'm having a wonderful time.

Я здесь прекрасно провожу время.
yah zdyehs' preeKRAHSnah prahvahZHOO VRYEHmyah

Where are you staying?

Где вы остановились?
gdyeh vih ahstahnahVEElees'

ESSENTIAL EXPRESSIONS

At the hotel...
В гостинице...
vgahsTEEneetseh
Are you married? *(m./f.)*

Вы женаты?/Вы замужем?
vih zhehNAHtih/vih ZAHmoozhehm
Yes, I am./No, I am not. *(m.)*

Да, женат./Нет, не женат.
dah, zhehNAHT/nyeht, nee zhehNAHT
Yes, I am./No, I am not. *(f.)*

Да, замужем./Нет, не замужем.
dah, ZAHmoozhehm/nyeht, nee ZAHmoozhehm
Do you have children?

У вас есть дети?
oo vahs yehst' DYEHtee

Making Oneself Understood

Russians are generally very kind-hearted towards
those who make an effort at trying to learn or use
Russian. Often they will go out of their way to try and
understand or to help you with the language.

Do you speak...
Вы говорите...
vih gahvahREEtyeh
...English?

...по-английски?
pahahngLEEskee
...Russian?

...по-русски?
pahROOSkee

…German?

…по-немецки?
pahneeMYEHtskee

…French?

…по-французски?
pahfrahnTSOOSkee

…Spanish?

…по-испански?
paheesPAHNskee

Only a little.

Только немного.
TOHL'kah neemNOHgah

None at all.

Нет, совсем нет.
nyeht, sahfSYEHM nyeht

I understand Russian, but I don't speak it well.

Я понимаю по-русски, но плохо говорю.
yah pahneeMAHyoo pahROOSkee, noh PLOHkhah gahvahRYOO

Do you understand?

Вы понимаете?
vih pahneeMAHeetyeh

No, I don't understand.

Нет, не понимаю.
nyeht, nee pahneeMAHyoo

Please speak more slowly.

Пожалуйста, говорите медленее.
pahZHAHLstah gahvahREEtyeh MYEHDleenyehyeh

Please repeat that.

Пожалуйста, повторите.
pahZHAHLstah pahftahREEtyeh

Please write it down.

Пожалуйста, напишите это.
pahZHAHLstah nahpeeSHEEtyeh EHtah

Translate this for me, please.

Переведите, пожалуйста.
peereeveeDEEtyeh pahZHAHLstah

What does this/that mean?

Что это значит?
shtoh EHtah ZNAHcheet

What did he/she say?

Что он/она сказал(a)?
shtoh ohn/ahNAH skahzAHL(ah)

UPON ARRIVAL

Passport Control

When you arrive in Russia, you first go through "Passport control," where they will check your passport and visa. Here they may ask you several questions to verify your identity.

As of November 2002, foreign visitors to Moscow are also required to fill out a migration card. Visitors will retain one half of the card and will turn it in when they leave Moscow. This is to allow the Russian government to keep a record of people who have outstayed their visa and are in Moscow illegally.

Your passport, please.
Ваш паспорт, пожалуйста.
vahsh PAHSpahrt pahZHAHLstah
Here it is.
Вот он.
voht ohn
How long are you staying?
На сколько времени вы здесь?
nah SKOHL'kah VRYEHmeenee vih zdyehs'
A few days.
Несколько дней.
NYEHskahl'kah dnyey
A week.
Неделю.
neeDYEHlyoo
Two weeks.
Две недели.
dvyeh neeDYEHlee

A month.
Месяц.
MYEHseets
Two months.
Два месяца.
dvah MYEHseetsah
I'm here...
Я здесь...
yah zdyehs'
...on vacation.
...в отпуске.
VOHTpooskyeh
...on business.
...по делам.
pahdeelAHM
...to study.
...учусь.
ooCHOOS'
I don't understand.
Я не понимаю.
yah nee pahneeMAHyoo
I don't know.
Я не знаю.
yah nee ZNAHyoo

Customs

You will have to fill out customs declarations upon
entering and leaving the country. Be sure to declare
all jewelry, computer, photographic equipment and
other valuables, so that you do not have to pay
duty fees on them when you leave. Also, remember
that you cannot bring out more money than you
brought in.

Customs.

Таможня.

tahMOHZHnyah

To pass through customs.

Проходить таможенный досмотр.

prahkhahDEET' tahMOHzhehnnihy dahsMOHTR

Customs Official.

Таможенник.

tahMOHZHehneek

Have you anything to declare?

Вы хотите что-нибудь декларировать?

vih khahTEEtyeh SHTOHneeboot'
dyehklahREErahvaht'

I have nothing to declare.

Мне нечего декларировать.

mnyeh NYEHchevah dyehklREErahvaht'

Open this suitcase.

Откройте этот чемодан.

ahtKROYtyeh EHtaht chehmahDAHN

What is this?

Что это?

shtoh EHtah

You'll have to pay duty on this.

Вам надо заплатить за это пошлину.

vahm NAHdah zahplahTEET' zah EHtah
POHSHleenoo

It's for my personal use.

Это для личного пользования.

EHtah dlyah LEECHnahvah POHL'zahvahneeyah

It's a gift.

Это подарок.

EHtah pahDAHrahk

May I bring this in?

Можно это провезти?

MOHZHnah EHtah prahveezTEE

Do you have any more luggage?
Есть у вас ещё багаж?
yehst' oo vahs yeeSHCHOH bahgAHSH
Is that all?
Это всё?
EHtah vsyoh
I have...
У меня...
oo meenYAH
...a carton of cigarettes.
...блок сигарет.
blohk seegahRYEHT
...a bottle of wine/whiskey.
...бутылка вина/виски.
booTIHLkah veeNAH/VEESkee
I don't understand.
Я не понимаю.
yah nee pahneeMAHyoo
Does anyone here speak English?
**Говорит здесь кто-нибудь по-
    английски?**
*gahvahREET zdyehs' KTOHneeboot' pahahng
LEEskee*

Baggage

Luggage claim.
Выдача багажа.
VIHdahchah bahgahZHAH
Porter.
Носильщик.
nahSEEL'shcheek
Are there any luggage carts?
Тележки есть?
teeLYEHSHkee yehst'

Please carry this...
Пожалуйста, возьмите...
pahZHAHLstah vahz'MEEtyeh

...luggage.
...багаж.
bahGAHSH

...suitcase.
...чемодан.
chehmahDAHN

That's mine, (too).
Это моё, (тоже).
EHtah mahYOH (TOHzheh)

This is all my luggage.
Это весь мой багаж.
EHtah vyes' moy bahGAHZH

There's a suitcase missing.
Одного чемодана не хватает.
ahdnahVOH chehmahDAHnah nee khvahTAHeet

Take these things to the...
Отнесите эти вещи к...
ahtneeSEEtyeh EHtee VYEHshchee k

...bus.
...автобусу
ahfTOHboosoo

...taxi.
...такси.
tahkSEE

...customs.
...таможне.
tahMOHZHneh

...baggage room.
...камере хранения.
KAHmeeryeh khrahNYEHneeyah

How much do I owe you? *(m./f.)*
Сколько я вам должен/должна?
SKOHL'kah yah vahm DOHLzhehn/dahlzhNAH
My luggage is lost.
Багажа нет.
bahgahZHAH nyeht

Currency Exchange

You can change money at the airport, at a currency
exchange office and sometimes at your hotel. You
will have to present your passport and currency
declaration form each time you change money. Be
wary of people who want to change money for you
on the street for a "better rate." They may be trying
to pass off pre-1998 currency that is no longer
used. You may bring in as much foreign currency as
you like, but Russian money is not allowed out of
the country.

Currency exchange.
Обмен валюты.
ahbMYEHN vahLYOOtih
Where can I change some money?
Где можно обменять валюту?
gdyeh MOHZHnah ahbmeeNYAHT' vahLYOOtoo
I'd like to change some dollars.
Я хочу обменять доллары.
yah khahCHOO ahbmeeNYAHT' DOHlahrih
Can you cash these traveler's checks?
**Можете вы обменять эти дорожные
    чеки?**
*MOHZHehtyeh vih ahbmeeNYAHT' EHtee
dahROHZHnihyeh CHEHkee*

Can you change this for rubles?

Можете вы обменять это на рубли?

MOHZHehtyeh vih ahbmeenYAHT' EHtah nah rooBLEE

What's the exchange rate?

Какой валютный курс?

kahKOY vahLYOOTnihy koors

Write it down, please.

Запишите, пожалуйста.

zahpiSHITyeh pahZHAHLstah

Can you give me smaller bills?

Можете вы дать мне мелкими купюрами?

MOHZHehtyeh vih daht' mnyeh MYEHLkeemee kooPYOOrahmee

ACCOMMODATIONS

The good news about finding a place to stay in Russia is that you now have some real choices. Motels and reasonable budget hotels are slowly beginning to spring up in Russia. Today's mid-range hotels are typically the best hotels left over from the Soviet days. Although many are showing their age, they are generally adequate accommodations. Quality and service can vary widely from one establishment to the next, but most will have private bathrooms, phones and TVs in the rooms. Reservations will make travel easier and are strongly advised, but you can usually walk in most hotels and get a room on the spot.

In the 1990s, luxury hotels were built in Moscow, St. Petersburg and a few of the other larger cities to accommodate business travelers and conferences. The prices are steep—especially in Moscow—but the service and amenities rival those found in five-star hotels around the world. A flurry of building in 2003 finally promises to provide a dozen or more brand new budget hotels in Moscow and St. Petersburg.

Other new economical alternatives include hostels, guest houses, dormitories and campgrounds. A favorite of students and academics are pre-arranged homestays with English-speaking families or the rental of private apartments. A quick search on the Web will turn up the URLs of associations and organizations that can help make these arrangements.

When choosing accommodations, common sense and caution should prevail. Remember that you usually get what you pay for.

Check In

Do you speak English?

Вы говорите по-английски?
vih gahvahREEtyeh pahahngLEEskee
Do you have any rooms available?

У вас есть свободные номера?
oo vas yest' svahBOHDneeyeh nahmeRAH
Do you have a reservation?

У вас есть броня?
oo vahs est' BROHNyah
I have a reservation./(f.)

Я заказал(а) заранее.
yah zahkahZAHL(ah) zahRAHNeeyeh
Here are my documents.

Вот мои документы.
voht mahEE dahkooMYEHNtih
My last name is...

Моя фамилия...
mahYAH fahMEEleeyah
I'd like a single/double room.

Я хочу номер на одного/на двоих.
yah khahCHOO NOHmeer nah ahdnahVOH/nah dvahEEKH
I'd like a room with...

Я хочу номер с...
yah khahCHOO NOHmeer s
...a double bed.

...двуспальной кроватью.
dvooSPAHL'nay krahVAHT'yoo
...two twin beds.

...двумя кроватями.
dvooMYAH krahVAHteemee

...a bath.

...ванной.
VAHNnay

...a shower.

...душем.
DOOshehm

...a private toilet.

...туалетом.
tooahLYEHtahm.

...a telephone.

...телефоном.
teeleeFOHnahm

...a television.

...телевизором.
teeleeVEEzahrahm

…a window.

...окном.
ahkNOHM

Is there...

Есть...
yehst'

...room service?

...обслуживание в номере?
ahpSLOOzheevahneeyeh VNOHmeeryeh

...a dining room?

...столовая?
stahLOHvahyah

...a restaurant?

...ресторан?
reestahRAHN

...air conditioning?

...кондиционер?
kahndeetsehahNYEHR

...heating?

...отопление?
ahtahpLYEHneeyeh
...hot water?

...горячая вода?
gahRYAHcheeyah vahDAH
May I see the room?

Можно посмотреть номер?
MOHZHnah pahsmahtRYEHT' NOHmeer
Good, I'll take it.

Хорошо, я беру.
kahrahSHOH yah beROO
No, I don't like it.

Нет, мне не нравится.
nyeht, mnyeh nee NRAHveetsah
Do you have anything else?

Есть ли у вас другой номер?
yehst' lee oo vas drooGOY NOHmeer
I asked for a room with a bath./(f.)

Я просил(а) номер с ванной.
yah prahSEEL(ah) NOHmeer SVAHNnay

Registration

No matter where you are staying, you must register
your visa at the Department of Visas and Registration
(OVIR) within three days of entering the country.
Your hotel will usually do it for you. Once your
reservation has been confirmed, you will be asked to
present your passport and visa, and to fill out a
registration form. Your passport may be kept
overnight for processing, but you should be able to
pick it up the next day. If you plan to exchange

money, be sure you do it before you register, since you will need your passport to carry out the transaction.

Registration.

Регистрация.
reegeeSTRAHtseeyah
Registration form.

Анкета для приезжающих.
ahnKYEHtah dlyah preeeeZHAHyooshcheekh
Fill out this form.

Заполните анкету.
zahPOHLneetyeh ahnKYEHtoo
Surname./First name./Patronymic.

Фамилия./Имя./Отчество.
fahMEELeeyah//EEMyah/OHTcheestvah
Date of birth.

Дата рождения.
DAHtah razhDYEHneeyah
Place of birth.

Место рождения.
MYEHStah razhDYEHneeyah
Marital status.

Семейное положение.
sehMYEYnahyeh pahlahZHENeeyeh
Age.

Возраст.
VOHZrahst
Sex.

Пол.
pohl
Nationality.

Гражданство.
grahzhDAHNtsvah

Sign here.

Подпишите тут.
pahtpeeSHEEtyeh toot

Your passport, please.

Ваш паспорт, пожалуйста.
vash PAHSpahrt pahZHAHLstah

How many people?

Сколько человек?
SKOHLkah chelahVEHK

How many nights?

Сколько суток?
SKOHL'kah SOOUtahk

What does this mean?

Что это значит?
shtoh EHtah ZNAHcheet

What's my room number?

Какой у меня номер?
kahKOY oo meeNYAH NOHmeer

My key, please.

Мой ключ, пожалуйста.
moy klyooch pahZHAHLstah

Take my luggage to my room.

Доставьте мой багаж в номер.
dahSTAHF'tyeh moy bahGAHSH VNOHmeer

Is there an elevator? Does it work?

Есть лифт? Он работает?
yehst' leeft? ohn rabOHTahyet

The Staff

Most old Soviet hotels still have a manager on duty on each floor. They may hold your key while you are out and can provide things like new lightbulbs and extra

ACCOMMODATIONS

towels. These older women can be very useful and it is
in your best interest to befriend them.

Hall monitor.
Дежурная.
dehZHURnahyah
Maid.
Горничная.
GOHRneechnahyah
Receptionist.
Секретарша.
seekreeTAHRshah
Switchboard operator.
Телефонистка.
teeleefahNEESTkah
Waiter.
Официант.
ahfeetseeAHNT
Waitress.
Официантка.
ahfeetseeAHNTkah
Manager.
Директор.
deeRYEHKtahr
Doorman.
Швейцар.
shveyTSAHR
Porter.
Носильщик.
nahSEEL'shcheek

ACCOMMODATIONS

Questions and Requests

The voltage in Russia is 220 A.C. The plugs and sockets are like those used in Europe (two round prongs), so Americans should bring adaptors and converters for their electrical appliances like hair dryers and electric razors. Unless you are staying in one of the five-star Western hotels, do not expect to find a hairdryer, scented soap, moisturizer or shampoo in your room.

Can you please bring me...
Прошу принесите мне...
prahSHOO preeneeSEEtyeh mnyeh
   ...a towel.

...полотенце.
pahlahTYEHNtseh
   ...a blanket.

...одеяло.
ahdeeYAHlah
   ...a pillow.

...подушку.
pahDOOSHkoo
   ...a pillowcase.

...наволочку.
NAHvahlahchkoo
   ...an ashtray.

...пепельницу.
PYEHpeel'neetsoo
   ...some hangers.

...несколько вешалок.
NYEHskahl'ka VYEHshahlahk
   ...some soap.

...мыло.
MIHlah

May I have another?

Можно ещё?
MOHZHnah yehSHCHhYOH
Where are the toilets?

Где уборная?
gdyeh ooBOHRnahyah
Where is the...

Где...
gdyeh
...restaurant? bar?

...ресторан? бар?
reestahRAHN bahr
...post office?

...почта?
POHCHtah
...information office?

...бюро обслуживания?
byooROH ahpSLOOzhehvahneeyah
...hairdresser/barber?

...парикмахерская?
pahreekMAHkheerskahyah
...currency exchange office?

...можно обменять валюту?
MOHZHnah ahbmeeNYAHT' vahLYOOtoo
...light switch?

...выключатель?
vihklyooCHAteel'
...electrical outlet?

...розетка?
rahzYEHTkah
Do you have a safe, where I can store my valuables?

У вас есть сейф, где я могу хранить
  свои цености?
oo vahs est' seyf, gdyeh yah mahGOO khraNIT'
svahEE TSYEHNnostee

ACCOMMODATIONS

Can I use the telephone?
Можно позвонить?
MOHZnah pahzvahNIT'

Problems and Complaints

It is common for the hot water to be turned off for
several hours for repairs during the day or in fact for
several weeks in most neighborhoods during the
summer.

The ... doesn't work.
...не работает.
nee rahBOHtaheet
....shower...
Душ...
doosh
....faucet...
Кран...
krahn
... toilet...
Туалет...
tooahLYEHT
...heating...
Отопление...
ahtahpLYEHneeyeh
...air conditioning...
Кондиционер...
kahndeetsehahNYEHR
...light...
Свет...
svyeht

…radio…

Радио...
RAHdeeoh

…television…

Телевизор...
teeleeVEEzahr

…telephone…

Телефон...
teeleeFOHN

…electrical socket…

Розетка...
rahZYEHTkah

There is no...

Нет...
nyeht

… (hot) water.

...(горячей) воды.
(gahRYAHchey) vahDIH

…toilet paper.

...туалетной бумаги.
tooahLYEHTnoy booMAHgee

…lamp.

...лампы.
LAHMpih

…light.

...света.
SVYEHtah

… fan.

...вентилятора.
veenteeLYAHtahrah

The sink is clogged.

Раковина засорена.
RAHkahveenah zahsahreeNAH

The door/window doesn't close.

Дверь/окно не закрывается.
dvyehr'/ahkNOH nee zahkrihVAHeetsah
The door doesn't lock.

Замок в двери не работает.
zahmOHK vdveeREE nee rahBOHtaheet
Can it be repaired?

Можно починить это?
MOHZHnah pahcheeNEET' EHtah
It's dirty. Change it, please.

Это грязное. Смените, пожалуйста.
EHtah GRYAHZnahyah. smeNEETtyeh, pahZHALstah
It's too hot/cold/noisy.

В комнате слишком жарко/холодно/
  шумно.
VKOHMnatyeh SLISHkahm
ZHARkah/KHOlahdnah/SHUMnah

Check Out

I'm leaving today/tomorrow morning.

Я уезжаю сегодня/завтра утром.
yah ooyeeZHAHyoo seeVOHdnyah/ZAHFtrah
OOtrahm
Please prepare my bill.

Приготовьте мне счёт, пожалуйста.
preegahTOHF'tyeh mnyeh shchoht pahZHAHLstah
Do you accept credit cards?

Можно оплатить кредитной карточкой?
MOHZHnah ahplahTEET' kreeDEETnay
KAHRtahchkay

May I have a receipt?

Можно получить квитанцию?
MOHZnah pahluCHIT' kviTAHNtseeyoo

There's a mistake in the bill.

В счёте ошибка.
VSHCHOtyeh ahSHEEBkah

Could you please send someone to get my bags?

Пришлите, пожалуйста, кого-нибудь вынести мой багаж.
preeSHLEEtyeh pahZHAHLstah kahVOHneeboot' VIHneestee moy bahGAHSH

Where can I get a cab?

Где можно поймать такси?
gdyeh MOHZHnah payMAHT' tahkSEE

Where is the metro?

Где метро?
gdyeh metROH

TRANSPORTATION

Public transportation in Russia is quite extensive and
relatively efficient. Buses, streetcars and trolleys all
run from six A.M. until one A.M. Tickets are usually
purchased beforehand at subway stations, some kiosks
and hotels, but it is not enough to simply have a ticket.
The paper ticket must be punched once on board by
puncher mechanisms located strategically throughout
the bus or trolley. If the bus is crowded, it is common
practice to merely pass your ticket towards the
direction of the box and the punched ticket will be
passed back to you. Spot checks are done occasionally
and passengers without punched tickets are fined and
sometimes expelled from the bus or trolley. Stops are
marked with an "A" for buses, "T" for trolleys and a
different capital "T" for street cars. These signs also
carry the name of the stop, the name of the terminal
stop and timetable or interval between buses. Numbers
denote the routes. If a passenger asks you if you are
getting off and you are not, it is expected that you will
move out of the passenger's way.

Buses, Street Cars and Trolleys

Bus.
Автобус.
ahfTOHboos
Street car.
Трамвай.
trahmVAY
Trolley.
Троллейбус.
trahLEYboos

Where is the bus/street car/trolley stop?

Где остановка автобуса/
  трамвая/троллейбуса?
gdyeh ahstahNOHFkah ahfTOHboosah
/trahmVAHyah /trahLEYboosah
When's the next bus?

Когда идёт следующий автобус?
kahgDAH eedYOHT SLYEHdooyooshcheey
ahfTOHboos
Where can I buy a ticket?

Где мне купить билет/талоны?
gdych mnyeh kooPEET' beeLYEHT/tahLOHnih
Bus driver.

Водитель.
vahDEEteel'
Inspector.

Контролёр.
kahntrahLYOHR
Fare.

Плата за проезд.
PLAHtah zah prahYEHST
Monthly pass.

Месячный билет.
MYEHseechnihy beeLYEHT
Cash box./Cashier.

Касса.
KAHsah
Pass me a ticket, please.

Передайте мне, пожалуйста, билет.
peereeDAYtyeh mnyeh pahZHAHLstah beeLYEHT
What bus do I take to get to Red Square?

Какой автобус идёт до Красной
  площади?
kahKOY ahfTOHboos eedYOHT dah KRAHSnay
PLOHshchahdee

How can I get to…

Как доехать до...
kahk dahEHKHaht' doh

What is the next stop?

Какая следующая остановка?
kahKAHyah SLYEHdooyooshchahyah
ahstahNOHFkah

Do I have to transfer?

Мне надо пересесть?
mnyeh NAHdah peereeSYEHST'

How many stops until we reach the center of town?

Сколько остановок до центра города?
SKOHL'kah ahstahNOHvahk dah TSEHNtrah
GOHrahdah

You've gotten on the wrong bus.

Вы сели не на тот автобус.
vih SYEHlee   nee nah toht ahfTOHboos

Can you tell me where to get off?

Вы не скажете, на какой остановке мне
    надо выйти?
vih nee SKAzhehtyeh nah kahKOY ahstahNOHFkyeh
mnyeh NAHdah VIHYtee

You've missed your stop.

Вы проехали свою остановку.
vih prahYEHkhahlee svahYOO ahstahNOHFkoo

Are you getting off?

Вы сейчас выходите?
vih seeCHAHS vihKHOHdeetyeh

I want to get off here/at the next stop.

Я хочу сойти здесь/на следующей
    остановке.
yah khahCHOO sayTEE zdyehs'/nah
SLYEHdooyooshchey ahstahNOHFkyeh

Excuse me, can I get through?

Извините, можно пройти?
eezveeNEEtyeh, MOHZHnah prahyTEE
Excuse me, I'm getting off at the next stop.

Извините, я выхожу на следующей.
eezveeNEEtyeh yah VIHkhahzhoo nah
SLYEHdooyooshchey

Subway

Russian subways are quick, safe and efficient. The stations are marked by a large red "M," which is illuminated at night. In order to get to the trains, you must drop a subway token into a turnstile. These tokens, which are different in Moscow and St. Petersburg, must be purchased from cashiers in the vestibules of the subway stations. Cards with magnetic strips are also being introduced as a form of payment. They are good for a set number of trips and may also be bought at the cashier's office at most subway stations. Trains run from six A.M. until one A.M. Smoking is prohibited. Subway cars in Moscow sometimes have subway maps—in both Cyrillic and Roman alphabets—inside the cars, but it is best to figure out your trip ahead of time and count the stops between stations. The Moscow system is a tourist attraction in itself, since each station is built from a different architectural design.

Subway.

Метро.
meetROH
Cashier's office.

Касса.
KAHsah

Tokens.

Жетоны.
zhehTOHnihy
Magnetic card.

Магнитная карта.
mahNEETnahyah KAHRtah
Entrance.

Вход.
fkhoht
Exit.

Выход.
VIHkhaht
No entrance.

Нет входа.
nyeht FKHOHdah
No exit.

Нет выхода.
nyeht VIHkhahdah
Way out.

Выход в город.
VIHkaht VGOHraht
To the trains.

К поездам.
kpaheezDAHM
Transfer.

Переход.
peereeKHOHT
Keep to the left/right.

Держитесь левой/правой стороны.
deerZHEEtyehs' LYEHvay/PRAHvay STOHrahnih
Please give me change.

Разменяйте, пожалуйста.
rahzmeeNYAYtyeh pahZHAHLstah

TRANSPORTATION

Where's the nearest subway stop?

Где ближайшая станция метро?
gdyeh bleeZHAYshahyah STAHNtseeyah meetROH

Does this line go to...

Эта линия идёт до...
EHtah LEEneeyah eedYOHT dah

What line should I take to...

По какой линии мне доехать до...
pah kahKOY LEEneeee mnyeh dahYEHkhaht' dah

Do I have to transfer?

Мне надо пересесть?
mnyeh NAHdah peereeSYEHST'

Can you tell me what the next station is?

**Скажите, пожалуйста, какая
   следующая станция?**
*skahZHEEtyeh pahZHAHLstah kahKAHyah
SLYEHdooyooshchahyah STAHNtseeyah*

The next station is...

Следующая станция...
SLYEHdooyooshchahyah STAHNtseeyah

Can you tell me where to get off?

Вы мне скажете когда надо сходить?
*vih mnyeh SKAHzhehtyeh kahgDAH NAHdah
skhahDEET'*

Careful, the doors are closing.

Осторожно, двери закрываются.
ahstahROHZHnah DVYEHree zahkrihVAHyootsah

The train goes as far as...

Поезд следует до станции...
POHeest SLYEHdooeet dah STAHNtseeee

This is the last stop.

Поезд дальше не пойдёт.
POHeest DAHL'sheh nee pahyDYOHT

Taxi

In addition to being ordered by phone, taxis can be found in front of major hotels and at taxi stands. Official cabs have a checkerboard pattern on the door or roof. A small, green light in the front window means that the cab is available. In recent years unofficial taxis have become common place in the larger cities. Simply stand on the side of the road and extend your arm. When a driver stops, negotiate the destination and fare before you get in. Do not try to take an unofficial cab if you do not speak enough Russian to negotiate. Use caution and common sense. Do not get into a car when there are other passengers already in the back.

Taxi./Private Cabs.

Такси./Частники.
tahkSEE/CHAHSneekee
Taxi stand.

Стоянка такси.
stahYAHNkah tahkSEE
Where can I get a taxi?

Где мне поймать такси?
gdyeh mnyeh pahyMAHT' tahkSEE
Where is the nearest taxi stand?

Где ближайшая стоянка такси?
gdyeh bleeZHAYshahyah stahYAHNkah tahkSEE
Please call me a taxi.

Пожалуйста, вызовите мне такси.
pahZHAHLstah VIHzahveetyeh mnyeh tahkSEE
Are you free?

Вы свободны?
vih svahBOHDnih

TRANSPORTATION

Where do you want to go?

Куда вам?
kooDAH vahm
Here's the address.

Вот адрес.
voht AHDrees
To the Bolshoi Theater, please.

Пожалуйста, к Большому театру.
pahZHAHLstah kbahl'SHOHmoo teeAHTroo
How much will the ride cost?

Сколько этот проезд будет стоить?
SKOHL'kah EHtaht prahYEHST BOOdeet STOHeet'
Can you get my bags, please.

Возьмите, пожалуйста, мои чемоданы.
vahz'MEEtyeh pahZHAHLstah mahEE chehmahDAHnih
I'm (not) in a hurry.

Я (не) спешу.
yah (nee) speeSHOO
Stop here.

Остановитесь здесь.
ahstahnahVEEtyehs' zdyehs'
Wait for me here.

Подождите меня.
pahdahzhDEEtyeh meenYAH
I'll be back in a couple of minutes.

Я вернусь через несколько минут.
yah veerNOOS' CHEHrees NYEHskahl'kah meeNOOT
Keep the change.

Сдачи не надо.
ZDAHchee nyeh NAHdah
Thank you. Good-bye.

Спасибо. До свидания.
spahSEEbah. dah sveeDAHneeyah

Car Rental and Driving

Driving in Russia is only for the very brave at heart. Since the 1990s, the number of Russians who own cars has risen dramatically. Roads that were constructed for mass transport are now packed with individual cars. Consequently, congestion and traffic accidents have increased. In Moscow and St. Petersburg, seven to nine A.M. and four to seven P.M. are considered rush hours *(часы пик/chahSIH peek)*.

Road regulations are complex and strictly enforced, even on foreigners, who are subject to the full severity of Russian law. Traffic police *(ГАИшники/ gahEESHneekee)* stop speeders, and check for sobriety and legality of drivers. When they point their stick at you, you are supposed to pull over and show them your documents. If they issue you a fine, never give them hard currency and be sure to get a receipt.

You can rent cars at the airport or through the better hotels, but you must have an international driver's license, international insurance, passport and credit card. Rental rates are high, gas stations can be difficult to find and gas is expensive.

Car rental.
Прокат машин.
prahKAHT mahSHEEN
I'd like to rent a car.

Я хочу взять машину в прокат.
yah khahCHOO vzyaht' mahSHEEnoo f prahKAHT

What's the rate...

Сколько это стоит...
SKOHL'kah EHtah STOHeet
...per day?

...в день?
vdyehn'
...per week?

...в неделю?
vneeDYEHlyoo
What's the charge per kilometer?

Сколько стоит километр?
SKOHL'kah STOHeet keelahMYEHTR
I need it for...

Она мне нужна...
ahNAH mnyeh noozhNAH
...a day.

...на день.
nah dyehn'

...three days.

...на три дня.
nah tree dnyah
...a week.

...на неделю.
nah neeDYEHlyoo
...two weeks.

...на две недели.
nah dvyeh neeDYEHlee
Here's my (international driver's) license.

Вот мои (международные

водительские) права.
voht mahEE (meezhdoonahROHDnihyeh
vahDEEteel'skeeyeh) prahVAH

Here's my credit card.

Вот моя кредитная карточка.
voht mahYAH kreeDEETnahyah KAHRtahchkah

I am not familiar/*(f.)* with this car.

Я не знаком(а) с этой машиной.
yah nee znahKOHM(ah) SEHtay mahSHEEnay

What is this?

Что это?
shtoh EHtah

Where can I buy gas/oil/a street map?

Где мне купить бензин/масло/
  карту дорог?
gdyeh mnyeh kooPEET' beenZEEN/
  MAHSlah/KAHRtoo dahROHK

I'm out of gas.

У меня кончился бензин.
oo meeNYAH KOHNcheelsyah beenZEEN

Self-service.

Самообслуживание.
sahmahahpSLUzheevahneeyeh

Gas pump.

Бензоколонка.
beenzahkahLOHNkah

Service station.

Автозаправочная станция.
ahftahzahPRAHvahchnahyah STAHNtseeyah

Parking lot.

Стоянка (для автомобиля).
stahYAHNkah (dlyah ahftahmahBEElyah)

Boats

Boat trips provide a different view of Moscow and St. Petersburg from their rivers and canals. Guided trips along the canals, hydrofoil rides or tours of the Neva during the summer in St. Petersburg can be very enjoyable. Riverboats usually operate from May to late September, but schedules often depend on the weather.

Boat.

Пароход.
pahrahKHOHT

Hydrofoil.

Ракета.
rahKYEHtah

Row boat.

Гребная лодка.
grehbNAHyah LOHTkah

Cruise.

Круиз.
krooEEZ

Tour.

Экскурсия.
ehksKOORseeyah

When does the next boat leave?

Когда отходит следующий пароход?
kahgDAH ahtKHOHdeet SLYEHdooyooshcheey pahrahKHOHT

Where do we get tickets?

Где можно купить билеты?
gdyeh MOHZHnah kooPEET' beelYEHTih

How much are the tickets?

Сколько стоят билеты?
SKOHL'kah STOHyeht beeLYEHtih

Where is the pier?

Где пристань?
gdyeh PREEstahn'

How long is the trip?

Сколько времени длится путешествие?
SKOHL'kah VRYEHmeenee DLEETsah pooteeSHEHSTveeyeh

Where do we stop?

В какие порты мы заходим?
fkahKEEyeh pahrTIH mih zahKHOHdeem

Deck.

Палуба.
PAHloobah

Cabin.

Каюта.
kahYOOtah

Life jacket.

Спасательный жилет.
spahSAHteel'nihy zheeLYEHT

Lifeboat.

Спасательная лодка.
spahSAHteel'nahyah LOHTkah

I feel seasick.

У меня морская болезнь.
oo meeNYAH mahrSKAHyah bahLYEHZN'

Trains

Like all long-distance travel in Russia, train trips must be reserved in advance. You can sometimes make reservations through your hotel. As with hotel rooms and museum entrance fees, foreigners are charged a significantly higher rate for train tickets than Russians pay.

Train is the most common form of travel between Moscow and St. Petersburg. There are ten departures a day. The trip takes about ten hours. Prices vary according to seating.

Long-distance train travel is considered everything three to four hours from Moscow. Local or suburban service is everything closer. Because Russia has eleven time zones, in order to avoid confusion, train schedules throughout Russia are posted according to Moscow time.

Although some food is usually available for purchase on the train, most Russians pack their own food and drinks for the trip.

Train.
Поезд.
POHeest
Train station.
Вокзал.
vahkZAHL
Ticket machine.
Автомат.
ahvtahMAHT
Schedule.
Расписание.
rahspeeSAHneeyeh
Ticket office.
Билетная касса.
beeLYEHTnahyah KAHsah

When does the ticket office open?

Когда откроется билетная касса?
kahgDAH ahtKROHeetsah beeLYEHTnahyah KAHsah

Reservation office.

Предварительная продажа билетов.
preedvahREEtyehl'nahyah prahDAHzhah beeLYEHtahf

Information office.

Справочное бюро.
SPRAHvahchnahyeh byooROH

Express long-distance trains.

Экспрессы поезда дальнего следования.
ehksPRYEHsih pahyehzDAH DAHL'nehvah SLYEHdahvahneeyeh

Standard long-distance train.

Скорый поезд.
SKOHrihy POHeest

Local (suburban) trains.

Электрички.
ehleekTREECHkee

Deluxe class.

Международный вагон.
meezhdoonahROHDnihy vahGOHN

First class.

Мягкий вагон.
MYAHKHkeey vahGOHN

Second class.

Купированный вагон.
kooPEErahvahnnihy vahGOHN

Third class.

Плацкартный вагон.
plahtsKAHRTnihy vahGOHN

One-way ticket.

Билет в один конец.
beeLYEHT vahDEEN kaNnYEHTS
Round-trip ticket.

Билет туда и обратно.
beeLYEHT tooDAH ee ahbRAHTnah
Timetable.

Расписание поездов.
rahspeeSAHneeyeh paheezDOHF
Departure time.

Время отправления.
VRYEHmyah ahtprahvLYEHneeyah
Arrival time.

Время прибытия.
VRYEHmyah preeBIHteeyah
When is the next train to Kiev?

Когда отходит следующий поезд на
Киев?
kahgDAH ahtKHOHdeet SLYEHdooyooshcheey
POHeest nah KEEeef
What's the cost of a ticket to Tblisi?

Сколько стоит билет до Тбилиси?
SKOHL'kah STOHeet beeLYEHT dah tbeeLEEsee
I'd like to reserve a seat.

Я хочу заказать платцкарту.
yah khahCHOO zahkahZAHT' plahtsKAHRToo
I'd like to reserve a berth in the sleeping car.

Я хочу купить билет в спальный вагон.
yah khaCHOO kooPEET' beeLlYEHT FSPAHL'nihy
vahGOHN
From what platform does the train leave?

С какой платформы отходит поезд?
skahKOY plahtFOHRmih ahtKHOHdeet POHeest

When does the train arrive in Erevan?

Когда поезд приходит в Ереван?
kahgDAH POHeest preeKHOHdeet veereeVAHN

Are we on time?

Поезд идёт по расписанию?
POHeest eedYOHT pah rahspeeSAHneeyoo

The train is twenty minutes late.

Поезд опаздывает на двадцать минут.
*POHeest ahPAHZdihvaheet nah DVAHTsaht'
meeNOOT*

Where are we now?

Где мы сейчас?
gdyeh mih seeCHAHS

How long do we stop here?

Сколько стоит здесь поезд?
SKOHL'kah stahEET zdyehs' POHeest

Is there time to get off?

Я успею сойти?
yah oosPYEHyoo sayTEE

Is this seat taken?

Это место занято?
EHtah MYEHstah ZAHneetah

This is my seat.

Это моё место.
EHtah mahYOH MYEHstah

Am I bothering you?

Я вам мешаю?
yah vahm meeSHAHyoo

Can I open/shut the window?

Можно открыть/закрыть окно?
MOHZHnah ahtKRIHT'/zahKRIHT' ahkNOH

Can I turn out/on the light?

Можно выключить/включить свет?
MOHZHnah VIHklyoocheet'/fklyooCHEET'svyeht

I'd like the top/bottom bunk.

Я хочу верхнюю/нижнюю полку.
yah khahCHOO VYEHRKHnyooyoo/NEEZHnyooyoo POHLkoo

We'd like some tea.

Принесите нам чай.
preeneeSEEtyeh nahm chay

Two glasses, please.

Два стакана, пожалуйста.
dvah stahKAHnah pahZHAHLstah

Where is the...

Где...
gdyeh

...baggage check?

...приём багажа?
preeYOHM bahgahZHAH

...lost and found?

...бюро находок?
byooROH nahKHOHdahk

...baggage room?

...камера хранения?
KAHmeerah khrahNYEHneeyah

...snackbar?

...буфет?
booFYEHT

...bathroom?

...туалет?
tooahLYEHT

...conductor?

...кондуктор?
kahnDOOKtahr

...ticket taker? *(m./f.)*

...проводник/проводница?
prahvahdNEEK/prahvahdNEEtsah

...ticket checker?

...контролёр?
kahntrahLYOHR

...porter?

...носильщик?
nahSEEL'shcheek

...platform?

...платформа?
plahtFOHRmah

...gate?

...вход?
fkhoht

...waiting room?

...зал ожидания?
zahl ahzheeDAHneeyah

...sleeping car?

...спальный вагон?
SPAHL'nihy vahGOHN

...dining car?

...вагон-ресторан?
vahGOHNreestahRAHN

...smoking car?

...вагон для курящих?
vahGOHN dlyah kooRYAHshcheekh

...my sleeping compartment?

...моё купе?
mahYOH kooPEH

Have a good trip!

Счастливого пути!
shahsLEEvahvah pooTEE

Planes

Aeroflot, the Russian airline, now flies directly out of the United States, so be sure to ask your travel agent about them. You may find that their rates to Russia are significantly less expensive than most other international carriers. Located about eightenn miles northwest of central Moscow, Sheremetevo-2 International Airport handles all foreign flights into Moscow. The city also has four other airports that handle domestic flights. Air travel within Russia is less regulated and often uncomfortable. Most Russians prefer to travel by train whenever possible.

Plane.

Самолёт.
sahmahLYOHT
Airport.

Аэропорт.
ahehrahPOHRT
Arrival./Departure.

Прибытие./Вылет.
preeBIHteeyeh/VIHlyeht
Boarding pass.

Посадочный талон.
pahSAHdahchnihy tahLOHN
I'd like to make a reservation.

Я хочу заказать билет.
yah khahCHOO zahkaZAIIT beeLYEHT
Is there a direct flight?

Есть ли прямой полёт?
yehst' lee preeMOY pahLYOHT
How long is the layover?

Как долго самолёт будет стоять?
kahk DOHLgah sahmahLYOHT BOOdeet stahYAHT'

When is the next flight?

Когда вылетает следующий самолёт?
*kahgDAH vihleeTAHeet SLYEHdooyooshcheey
sahmahLYOHT*

One-way ticket.

Билет в один конец.
beeLYEHT vahDEEN kaNYEHTS

Round-trip ticket.

Билет туда и обратно.
beeLYEHT tooDAH ee ahbRAHTnah

Is flight (number five) on time?

Рейс (номер пять) идёт по расписанию?
*reys (NOHmeer pyaht') eedYOHT pah rahspee-
SAHneeyoo*

I'd like to change/confirm my flight.

Я хочу поменять/подтвердить рейс.
yah khatCHOO pahmeeNYAHT'/pahttveerDEET' reys

I'd like to cancel my reservation.

Я хочу отказаться от билета.
yah khatCHOO ahtkahZAHT'sah aht beeLYEtah

How much luggage am I allowed?

**Какой вес багажа разрешается
   провозить?**
*kahKOY vyehs bahgahZHAH rahzreeSHAHeetsah
prahvahZEET'*

What's the flight number?

Какой номер рейса?
kahKOY NOHmeer REYsah

Which gate do we leave from?

**Через какой выход посадка на наш
   рейс?**
*CHEEryehz kahKOY VIHkhaht pahSAHTkah nah
nahsh reys*

Boarding gate.

Выход на посадку.
VIHkhaht nah pahSAHTkoo

What time do we leave/arrive?

Когда вылет/прибытие?
kahgDAH VIHlyeht/ preeBIHTeeyeh

What time should I check in?

**Во сколько надо регистрировать
  багаж?**
*vah SKOHL'kah NAHdah reegeestREErahvaht'
bahGAHSH*

Call the stewardess.

Вызовите стюардессу.
VIHzahveetyeh styooahrdYEHsoo

Fasten your seat belts.

Пристегните ремни.
preesteegNEEtyeh reemNEE

Will there be food served?

Будут ли кормить в самолёте?
BOOdoot lee kahrMEET' fsahmahLYOHtyeh

Can I smoke on board?

Можно курить в полёте?
MOHZHnah kooREET' vpahLYOHtyeh

Is there a bus from the airport into the city?

**Есть ли автобус от аэропорта до
  города?**
*yehst' lee ahfTOHboos aht ahehrahPOHRtah dah
GOHrahdah*

BANKING

At the Bank

You can exchange money at the airport, in your hotel, at currency exchange offices, or local banks. If you are not in a hurry, shop around for the best rates. Remember that you will need your passport and customs declaration to carry out the transaction. Be sure to receive a receipt of the transaction. You will need to attach it to your customs declaration when you leave the country. Old, ripped or defaced bills will not be accepted for exchange, so be sure you check the condition of your money before you leave home.

There are one hundred kopecks in one ruble. Kopeck coins exist in one, ten and fifty kopeck denominations. Ruble coins exist in the amounts of one, two and five rubles. Paper rubles are issued in the values of ten, fifty, one hundred and five hundred. If you encounter larger bank notes, they are left over from the currency devaluation of 1998 and are no longer accepted.

ATMs have sprung up everywhere but not all machines work and most ATMs distribute only rubles.

Traveler's checks are difficult to cash except at banks. Credit cards are also not widely accepted except at larger hotels, expensive boutiques and some high-end restaurants. However, you can use your credit cards to obtain cash advances at banks and larger hotels.

Currency exchange.

Обмен валюты.
ahbMYEHN vahLYOOtih

Where can I exchange money?

Где можно обменять валюту?
gdyeh MOHZHnah ahbmeeNYAHT' vahLYOOtoo

Where can I find the nearest bank?

Где находится ближайший банк?
gdyeh nahKHOHdeetsah bleeZHAYsheey bahnk

When does the bank open?

Во сколько открывается банк?
vahSKOHL'kah ahtkrihVAHeetsah bahnk

How late is the bank open?

Во сколько закрывается банк?
vahSKOHL'kah zahkrihVAHeetsah bahnk

The bank is open from nine thirty A.M. to one P.M.

Банк работает с половина десятого до
**   часа дня.**
bahnk rahBOHtaheet spahlahVEEnah
deesYAHtahvah dah CHAHsah dnyah

What is the exchange rate for dollars today?

Какой сегодня обменный курс доллара?
kahKOY seeVOHnyah ahbMYEHnihy koors
DOHlahrah?

Can you write it down, please.

Запишите, пожалуйста.
zahpeesSHEEtyeh pahZHALstah

I'd like to change some dollars.

Я хочу обменять доллары.
yah khahtCHOO ahbmeenYAHT' DOHlahrih

I'd like to cash some traveler's checks.

Я хочу разменять дорожные чеки.
yah khahtCHOO rahzmeeNYAHT' dahROHZHnihyeh
CHEHkee

Can I purchase an international money order here?

Можно здесь купить международный почтовый перевод?

*MOHZHnah zdyehs' kooPEET' meezhdoo-
nahROHDnihy pahchTOHvihy peereeVOHT*

What's the charge?

Сколько стоит?

SKOHL'kah STOHeet

I'm expecting money from America.

Для меня должны быть деньги из Америки.

*dlyah meeNYAH dahlzhNIH biht' DYEHN'gee ees
ahMYEHreekee*

Has it arrived?

Они уже пришли?

ahNEE ooZHEH preeSHLEE

Go to the cashier's office.

Идите в кассу.

eeDEEtyeh FKAHsoo

Where is the cashier's office?

Где касса?

gdyeh KAHsah

When is the cashier open?

Когда касса открыта?

kahgDAH KAHsah ahtKRIHtah

Are you the cashier?/(f.)

Вы кассир(ша)?

vih kahSEER(shah)

Here's my identification.

Вот моё удостоверение личности.

*voht mahYOH oodahstahveeRYEHneeyeh
LEECHnahstee*

Here's my passport.

Вот мой паспорт.
voht moy PAHSpahrt

Where do I sign?

Где мне подписать?
gdyeh mnyeh pahtpeeSAHT'

May I please have large bills?

Дайте мне, пожалуйста, крупными купюрами.
DAYtyeh mnyeh pahZHAHLstah KROOPnihmee kooPYOOrahmee

May I please have small bills?

Дайте мне, пожалуйста, мелкими купюрами.
DAYtyeh mnyeh pahZHAHLstah MYEHLkeemee kooPYOOrahmee

Can you give me small change?

Дайте мне, пожалуйста, мелкими монетами.
DAYtyeh mnyeh pahZHAHLstah MYEHLkeemee mahNYEHtahmee

I think you've made a mistake.

Мне кажется, что вы ошиблись.
mnyeh KAHzhehtsah shtoh vih ahSHEEBlees'

Where's the nearest ATM?

Где ближайший банкомат?
gdyeh bleeZHAYshee bahnkahMAHT

The ATM ate my card.

Банкомат проглотил мою карточку.
bahnkahMAHT prahglahTEEL mahYOO KAHRtachkoo

COMMUNICATION

Mail

In addition to the regular postal services, the main
branch post office provides international telegram,
telephone, fax services as well as access to the
Internet. You may also buy postcards, stationery,
envelopes and prepaid phone cards at the main post
office. Packages to be sent out of Russia must be
brought to a post office unwrapped. There they will be
weighed, inspected, wrapped and stamped. Anything
other than paper mail must be checked by customs.
International mail is notoriously slow and inefficient.
Federal Express and DHL have offices in both
Moscow and St. Petersburg.

Post office.
Почта.
POHCHtah
Letter./Letters.

Письмо./Письма.
pees'MOH/PEES'mah
Where's the nearest post office?

Где ближайшая почта?
gdyeh bleeZHAYshahyah POHCHtah
Where's the main post office?

Где главпочтамт?
gdyeh glahfpahchtAHMT
When does the post office open/close?

**Во сколько открывается/закрывается
    почта?**
*vahSKOHL'kah ahtkrihVAHeetsah
/zahkrihVAHeetsah POHCHtah*

COMMUNICATION

The post office is open from nine to six.

Почта работает с девяти до шести.
POHCHtah rahBOHtaheet sdeevyahTEE dah shehsTEE

Where can I find a mailbox?

Где можно найти почтовый ящик?
gdyeh MOHZHnah nayTEE pahchTOHvihy YAHshcheek

Can I buy ... here?

Можно здесь купить...
MOHZHnah zdyehs' kooPEET'

...envelopes...

...конверты?
kahnVYEHRtih

...postcards...

...открытки?
ahtKRIHTkee

...stamps...

...марки?
MAHRkee

Please give me ten airmail stamps for letters/postcards to the USA.

Дайте мне, пожалуйста, десять марок для авиаписем/авиаоткрыток в США.
DAYtyeh mnyeh pahZHALstah DYEHseet' MAHrahk dlyah AHveeahPEEseem/AHveeahahtKRIHtahk vsshah

I'd like to send this letter/postcard by...

Я хочу послать это письмо/эту открытку...
yah khahTCHOO pahSLAHT' EHtah pees'MOH/ EHtoo ahtKRIHTkoo

...surface mail.

...простой почтой.
prahsTOY POHCHtay

…airmail.

…авиапочтой.
ahveeahPOHCHtay

…registered mail.

…заказной почтой.
zahkahzNOY POHCHtay

…insured.

…ценной почтой.
TSYEHnay POHCHtay

How much do you want to insure your letter for?

Во сколько вы оцениваете ваше
письмо?
vah SKOHL'kha vy ahTSYEHneevahyehteh VAsheh
pees'MOH

Will this go out today?

Это уйдёт сегодня?
EHtah ooyDYOHT seeVOHdnyah

I'd like to send this to…

Я хочу послать это в…
yah khahTCHOO pahSLAHT' EHtah f

…America.

…Америку.
ahMYEHReekoo

…Canada.

…Канаду.
kahNAHdoo

…England.

…Англию.
AHNgleeyoo

…Germany.

…Германию.
geerMAHneeyoo

…France.

…Францию.
FRAHNtseeyoo
I'd like to send this parcel.

Я хочу послать эту посылку.
yah khaCHOO pahSLAHT' EHtoo pahSIHLkoo
It contains books/souvenirs/fragile material.

Она содержит книги/сувениры/
хрупкий материал.
ahNAH sahDYEHRzheet KNEEgee/sooveeNEErih/
KHROOPkeey mahteereeAHL
Wrap it up, please.

Заверните, пожалуйста.
zahveerNEEtyeh pahZHAHLstah
Write the address here.

Напишите адрес вот здесь.
nahpeeSHEEtyeh AHDrees voht zdyehs'
Return address.

Обратный адрес.
ahbRAHTnihy AHDrees
Have I received any mail?

Есть ли для меня письма?
yehst' lee dlyah meeNYAH PES'mah
My last name is...

Моя фамилия...
mahYAH fahMEEleeyah
Here's my passport.

Вот мой паспорт.
voht moy PAHSpahrt

Telephones

Phone calls tend to be brief as Russians prefer to
speak face to face. Since the 1990s, business

phone books have begun to be published. O9 is
the number for directory assistance in Moscow,
but the operator most likely will only speak
Russian.

Just like in the West, phone calls made from your
hotel can be very expensive. It is more
economical to make phone calls from public
phones using pre-paid phone cards, which are
available at metro token booths, kiosks and the
main post office. There are different calling cards
for different kinds of calls. Phone tokens may
also be used to make calls and may be purchased
in the same places as the phone cards.

International direct-dialing is now available at
the larger hotels and at the blue and white
Moscow State Telephone Network *(МГТС)*
phones or St. Petersburg Telephone Network
(ПТС) phones often found near metro stations
and at the Central Telegraph Office.

Cell phones are popular among the wealthy, but
are not in widespread use yet in Russia.

Pay phone.

Таксофон.
tahksahFOHN

Where's the nearest telephone?

Где ближайший телефон?
gdyeh bleeZHAYsheey teeleeFOHN

May I use your phone?

Можно от вас позвонить?
MOHZHnah aht vahs pahzvahNEET'

Phone card.

Телефонная карточка.
tehlehFOHnahyah KAHRtachkah

Hello (on the phone).

Алло./Слушаю.
ahLOH/SLOOshahyoo

Who is this?

Кто говорит?
ktoh gahvahREET

This is...

Это говорит...
EHtah gahvahREET

My name is...

Меня зовут...
meeNYAH zahVOOT

I'd like to speak to...

Я хочу поговорить с...
yah khahCHOO pahgahvahREET' s

He/She isn't in.

Его/Её нет.
yeeVOH/yeeYOH nyeht

When will he/she return?

Когда он/она вернётся?
kahgDAH ohn/ahNAH veerNYOHTsah

Tell him/her that I called./(f.)

Передайте ему/ей, что я звонил(а).
*peereeDAYtyeh yehMOO/yehyshtoh yah
zvahNEEL(ah)*

Take a message, please.

Передайте, пожалуйста, что...
peereeDAYtyeh pahZHAHLstah shtoh

My number is...

Мой номер телефона...
moy NOHmeer teeleeFOHnah

I'll call back later.

Я перезвоню позже.
yah pehrehzvahNYOO POHZHeh

Ask him/her to call me back.

Попросите его/её позвонить мне.
*pahprahSEEtyeh yeeVOH/yeeYOH pahzvahNEET'
mnyeh*

I don't understand.

Я не понимаю.
yah nyeh pahneeMAHyoo

Do you speak English?

Вы говорите по-английски?
vih gahvahREEtyeh pahahngLEEskee

I can't hear you.

Я вас не слышу.
yah vahs nee SLIHshoo

Can you please speak slowly/louder?

**Говорите помедленнее/громче,
    пожалуйста.**
*gahvahREEtyeh pahMYEHDlennehyeh/GROHMcheh
pahZHAHLstah*

With whom do you want to speak?

С кем вы хотите говорить?
skyehm vih khahTEEtyeh gahvahREET'

You've got the wrong number.

Вы не туда попали.
vy nyeh tooDAH pahPAHlee

Dial again.

Наберите ещё раз.
nahbeeREEtyeh yeeSHCHOH rahs

The number has been changed.

Номер телефона поменялся.
NOHmeer teeleeFOHnah pahmeeNYAHLsah

The phone is broken.

Телефон не работает.
teeleeFOHN nee rahBOHtaheet

Long-distance phone call.

Междугородный разговор.
meezhdoogahROHDnihy rahzgahVOHR
International phone call.

Международный разговор.
meezhdoonahROHDnihy rahzgahVOHR
Can I *(f.)* dial direct?

Могу ли я сам(а) набрать?
mahGOO lee yah sahm(AH) nahbRAHT'
Operator, please connect me to this number.

Телефонистка, пожалуйста,
  соедините меня с этим номером.
teeleefahnEESTkah pahZHAHLstah saheedeeNEEtyeh
meeNYAH SEHteem NOHmeerahm
What number are you calling?

Какой номер?
kahKOY NOHmeer
Wait a minute!

Подождите минуточку!
pahdahzhDEEtyeh meeNOOtahchkoo
Your time is up.

Время кончилось.
VRYEHmyah KOHNcheelahs'
There's a call for you.

Вас вызывают по телефону.
vahs vihzihVAHyoot pah teeleeFOHnoo
Hold on.

Не вешайте трубку.
nee VEEshaytyeh TROOPkoo
It's busy.

Номер занят.
NOHmyehr ZAHnyaht
There's no answer.

Никто не отвечает.
neeKTOH nee ahtveeCHAHyeht

I can't get through.

Я не могу дозвониться.
yah nee mahGOO dahzvahNEEtsah
We've been cut off.

Нас разъединили.
nahs rahz"eedeeNEElee

Telegram and Fax Services

The main post office, the central telegraph agency
and better hotels offer telegram and fax services.

I'd like to send a telegram/fax.

Я хочу послать телеграмму/факс.
yah khahCHOO pahSLAHT' teeleeGRAHmoo/fahks
Where can I send a telegram/fax?

**Откуда можно послать телеграмму/
    факс?**
*ahtKOOdah MOHZHnah pahsLAHT'
teeleeGRAHmoo/fahks*
May I have an international telegram form?

**Дайте мне, пожалуйста, бланк
    международной телеграммы.**
*DAYtyeh mnyeh pahZHAHLstah blahnk
meezhdoonahROHDnay teeleeGRAHmih*
What is the rate per word/per page?

Сколько стоит слово/страница?
SKOHL'kah STOHeet SLOHvah/STRAHneetsah
What will the telegram/fax cost?

Сколько будет стоить телеграмма/факс?
*SKOHL'kah BOOdeet STOHeet' teeleeGRAHmah
/fahks*

How long will it take to reach the USA/England?

Сколько времени идёт телеграмма в
   США/Англию?

*SKOHL'kah VRYEHmeenee eedYOHT
teeleeGRAHmah vsshah/VAHNgleeyoo*

E-Mail and Internet Access

Cybercafes are quickly springing up all over Russia
and Eastern Europe. Many are open around the clock.
The Internet is an excellent way to get up-to-date
travel and visa information about Russia. For starters,
try the Washington D.C. Consular Information Sheet
found at travel-state.gov/russia.html.

E-mail.

Электронная почта.
ehlyehkTROHnnahyah POCHtah

I want to check my E-mail.

Я хочу проверить мою электронную
   почту.
*yah khahCHOO prahVYEHreet' mahYOO
ehlyehkTROHNnooyoo POCHtoo*

How much does an hour cost?

Сколько стоит час?
SKOHL'kah STOHeet chahs

Computer.

Компьютер.
kahmp'YOOtehr

Screen.

Экран.
ehkRAHN

Monitor.

Монитор.
mahneeTOHR

Keyboard.

Клавиатура.
klahveeahTOOrah

Mouse.

Мышь.
mysh'

Printer.

Принтер.
PREENtehr

Disks.

Дискеты.
deesKYEHtih

Fonts.

Фонты.
fahnTIH

EATING OUT

Except for celebrating major occasions like weddings, most Russians prefer entertaining at home. When they do go to a restaurant, they expect to make a full evening of it. Thus, except for the new fast-food places, most dining establishments serve meals slowly and in multiple courses. Many restaurants still do not accept credit cards. Russians tend to dress more formally than Westerners, so attire will range from casual to semi-formal in restaurants.

Before the 1990s, there were few restaurants to choose from and little variety. These days in Moscow and St. Petersburg you can find a wide array of ethnic restaurants including Chinese, Indian, Irish, Italian, Japanese, German, American, French as well as Georgian, Armenian, Ukrainian and traditional Russian. Quality and cost vary as widely as variety. Prices in Moscow can be downright exorbitant, but there is also the Russkoe Bistro chain, Russia's version of a fast-food restaurant. It's definitely worth a try.

Beware of food and alcohol sold at street kiosks, where the quality of foodstuffs is questionable at best.

Non-smoking sections, disabled facilities and special children's menus are usually not available.

The Preliminaries

I'm hungry. *(m./f.)*
Я голоден./Я голодна.
yah GOHlahdeen/yah gahlahdNAH
Can you recommend a good restaurant?
**Можете ли вы рекомендовать хороший
   ресторан?**
*MOzhehtyeh lee vih reekahmyehndahVAHT'
khahROHshee reestahRAHN?*
Do you serve breakfast/lunch/dinner?
Подаёте ли вы завтрак/обед/ужин?
*pahdahYOHtyeh lee vih
ZAHFtrahk/ahBYEHT/OOzheen*
I'd like to make a reservation.
Я хочу заказать столик.
yah khahCHOO zahkahZAHT' STOHleek
There are two/three/four of us.
Нас двое/трое/четверо.
nahs DVOHyeh/TROHyeh/CHEHTveerah
We'll come at six/seven/eight.
Мы будем в шесть/семь/восемь.
mih BOOdeem vshesht'/vsyem'/vVOHsyem'
Where is the coat check?
Где гардероб/раздевалка?
gdyeh gahrdeeROHP/rahzdeeVAHLkah
coat check number
Номерок.
nahmehROHK
Where is the bathroom?
Где уборная?
gdyeh ooBOHRnahyah

Is this place taken/reserved/free?

Это место занято/заказано/свободно?
*EHtah MYEHstah ZAHneetah/zahKAzZahnah/
svahBOHDnah*
It's taken/reserved/free.

Оно занято/заказано/свободно.
ahNOH ZAHneetah/ zahKAHzahnah/svahBOHDnah
Have a seat!

Садитесь!
sahDEEtees'
We'd prefer a table…

Мы предпочитаем столик...
mih preedpahcheeTAHeem STOHleek
…in the corner.

...в углу.
voogLOO
…by the window.

...у окна.
oo ahkNAH
…outside.

...на открытом воздухе.
nah ahtKRIHtahm VOHZdookhyeh
May we have another table, please?

Дайте нам, пожалуйста, другой столик.
DAYtyeh nahm pahZHALHstah drooGOY STOHleek
Is smoking permitted here?

Можно здесь курить?
MOHZnah zdyehs' kooREET'

Ordering

Except in the five-star hotels, few Russian waiters and
waitresses speak more than a little English, if any at

all. Restaurants that cater to foreigners may have
menus in English or at least a summary in English.
Unless you want to order by pointing, be prepared
with a few key phrases.

Waiter./Waitress.

Официант./Официантка.
ahfeetseeAHNT/ahfeetseeAHNTkah

This way please.

Сюда, пожалуйста.
syooDAH pahZHAHLstah

May I have a menu, please.

Принесите, пожалуйста, меню.
preeneeSEEtyeh pahZHAHLstah meeNYOO

Have you decided?

Вы уже выбрали?
vih ooZHEH VIHbrahlee

What do you recommend?

Что вы посоветуете?
shtoh vih pahsahVYEHtooyehtyeh

I recommend...

Я советую вам взять...
yah sahVYEHtooyoo vahm vzyaht'

Unfortunately, we don't have that.

К сожалению, у нас нет этого.
ksahzhahLYEHneeyoo oo nahs nyeht EHtahvah

Why not take this instead.

Лучше возьмите вот это.
LOOCHsheh vahz'MEEtyeh voht EHtah

What would you like?

Что вы хотите?
shtoh vih khahTEEtyeh

Go ahead.

Слушаю вас.
SLOOshahyoo vahs
I'll have…

Я хочу…
yah khahCHOO
…for appetizers…

…на закуску…
nah zahKOOSkoo
…for the first course…

…на первое…
nah PYEHRvahyeh
…for the second course…

…на второе…
nah vtahROHyeh
…for the third course/dessert…

…на третье/на сладкое…
nah TRYET'yeh/nah SLAHTkahyeh
…a small portion.

…маленькую порцию.
MAHleen'kooyoo POHRtseeyoo
What would you like to drink?

Что бы вы хотели выпить?
shtoh bih vih khahtYEHlee VIHpeet'
That's all, thank you.

Это всё, спасибо.
EHtah vsyoh, spahSEEbah

Special Orders

Vegetarianism is a novel concept in Russia. The introduction of many new ethnic restaurants, however, gives vegetarians a few more options.

Does this dish contain meat?

Это блюдо мясное?
EHtah BLYOOdah myahsNOHyeh
I don't eat meat/dairy.

Я не ем мясного/молочного.
ya nyeh yehm myasNOHvah/mahLOCHnahvah
Does this contain eggs/nuts?

В этом блюде есть яйца/орехи?
VEHtahm BLYOOdeh yehst' YAYtsah/ahRYEHkhee
I'm allergic to eggs/milk/nuts.

У меня аллергия на яйца/молоко/орехи.
oo meeNYAH alehrGEEyah nah YAYtsah/
mahlahKOH/ahRYEHkhee
Is this dish kosher?

Это блюдо кошерное?
EHtah BLOOdah kaSHEHRnahyeh

Preparation

How is this dish prepared?

Как это блюдо приготовлено?
kahk EHtah BLYOOdah preegahTOHVlyehnoh
It's...

Оно...
ahNOH
...baked.

...печёное.
peeCHOHNahyeh
...boiled.

...варёное.
vahRYOHNahyeh

…braised.

…тушёное.

tooshOHnahyeh

…breaded.

…панированное.

pahneeROHvahnahyeh

…chopped.

…рубленое.

ROObleenahyeh

…fried.

…поджаренное.

pahdZHAHreenahyeh

…ground.

…молотое.

MOHlahtahyeh

…marinated.

…маринованное.

mahreeNOHvahnahyeh

…poached.

…отварное.

ahtvahrNOHyeh

…raw.

…сырое.

sihROHyeh

…roasted.

…жареное.

ZHAHreenahyeh

…smoked.

…копчёное.

kahpCHOHnahyeh

…steamed.

…паровое.

pahrahVOHyeh

...stuffed.

...**фаршированное.**
fahrsheeROHvahnahyeh

The Meal

Enjoy your meal!

Приятного аппетита!
preeYAHTnahvah ahpeeTEEtah

How is it?

Как вам нравится?
kahk vahm NRAHveetsah

It's very tasty.

Очень вкусно.
OHcheen' VKOOSnah

Please pass me...

Передайте, пожалуйста...
peereeDAYtyeh pahZAHLstah

Please bring me...

Принесите мне, пожалуйста...
preeneeSEEtyeh mnyeh pahZHAHLstah

...a cup.

...**чашку.**
CHAHSHkoo

...a glass.

...**стакан.**
stahKAHN

...a fork.

...**вилку.**
VEELkoo

…a knife.

…нож.
nohsh

…a spoon.

…ложку.
LOHSHkoo

…a plate.

…тарелку.
tahRYEHLkoo

…a napkin.

…салфетку.
sahlFYEHTkoo

…an ashtray.

…пепельницу.
PYEHpeel'neetsoo

…salt.

…соль.
sohl'

…pepper.

…перец.
PYEHreets

…sugar.

…сахар.
SAHlhar

…water.

…воду.
VOHdoo

…bread and butter.

…хлеб и масло.
khlyehp ee MAHSlah

Please bring me some more of this.

Принесите ещё немного этого.
*preeneeSEEtyeh yeeSHCHOH neeMNOggah
EHtahvah*

Would you like anything else?
Что-нибудь ещё?
SHTOHneeboot' yeeSHCHOH

Complaints

The service industry is a relatively new concept in Russia. Although the situation is much better than it once was, waiters and waitresses can be downright surly. Do not let this stop you from asking for better service.

I have a complaint.
У меня жалоба.
oo meenYAH ZHAHlahbah
This is…

Это…
EHtah
…cold.

…холодное.
KHOHlahdnahyeh
…hot.

…горячее.
gahRYAcheeyeh
…too spicy.

…слишком острое.
SLEESHkahm OHStrahyeh
…too sweet/salty.

…слишком сладкое/пересолено.
SLEESHkahm SLAHTkahyeh/peereeSOHleenah

...sour.

...кислое.
KEESlahyeh
...stale.

...не свежее.
nee SVYEHzheeyeh
...tough.

...жесткое.
ZHOHSTkahyeh
...overdone.

...пережарено.
peereeZHAHreenah
...underdone.

...недожарено.
needahZHAHreenah
This is dirty.

Это грязное.
EHtah GRYAHZnahyeh
I don't like this.

Это мне не нравится.
EHtah mnyeh nee NRAHveetsah
You can take this away.

Можно это убрать.
MOHZHnah EHtah ooBRAHT'
Have you made a mistake?

Вы не ошиблись?
vih nee ahSHEEBlees'
This isn't what I ordered. *(f.)*

Я этого не заказывал(а).
yah EHtahvah nee zahKAHzihvahl(ah)
I ordered... *(f.)*

Я заказал(а)...
yah zahkahZAHL(ah)

I don't want it.

Я этого не хочу.
yah EHtahvah nee khahCHOO

The Check

Prices may be listed on the menu in dollars or other currencies, but the bill is supposed to be paid in rubles. Most Russian restaurants still do not accept credit cards. A tip of ten to fifteen percent is expected nowadays at any dining establishment with a wait staff.

We're finished.

Мы закончили.
mih zahKOHNcheelee

I have had enough.

Мне хватит.
mnyeh KHVAHteet

Bring me the check, please.

Принесите мне счёт, пожалуйста.
preeneeSEEtyeh mnyeh shchoht pahZHAHLstah

Have you made a mistake?

Вы не ошиблись?
vih nee ahSHEEBlees'

How did you get this total?

Что входит в эту сумму?
shtoh FKHOHdeet VEHtoo SOOmoo

Is a tip included?

Чаевые включены в счёт?
chaheeVIHyeh fklyoochehNIH fshchoht

Pay the cashier.

Платите в кассу.
plahTEEtyeh FKAHSsoo

We'd like to pay separately.

Мы хотели бы платить отдельно.
mih khahTYEHLee bih plahTEET' ahdDYEHL'nah

Do you accept...

Вы принимаете...
vih preeneeMAHyehteh

...traveler's checks?

...дорожные чеки.
dahROHZHnihyeh CHHEHkee

...credit cards?

...кредитные карточки.
kreeDEETnihyeh KAHRtahchkee

Thank you, this is for you.

Спасибо, это для вас.
spahSEEbah EHtah dlyah vahs

Snack Bars, Take-Out & Food Stands

At Russian snack bars, just like in the U.S., you usually pick up what you want yourself or else ask someone behind the counter for it. Be sure to carry small
bills with you because the cashiers very often will not
accept large ruble notes. Take-out restaurants, especially sandwich shops and Chinese, have appeared in
Moscow and St. Petersburg, but delivery is still
scarce.

What's this?

Что это такое?
shtoh EHtah tahKOHyeh

Please give me one of those.

Дайте, пожалуйста, один такой.
DAYtyeh pahZAHLstah ahDEEN tahKOY
I'd like (that), please.

Я хочу (это), пожалуйста.
yah khaCHOO (EHtah) pahZHAHLstah
Please give me a piece of that.

Дайте, пожалуйста, кусок этого.
DAYtyeh pahZHAHLstah kooSOHK EHtahvah
May I help myself? *(f.)*

Могу я взять сам(а)?
mahGOO yah vzyaht' sahm(AH)
Just a little.

Только немного.
TOHL'kah neeMNOHgah
A little more, please.

Побольше, пожалуйста.
pahBOHL'she pahZHALstah
Enough?

Достаточно?
dahsTAHtahchnah
Anything else?

Что-нибудь ещё?
SHTOHneeboot' yeeSHCHOH
That's all, thank you.

Это всё, спасибо.
EHtah vsyoh, spahSEEbah
How much is it?

Сколько это стоит?
SKOHL'kah EHtah STOHeet
Is that to go?

Эта на вынос?
EHtah nah VIHnahs

FOOD AND DRINK

This chapter provides the names of products and dishes that are common to Russia and Eastern Europe. The main thing to keep in mind with regards to the various foods and drinks provided here are their limited availability. Not everything will be available everywhere you go, so be prepared to experience new foods and methods of preparation.

Breakfast

Where can I have breakfast?

Где можно позавтракать?
gdyeh MOHZHnah pahZAHFtrahkat'

What time is breakfast served?

Во сколько завтрак?
vahSKOHL'kah ZAHFtrahk

How late is breakfast served?

До которого часа можно завтракать?
dahkahTOHrahvah CHAHsah MOHZHnah ZAHFtrahkat'

I'd like...

Я хочу...
yah khahCHOO

...(black) coffee.

...(чёрный) кофе.
(CHOHRnihy) KOHfyeh

    ...with milk.

    ...с молоком.
    smahlahKOHM

…with sugar.

…с сахаром.
SSAHkhahrahm

…without sugar.

…без сахара.
byehs SAHkhahrah

…tea.

…чай.
chay

…with lemon.

…с лимоном.
sleeMOHnahm

…with milk.

…с молоком.
smahlahKOHM

…with honey.

…с мёдом.
SMYOHdahm

…cocoa.

…какао.
kahKAHoh

…milk.

…молоко.
mahlahKOH

…juice.

…сок.
sohk

…orange juice.

…апельсиновый сок.
ahpeel'SEEnahvihysohk

…grapefruit juice.

…грейпфрутовый сок.
greypFROOtahvihy sohk

…tomato juice.

…томатный сок.
tahMAHTnihy sohk

…kefir (a yogurt drink).

…кефир.
keeFEER

…bread.

…хлеб
khlyehp

…toast.

…поджаренный хлеб.
pahdZHAHreenihy khlyehp

…a roll.

…булочку.
BOOlahchkoo

…butter.

…масло.
MAHSlah

…cheese.

…сыр.
sihr

…cottage cheese.

…творог.
tvahROHK

…jam.

…варенье.
vahRYEHN'yeh

…hot cereal.

…кашу.
KAHshoo

…oatmeal.

…овсяную кашу.
ahfSYAHnooyoo KAHshoo

…eggs.
…яйца.
YAYtsah

…scrambled eggs.
…яичницу-болтунью.
yahEECHneetsoobahlTOON'yoo

…a fried egg.
…яичницу.
yahEECHneetsoo

…a boiled egg.
…варёное яйцо.
vahRYOHnahyeh yayTSOH

…a hard-boiled egg.
…крутое яйцо.
krooTOHyeh yayTSOH

…salt./pepper.
…соль./перец.
sohl'/PYEHreets

Appetizers

Russians have a variety of very tasty hot and cold
appetizers. They can be quite hearty and may often
seem like an entire meal onto themselves.
Unfortunately for vegetarians, most Russian
appetizers contain meat.

Appetizers.
Закуски.
zahKOOSkee

For an appetizer I want…
На закуску я хочу…
nah zahKOOSkoo yah khahCHOO

…(black/red) caviar.

… (зернистую/кетовую) икру.
zeerNEEStooyoo/keeTOHvooyoo eekROO
…cold, boiled pork with vegetables.

…буженину с гарниром.
boozhehNEEnoo zgahrNEErahm
…cold roast beef with vegetables.

…ростбиф с гарниром.
ROHSTbeef zgahrNEErahm
…assorted meat/fish plate.

…мясное/рыбное ассорти.
meesNOHyeh/RIHBnahyeh ahssahrTEE
…smoked/pickled herring.

…копчёную/маринованную селёдку.
kahpCHOHnooyoo/ mahreeNOHvahnooyoo seeLYOHTkoo
…meat/fish in aspic.

…мясное/рыбное заливное или студень.
meesNOHyeh/RIHBnahyeh zahleevNOHyeh EElee STOOdeen'
…sausage.

…колбасу.
kahlbahSOO
…sturgeon.

…осетрину.
ahseetREEnoo
…lox.

…сёмгу.
SYOHMgoo
…pancakes with…

…блины…
bleeNIH
   …caviar.

   …с икрой.
   seekROY

…herring.

…с сельдью.
SSYEHL'd'yoo

…sour cream.

…со сметаной.
sahsmeeTAHnay

…jam.

…с вареньем.
zvahRYEHN'yehm

…small pies filled with…

…пирожки…
peerahshKEE

…meat.

…с мясом.
SMYAHsahm

…cabbage.

…с капустой.
skahPOOstay

…rice.

…с рисом.
SREEsahm

…potatoes.

…с картошкой.
skahrTOHSHkay

…meat-filled dumplings.

…пельмени.
peel'MYEHnee

…marinated/salted mushrooms.

…маринованные/солёные грибы.
mahreeNOHvahnihyeh/sahLYOHnihyeh greeBIH

…mushrooms baked in a sour cream sauce.

…жульен из грибов.
zhool'YEHN ees greeBOHF

…chicken baked in a sour cream sauce.

…жульен из курицы.
zhool'YEHN ees KOOreetsih
…Russian vegetable salad.

…винегрет.
veeneeGRYEHT
…cucumber salad.

…салат из огурцов.
sahLAHT ees ahgoorTSOF
…tomato salad.

…салат из помидоров.
sahLAHT ees pahmeeDOHrahf
…cabbage salad.

…салат из капусты.
sahLAHT ees kahPOOstih
…potato salad.

…картофельный салат.
kahrTOHfeel'nihy sahLAHT
…meat salad.

…столичный салат.
stahLEECHnihy sahLAHT
…sauerkraut.

…кислую капусту.
KEESlooyoo kahPOOstoo
…liver pâté.

…паштет из печёнки.
pashTYEHT ees peeCHOHNkee
…olives.

…маслины.
mahsLEEnih
…radishes.

…редис.
reeDEES

Soups

After your appetizers, try a steaming bowl of
borscht—a savory beet soup flavored with beef
and often served with a dollop of sour cream.

For the first course I want...

На первое я хочу...
nah PYEHRvahyeh yah khahCHOO
Please bring me some...

Принесите мне, пожалуйста...
preeneeSEEtyeh mnyeh pahZHAHLstah
...borscht.

...борщ.
bohrshch
...bouillon.

...бульон.
bool'YOHN
...cabbage soup.

...щи.
shchee
...chicken soup...

...куриный суп...
kooREEnihy soop
  ...with noodles.

  ...с лапшой.
  slahpSHOY
  ...with rice.

  ...с рисом.
  SREEsahm
...cold kvas soup.

...окрошку.
ahkROHSHkoo

…cold beet soup.

…свекольник.
sveeKOHL'neek

…fish soup.

…уху.
ooKHOO

…mushroom soup.

…грибной суп.
greebNOY soop

…pea soup.

…гороховый суп.
gahROHkhahvihy soop

…pickled cucumber soup.

…рассольник.
rahsSOHL'neek

…potato soup.

…картофельный суп.
kahrTOHfeel'nihy soop

…spicy Georgian beef soup.

…харчо.
khahrCHOH

…tart meat/fish soup.

…мясную/рыбную солянку.
meesNOOyoo/RIHBnooyoo sahLYAHNkoo

…vegetable soup.

…овощной суп.
ahvahshchNOY soop

Grains and Cereals

I want...

Я хочу...
yah khahCHOO

…rice.
...рис.
rees
…pilaf.
...плов.
plohf
…pasta.
...макароны.
mahkahROHnih
…potatoes.
...картофель.
kahrTOHfeel'
  …fried.
  ...жареный.
  ZHAHreenihy
  …boiled.
  ...отварной.
  ahtvahrNOY
  …mashed.
  ...пюре.
  pyoorYEH
  …baked.
  ...печёный.
  pyehCHOHnih

Vegetables

Today Russia has no shortage of fresh vegetables and fruits. Some of the best deals can be struck with venders in stalls outside of various metro stations.

What kind of vegetables are available?
Какие у вас овощи?
kahKEEyeh oo vahs OHvahshchee

Cabbage.
Капуста.
kahPOOstah

Red cabbage.
Красная капуста.
KRAHSnahyah kahPOOstah

Beets.
Свёкла.
SVYOHKlah

Tomatoes.
Помидоры.
puhmeeDOHrih

Potatoes.
Картофель.
kahrTOHfeel'

Radishes.
Редис.
reeDEES

Cucumbers.
Огурцы.
ahgoorTSIH

Eggplants.
Баклажаны.
bahklahZHAHNih

Mushrooms.
Грибы.
greeBIH

Peas.
Горох.
gahROHKH

Green beans.
Фасоль.
fahSOHL'

FOOD AND DRINK

Wax beans.
Жёлтая фасоль.
ZHOHLtahyah fahSOHL'
Carrots.
Морковь.
mahrKOHF'
Onions.
Лук.
look
Leeks.
Зелёный лук.
zeeLYOHnihy look
Corn.
Кукуруза.
kookooROOzah
Green peppers.
Сладкий перец.
SLAHTkeey PYEHrehts
Red peppers.
Красный перец.
KRAHSnihy PYEHrehts
Parsley.
Петрушка.
peetROOSHkah
Turnips.
Репа.
RYEHpah
Garlic.
Чеснок.
cheesNOHK
Cauliflower.
Цветная капуста.
tsveetNAHyah kahPOOstah

Horseradish.
Хрен.
khryehn

Meat and Meat Dishes

What kind of meat dishes do you have?
Какие у вас мясные блюда?
kahKEEyeh oo vahs meesNIHyeh BLYOOdah
What kind of meat do you have?

Какое у вас мясо?
kahKOHyeh oo vahs MYAHsah
For the second course I want...

На второе я хочу...
nah ftahROHyeh yah khahCHOO
...mutton.

...баранину.
bahRAHNeenoo
...lamb.

...молодую баранину.
mahlahDOOyoo bahRAHneenoo
...lamb chop.

...баранью отбивную.
bahRAHN'yoo ahtbeevNOOyoo
...beef.

...говядину.
gahVYAHdeenoo
...pork.

...свинину.
sveeNEEnoo
...pork chop.

...свиную отбивную.
sveeNOOyoo ahtbeevNOOyoo

…veal.

…телятину.
teeLYAHteenoo

…veal cutlet.

…телячью отбивную.
teeLYAHCH'yoo ahtbeevNOOyoo

…ham.

…ветчину.
veetcheeNOO

…roast beef.

…ростбиф.
ROHSTbeef

…pot roast.

…тушёную говядину.
tooSHOHnooyoo gahVYAHdeenoo

…meat patties.

…котлеты.
kahtLYEHtih

…beefsteak.

…бифштекс.
beefSHTEHKS

…bacon.

…бекон.
beeKOHN

…meat loaf.

…мясной рулет.
meesNOY rooLYEHT

…meatballs.

…тефтели.
teefTYEHlee

…sausages.

…сосиски.
sahSEEskee

…shnitzel.

…шницель.
SHNEEtsehl'

…meat stew.

…рагу.
rahGOO

…liver.

…печёнку.
peeCHOHNkoo

…kidneys.

…почки.
POHCHkee

…cutlet.

… отбивную котлету.
ahtbeevNOOyoo kahtLYEHtoo

…tongue.

…язык.
yeeZIHK

…shish kebob.

…шашлык.
shahshLIHK

…ground lamb kebob.

…люля-кебаб.
lyooLYAHkeeBAHP

…goulash.

…гуляш.
gooLYAHSH

…beef casserole.

…жаркое.
zhahrKOHyeh

…chopped meat in a sauce.

…азу.
ahZOO

…beef stroganoff.

...бефстроганов.
beefSTROHgahnahf

…cabbage rolls with meat.

...голубцы.
gahloopTSIH

Poultry and Game

What kind of poultry/wild game dishes do you have?

Какие у вас блюда с птицей/дичью?
kahKEEyeh oo vahs BLOOdah spteeTSEY/
DEECH'yoo

Chicken.

Курица.
KOOreetsah

Duck.

Утка.
OOTkah

Goose.

Гусь.
goos'

Hare.

Заяц.
ZAHeets

Hazel grouse.

Рябчик.
RYAHPcheek

Pigeon.

Голубь.
GOHloop'

Rabbit.

Кролик.
KROHleek

Turkey.

Индейка.
eenDEYkah

Venison.

Оленина.
ahleeNEEnah

Chicken Kiev.

Котлеты по-киевски.
kahtLYEHtih pahKEEeefskee

Georgian fried chicken.

Цыплёнок табака.
tsihpLYOHnahk tahbahKAH

Chicken cutlets.

Пожарские котлеты.
pahZHAHRskeeyeh kahtLYEHtih

Fish and Seafood

What kind of fish do you have?

Какая у вас рыба?
kahKAHyah oo vahs RIHbah

I'll take...

Я возьму...
yah vahz'MOO

...sturgeon.

...осетрину.
ahseetREEnoo

...trout.

...форель.
fahRYEHL'

...pike.

...щуку.
SHCHOOkoo

...flounder.

...камбалу.
KAHMbahloo

...carp.

...карпа.
KAHRpah

...halibut.

...палтус.
PAHLtoos

...cod.

...треску.
treesKOO

...salmon.

...лососину.
lahsahSEEnoo

...tuna.

...тунца.
toonTSAH

...herring.

...сельдь.
syehl't'

...seafood.

...дары моря.
dahRIH MOHryah

...prawns.

...креветки.
kreeVYEHTkee

…crayfish.

…раков.
RAHkahf

…oysters.

…устрицы.
OOStreetsih

Groceries

Groceries.

Продукты.
prahDOOKtih

I'd like…

Я хочу…
yah khahCHOO

…a piece of that.

…кусок этого.
kooSOHK EHtahvah

…a half kilo…

…полкило…
pohlkeeLOH

…a kilo…

…килограмм…
keelahGRAHM

…one-and-a-half kilos…

…полтора кило…
pohltahRAH keeLOH

…fifty grams…

…пятьдесят грамм…
peet'deeSYAHT grahm

…one hundred grams…

…сто грамм…
stoh grahm

…a liter of...

…литр...

leetr

…a bottle of...

…бутылку...

booTIHLkoo

…ten eggs.

…десяток яиц.

deeSYAHtahk yahEETS'

…a packet of cookies/tea.

…пачку печенья/чая.

PAHCHkoo peeCHEHN'yah/CHAHyah

…a can of pears.

…банку консервированных груш.

BAHNkoo kahnseerVEErahvahnih groosh

…a jar of sour cream.

…банку сметаны.

BAHNkoo smeeTAHnih

…a loaf of bread.

…буханку хлеба.

booKHAHNkoo KHLYEHbah

…a box of candy.

…коробку конфет.

kahROHPkoo kahnFYEHT

…a bar of chocolate.

…плитку шоколада.

PLEETkoo shahkahLAHdah

FOOD AND DRINK

Fruit

Public markets and street stalls offer a good selection
of fruit in season. You can usually negotiate a bit over
the prices.

What kind of fruit do you have?

Какие у вас фрукты?
kahKEEyeh oo vahs FROOKtih

Are they fresh?

Они свежие?
ahNEE SVYEHzhehyeh

Apples.

Яблоки.
YAHBlahkee

Oranges.

Апельсины.
ahpeel'SEEnih

Tangerines.

Мандарины.
mahndahREEnih

Pears.

Груши.
GROOshee

Peaches.

Персики.
PYEHRseekee

Plums.

Сливы.
SLEEvih

Watermelon.

Арбуз.
ahrBOOS

Bananas.
Бананы.
bahNAHnih
Apricots.
Абрикосы.
abreeKOHsih
Pineapple.
Ананас.
ahnahNAHS
Grapes.
Виноград.
veenahGRAHT
Raisins.
Изюм.
eeZYOOM
Figs.
Финики.
FEEneekee
Lemon.
Лимон.
leeMOHN
Grapefruit.
Грейпфрут.
GREYPfroot
Prunes.
Черносливы.
cheernahSLEEvih
Currants.
Смородина.
smahROHdeenah
Strawberries.
Клубника.
kloobNEEkah

Wild strawberries.

Земляника.
zeemleeNEEkah

Cherries.

Черешня.
cheeRYEHSHnyah

Blackberries.

Ежевика.
yeezhehVEEkah

Cranberries.

Клюква.
KLYOOKvah

Raspberries.

Малина.
mahLEEnah

Blueberries.

Черника.
chehrNEEkah

Dessert

Russians claim that their ice cream, sold at kiosks year-round, is the best in the world. Whether you agree or not, it is certainly worth a taste.

What do you have for dessert?

Что у вас на десерт?
shtoh oo vas nah deeSYEHRT

I'd like/(f.)...

Я хотел(а) бы...
yah khaTYEHL(ah) bih

...ice cream.

...мороженое.
mahROHzhehnahyeh

...a cookie.

...печенье.
peeCHEHN'yeh

...pie.

...пирог.
peeROHK

...pastry.

...пирожное.
peeROHZHnahyeh

...honey cake.

...медовый пряник.
meeDOHvihy PRYAHneek

...cake.

...торт.
tohrt

...stewed fruit.

...компот.
kahmPOHT

...thin pancakes with jam.

...блинчики.
BLEENcheekee

...thin fruit jelly.

...кисель.
keeSYEHL'

...marzipan.

...марципан.
mahrtseePAHN

...filled doughnuts.

...пончики.
POHNcheekee

...chocolate.

...шоколад.
shahkahLAHT

FOOD AND DRINK

Drinks

Russians are a tea-drinking people. Tea is usually
served black but pre-sweetened with honey, jam or
sugar. Although coffee has gained in popularity, it is
still more expensive and less common than tea.
Bottled fruit juices and waters are also very popular,
as are soft drinks. Drinking unboiled tap water,
especially in St. Petersburg, is not a good idea.

What do you have to drink?

Какие у вас напитки?
kahKEEyeh oo vas nahPEETkee
Please bring me...

Пожалуйста, принесите мне...
pahZHAHLstah preeneeSEEtyeh mnyeh
...(black) coffee.

...(чёрный) кофе.
(CHOHRnihy) KOHfyeh
   ...with milk.

   ...с молоком.
   smahlahKOHM
   ...with sugar.

   ...с сахаром.
   SSAHkhahrahm
   ...without sugar.

   ...без сахара.
   byehs SAHkhahrah
...tea.

...чай.
chay
   ...with lemon.

   ...с лимоном.
   sleeMOHnahm

…with milk.

…с молоком.
smahlahKOHM

…with honey.

…с мёдом.
SMYOHdahm

…with jam.

…с вареньем.
svahRYEHN'ehm

…a Pepsi.

…пепси.
PYEHPsee

I'd like a glass of…

Я хочу стакан…
yah khahCHOO stahKAHN

…milk.

…молока.
mahlahKAH

…lemonade.

…лимонада.
leemahNAHdah

I'd like a bottle of…

Я хочу бутылку…
yah khahCHOO booTIHLkoo

…mineral water.

…минеральной воды.
meeneeRAHL'nay vahDIH

…apple juice.

…яблочного сока.
YAHBlahchnahvah SOHkah

…cherry juice.

…вишнёвого сока.
veeshNYOHvahvah SOHkah

FOOD AND DRINK

Alcoholic Drinks

Since the early 1990s, beer has grown in popularity among Russians. In fact, in 2002, beer consumption among young Russians surpassed that of vodka for the first time ever. Heineken is the favorite import, but Baltika, the most popular local brew, is gaining in popularity. The favorite wines of the region come from Georgia and the Crimea. Sweet and similar to a sparkling wine, Russian champagne is a good choice with dessert. Vodka comes in a variety of flavors and is most often served chilled in fifty gram shot glasses. It is the custom to drink the shot all at once and chase it with bread or raw vegetables. Hard liquor is now available for purchase from kiosks on the street in Russia, but these offerings should be avoided.

Do you serve alcohol?

У вас есть алкогольные напитки?
oo vahs yehst' ahlkahGOHL'nihyeh nahPEETkee
Which wine would you recommend?

Какое вино вы рекомендуете?
kahKOHyeh veeNOH vih reekahmeenDOOeetyeh
How much is a bottle of...

Сколько стоит бутылка...
SKOHL'kah STOHeet booTIHLkah
I'd like a glass/bottle of...

Я хочу стакан/бутылку...
yah khaCHOO stahKAHN booTIHLkoo
...wine.

...вина.
veenAH
...red wine.

...красного вина.
KRAHSnahvah veeNAH
...white wine.

...белого вина.
BYEHlahvah veeNAH
...dry wine.

...сухого вина.
sookhOHvah veeNAH
...sweet wine.

...сладкого вина.
SLAHTkahvah veeNAH
...Georgian wine.

...грузинского вина.
grooZEENskahvah veeNAH
...Russian champagne (sparkling wine).

...российского шампанского.
rahSEEYskahvah shahmPAHNskahvah
...beer.

...пива.
PEEvah
...vodka.

...водки.
VOHTkee
...pepper-flavored vodka.

...перцовки.
peerTSOHFkee
...lemon-flavored vodka.

...лимонной.
leeMOHNnay
...cherry-flavored vodka.

...вишнёвки.
veeshNYOHFkee
...dark, smooth, old vodka.

...старки.
STAHRkee

...Azerbaijani/Armenian brandy.

...азербайджанский/армянский коньяк.
ahzeerbayDZHAHNskeey/ahrMYAHNskeey
kahn'YAHK

...a gin (and tonic).

...джин (с тоником).
dzheen (STOHneekahm)

...whiskey./scotch.

...виски./шотландское виски.
VEESkee/shahtLAHNTskahyeh VEESkee

...straight up.

...чистого.
CHEEStahvah

...with ice.

...со льдом
sahL'DOHM

...with soda.

...с содовой.
seSOHdahvay

Toasts

Russians love to make toasts before each round of
drinks. The first one is usually reserved for the host.
Be sure to have a toast ready because even foreign
guests are asked to make them.

To the host/hostess!

За хозяина/хозяйку!
zah khahZYAHeenah/khahZYAHkYoo

To your health!

За ваше здоровье!
zah VAHsheh zdahROHV'yeh

To eternal friendship!

За вечную дружбу!
zah VYECHnooyoo DROOSHboo

I wish you happiness/health/success!

Желая вам счастья/здоровья/успеха!
zheLAHyoo vahm SHCHAST'yah/ zdahROHV'yah/ oosPYEHkhah

Congratulations!

Поздравляю вас!
pahzdrahvLYAHyoo vahs

ENTERTAINMENT

Tickets

Usually, tickets can be purchased from the ticket office of the establishment the day of the show. Larger hotels may also have a ticket office, but the prices will be marked up and you may be asked to pay in hard currency. You can also try your luck at buying tickets from kiosks on the street, but do not expect to get your first choice. Russians are avid theatergoers and most performances sell out quickly. If you really want to see a particular performance, go down to the theater a little early and try to buy spare tickets *(лишние билеты /LEESHneeyeh beelYEHTih)* from people outside the theater. This is accepted and very common behavior. Be sure, however, that the ticket you buy is for the right date and time. From late June to early September, many Russian entertainers and troupes go on tour, so performances are limited.

Tickets.
Билеты.
beeLYEHtih
(Theater) box office.

(Театральная) касса.
(teeahTRAHL'nahyah) KAHsah
Ticket window.

Билетная касса.
beeLYEHTnahyah KAHsah
Can you recommend a(n) opera/concert/play?

**Можете ли вы посоветовать мне оперу/
концерт/пьесу?**
*MOHzhehtyeh lee vih pahsahVYEHtahvaht' mnyeh
OHpeeroo/kahnTSEHRT/P'YEHsoo*

Have you any tickets for tonight's performance?

У вас есть билеты на сегодняшний спектакль?

oo vahs yehst' beeLYEHtih nah seeVOHdneeshneey speekTAHKL'

How much are they?

Сколько они стоят?

SKOHL'kah ahNEE STOHyaht

I'd like two for...

Я хочу два на...

yah khahCHOO dvah nah

We're sold out.

Все билеты проданы.

vsyeh beeLYEHtih PROHdahnih

At what time does it begin?

Во сколько начинается спектакль?

vah SKOHL'kah nahcheeNAHeetsah speekTAHKL'

How do I get to the Bolshoi Theater?

Как мне добраться до Большого театра?

kahk mnyeh dahBRAHT'sah dah bahl'SHOHvah teeAHTrah

No admittance after the third bell.

Вход в зрительный зал после третьего звонка воспрещён.

fxhoht VZREEteel'nihy zahl POHSlee TRYEHT'ehvah zvahnKAH vahspreeSHCHOHN

Seating and Signs

Orchestra stalls.

Партер.

pahrtTEHR

Amphitheater.

Амфитеатр.

ahmfeeteeAHTR

Balcony.

Балкон.

bahlKOHN

Box.

Ложа.

LOHzhah

Left side.

Левая сторона.

LYEHvahyah stahrahNAH

Right side.

Правая сторона.

PRAHvahyah stahrahNAH

Middle.

Середина.

seereeDEEnah

Lobby.

Фойе.

foyYEH

Snack bar.

Буфет.

booFYEHT

Smoking room.

Курительная комната.

kooREEteel'nahyah KOHMnahtah

Cloakroom.

Гардероб.

gahrdeeROHP

Cloakroom attendant. *(m./f.)*

Гардеробщик/Гардеробщица.

gahrdeeROHPshcheek/gahrdeerOHPshcheetsah

Entrance to auditorium.

Вход в зрительный зал.
fxoht VZREEteel'nihy zahl

Exit.

Выход.
VIHkhat

Opera, Concerts and Ballet

Tickets to Moscow's Bolshoi Theater and
St. Peterburg's Kirov Theater are expensive and often
hard to obtain. They are usually sold well in advance
of the performance. Sometimes you can buy them
from Hotel ticket offices, even if you are not a guest
in their hotel. Most major cities in Russia, however,
have their own excellent ballets, operas and
symphonies. Rock and popular music concerts are
most often advertised on posters around town.

Opera.

Опера.
OHpeerah

Concert.

Концерт.
kahnTSEHRT

Ballet.

Балет.
bahLYEHT

Orchestra.

Оркестр.
ahrKYEHSTR

Folk songs/dances.

Народные песни/танцы.
nahROHDnihyeh PYEHSnee/TAHNtsih

Here is my ticket.

Вот мой билет.
voht moy beeLYEHT

Where is my seat?

Где моё место?
gdyeh mahYOH MYEHstah

Follow me.

Следуйте за мной.
SLYEHdooytyeh zah mnoy

How much for a program?

Сколько стоит программа?
SKHOL'kah STOHeet prahGRAHmah

May I have a program, please?

Дайте, пожалуйста, программу.
DAYtyeh pahZHAHLstah prahGRAHmoo

Do you want to rent opera glasses?

Бинокль вам нужен?
beeNOHKL' vahm NOOzhehn

No, thank you. I don't need them.

Нет, спасибо. Он мне не нужен.
nyeht spahSEEbah. ohn mnyeh nee NOOzhehn

Who is the conductor?

Кто дирижёр?
ktoh deereeZHOHR

Who is dancing the lead?

Кто танцует главную партию?
ktoh tahnTSOOeht GLAHVnooyoo PAHRteeyoo

Who is the soloist?/(f.)

Кто солист(ка)?
ktoh sahLEEST(kah)

When is the intermission?

Когда антракт?
kahgDAH ahnTRAHKT

How long is the intermission?

Сколько длится антракт?
SKOHL'kah DLEETsah ahnTRAHKT
Pardon me, can I get by?

Простите, можно пройти?
prahsTEEtyeh, MOHZHnah prahyTEE
That's my seat.

Это моё место.
EHtah mahYOH MYEHstah

Theater and Movies

Russian theater is often first-rate and tickets are relatively inexpensive compared to western standards. Movies are shown all day long at most movie theaters. No one is admitted after the lights are turned off and Russians typically keep their coats on in movie theaters, but leave them in coatrooms while at plays or concerts.

Play.

Пьеса.
P'YEHsah
Performance.

Спектакль.
speekTAHKL'
Movie.

Кино.
keeNOH
Theater.

Театр.
teeAHTR

What's playing at the... ?

Что идёт в... ?
shtoh eeDYOHT f

What kind of play/movie is it?

Что это за пьеса/фильм?
shtoh EHtah zah P'YEHsah feel'm

It's a...

Это...
EHtah

...cartoon.

...мультфильм.
mool'tFEEL'M

...comedy.

...комедия.
kahMYEHdeeyah

...documentary.

...документальный фильм.
dahkoomeenTAHL'nihy feel'm

...drama.

...драма.
DRAHmah

Who's the director?

Кто режиссёр?
ktoh reezheeSYOHR

Who's playing the lead?

Кто играет главную роль?
ktoh eeGRAHeet GLAHVnooyoo rohl'

Are there any tickets left?

Остались ли лишние билеты?
ahSTAHlees' lee LEESHneeyeh beeLYEHtih

Is there a matinee?

Есть ли дневной спектакль?
yehst' lee dneevNOY speekTAHKL'

When does the show begin?

Когда начинается спектакль?
kahgDAH nahcheeNAHeetsah speekTAHKL'

Do you have any extra tickets?

У вас есть лишние билеты?
oo vahs yehst' LEESHneeyeh beeLYEHtih

Circus and Puppet Show

Russians love the circus. Most cities have one, but the Moscow Circus is the premiere troupe. It's well worth a visit.

Circus.

Цирк.
tseerk

Puppet theater.

Кукольный театр.
KOOkahl'nihy teeAHTR

Do you have tickets for the circus/puppet theater?

У вас есть билеты в цирк/кукольный театр?
oo vahs yehst' beeLYEHtih vtseerk/VKOOkahl'nihy teeAHTR

How do I get to the circus?

Как мне добраться до цирка?
kahk mnyeh dahBRAHT'sah dah TSEERkah

Is there a matinee today?

Есть ли сегодня дневной спектакль?
yehst' lee seeVOHdnyah dneevNOY speekTAHKL'

Do you have a spare ticket?

У вас есть лишний билет?
oo vahs yehst' LEESHneey beeLYEHT

Give me a program, please.

Дайте мне, программу, пожалуйста.
DAYtyeh mnyeh prahgRAHmoo pahZHAHLstah

Museums

Most of the larger, better-known museums in Russia provide guides or brochures in English as well as in Russian. Smaller literary museums, however, usually have no English-language materials available.

Entrance.

Вход.
fxoht
Exit.

Выход.
VIHkhaht
What is the admission fee?

Сколько стоит билет?
SKOH'Lkah STOHeet beeLYEHT
Free Admission.

Вход бесплатный.
fxoht byehsPLAHTnihy
When does it open/close?

Когда открывается/закрывается?
kahgDAH ahtkrihVAHyetsyah/zahkrihVAHyetsyah
Is there a guidebook (in English)?

Есть путеводитель (на английском языке)?
yehst' pootahvahDEEtyehl' (nah ahnGLEEYskahm yehzeeKEH)

Can I buy a catalogue?

Можно купить каталог?
MOHZHnah kooPEET' kahtahLOHK

When is the tour?

Когда экскурсия?
kahgDAH ehksKOORseeyah?

Can I take photos?

Можно снимать фотографии?
MOHZHnah sneeMAHT' fahtahGRAHFeeee

No photographs allowed.

Фотографировать воспрещается.
fahtahgrahfEERahvaht' vahsprehSHCHAHyetsyah

Where can I find…?

Где находится…?
gdyeh naKHODeetsyah

Is this the way to the exhibit/the entrance/the exit?

Сюда к выставке/входу/выходу?
sooDAH KVEEstahfkeh/KFXOHDoo/KVIHkhahdoo

Is there an elevator?

Есть лифт?
yehst' leeft

Where are the bathrooms?

Где туалеты?
gdyeh tooahLYETih

Is there a café?

Есть кафе?
yehst' kahFEH

Sporting Events

Soccer (football in Russia) and ice hockey are the
big draws in Russia, but chess is also considered a
national sport. Tickets for sporting events can
usually be purchased at the stadium before the game.

Sporting events.

Спортивные соревнования.
spahrTEEVnihyeh sahreevnahVAHneeyah

Sports fan.

Болельщик.
bahLYEHL'shcheek

I want to see a hockey/soccer game.

Я хочу посмотреть хоккейный/
   футбольный матч.
yah khahCHOO pahsmahTRYEHT' khahKEYnihy/
footBOHL'nihy mahtch

How much are the tickets?

Сколько стоят билеты?
SKOHL'kah STOHyaht beeLYEHtih

Are there any tickets for today's game?

Есть ли билеты на сегодняшний матч?
yehst' lee beeLYEHtih nah seeVOHdnyeeshneey
mahtch

How do I get to the stadium?

Как мне доехать до стадиона?
kahk mnyeh dahYEHkhat' dah stahdeeOHnah

Who is playing?

Кто играет?
ktoh eeGRAHyeht

Scoreboard.

Табло.
tahbLOH

Who is winning?

Кто выигрывает?
ktoh vihEEgrihvaheet

What's the score?

Какой счёт?
kahKOY shchoht

Dynamo are ahead three to one.

Три-один в пользу Динамо.
tree ahdEEN FPOHL'zoo deeNAHmoh

It's scoreless.

Ноль-ноль.
nohl'-nohl'

Score a point.

Выиграть очко.
VIHeegraht' ahchKOH

Score a goal.

Забить гол.
zahBEET' gohl

Who won?

Кто выиграл?
ktoh VIHeegrahl

Scoreless tie.

Нулевая ничя.
nooleeVAHyah neechYAH

Do you want to play chess?

Вы хотите играть в шахматы?
vih khahTEEtyeh eeGRAHT' FSHAHKHmahtih

Check.

Шах.
shakh

Checkmate.

Мат.
maht

King.

Король.
kahROHL'

Queen.

Ферзь.
fyehrz'

Bars, Clubs and Casinos

The bar scene in Moscow and St. Petersburg offers a
look at the other side of the entertainment industry in
Russia. Since there was no pub scene in the former
Soviet Union, most bars are new and reflect the values
of the new Russians. Many have cover charges and
live music. Big-name Russian rock bands can often be
found performing at the more well-known nightclubs
around town. No set closing time is enforced. Strip
shows and open prostitution are common at the wilder
establishments.

In the 1990s in Russia, casinos sprang up like
mushrooms. They range widely in size and glamour.
Most of the large, Western-style hotels have their own
gambling parlors as well.

Bet.

Ставка.
STAHFkah

I want to bet twenty dollars.

Я хочу ставить на двадцать долларов.
*yah khaCHOO STAHVeet' nah DVAHTsaht'
DOHlahrof*

Roulette.

Рулетка.
rooLYEHTkah

Blackjack.

Очко.
ahchKOH

Cards.

Карты.
KAHRtih

Do you want to play poker?

Вы хотите играть в покер?
vy xahTEEtyeh eeGRAHT' FPOHkehr

I raise you.

Я повышаю ставку.
yah pahvihSHAHyoo STAHFkoo

Diamonds.

Бубны.
BOOBnih

Spades.

Пики.
PEEkee

Clubs.

Трефы.
TREHfih

Hearts.

Черви.
CHEHRvee

Chips.

фишки.
FEESHkee

I've won! (f.)

Я выиграл(а)!
yah VIHeegrahl(ah)

I've lost (f.) everything.

Я проиграл(а) всё.
yah praheeGRAHL(ah) fsyoh

Time to go home.

Пора домой.
pahRAH dahMOY

SIGHTSEEING AND RELAXING

Asking Directions and Exploring

Russians are usually tremendously helpful and will often do all they can to help you get where you are going; so do not be afraid to wander around and ask for information from people on the street.

I'm lost. *(m./f.)*
Я заблудился/заблудилась.
yah zahblooDEELsah/zahblooDEElahs'
Excuse me.

Простите./Извините.
prahsTEEtyeh/eezveeNEEtyeh
Can you tell me how to get to...

Скажите пожалуйста, как попасть...
skahZHEEtyeh pahZHAHLstah kahk pahPAHST'
...Tverskaya Street?

...на улицу Тверскую.
nah OOleetsoo tveerSKOOyoo
...the center of town?

...в центр города.
vtsehntrGOHrahdah
I'm looking for...

Я ищу...
yah eeSHCHOO
Am I going in the right direction?

Я иду в правильном направлении?
yah eeDOO VPRAHveel'nahm nahprahvLYEHneeee
Do you know where ... is?

Вы знаете где находится...?
vih ZNAHeetyeh gdyeh nahKHOHdeetsah

Is it far?

Это далеко?
EHtah dahleeKOH
Is it close?

Это близко?
EHtah BLEESkah
Can I walk there?

Можно дойти туда пешком?
MOHZHnah dahyTEE tooDAH peeshKOHM
It would be best to take a bus or the metro.

**Вам лучше доехать или на метро или на
    автобусе.**
*vahm LOOCHsheh dahYEHkhaht' eelee nah
meetROH eelee nah ahfTOHboosyeh*
What bus can I take to get to...?

Каким автобусом можно доехать до...?
*kahKEEM ahfTOHboosahm MOHZHnah
dahYEHkhaht' dah*
What street is this?

Какая это улица?
kahKAHyah EHtah OOleetsah
Please show me on the map where I am.

**Покажите мне, пожалуйста, на карте,
    где я нахожусь.**
*pahkahZHEEtyeh mnyeh pahZHAHLstah nah
KAHRtyeh gdyeh yah nahkhahZHOOS'*
Go straight ahead.

Идите прямо.
eeDEEtyeh PRYAHmah
Go in this/that direction.

Идите в эту/ту сторону.
eeDEEtyeh VEHtoo/ftoo STOHrahnoo
Turn left/right...

Поверните налево/направо...
pahveerNEEtyeh nahLYEHvah/nahPRAHvah

…at the next corner.

…на следующем углу.
nah SLYEHdooyooshchem oogLOO

…at the light.

…у светофора.
oo sveetahFOHrah

Take this road.

Поезжайте по этой улице.
paheezhZHAYtyeh pah EHtay OOleetseh

You have to go back.

Вам надо вернуться.
vahm NAHdah veerNOOT'syah

You're on the wrong bus.

Вы сели не на тот автобус.
vih SYEHlee nee nah toht ahfTOHboos

Do I have to transfer?

Мне надо пересесть?
mnyeh NAHdah peereeSYEHST'

North./South.

Север./Юг.
SYEHveer/yook

East./West.

Восток./Запад.
vahsTOHK/ZAHpaht

It's there…

Это там…
EHtah tahm

…on the right./left.

…направо/налево.
nahPRAHvah/nahLYEHvah

…after/behind…

…после/позади…
POHSlee/pahzahDEE

...next to/opposite...

...**рядом/напротив**...
RYAHdahm/nahPROHteef
There it is. *(m./f./nt.)*

Вот он/она/оно.
voht ohn/ahNAH/ahNOH
This way./That way.

Сюда./Туда.
syooDAH/tooDAH

Taking a Bus Trip

What sights should we see?

**Какие достопримечательности стоит
    осмотреть?**
*kahKEEyeh dahstahpreemeeCHAHteel'nahstee
STOHeet ahsmahTRYEHT'*
Where can I sign up for an excursion?

Где можно записаться на экскурсию?
*gdyeh MOHZHnah zahpeeSAHTsah nah
ehksKOORseeyoo*
Which excursion do you suggest?

Какую экскурсию вы мне посоветуете?
*kahKOOyoo ehksKOORseeyoo vih mnyeh
pahsahVYEHtooeetyeh*
I want to take a bus trip around the city.

**Я хочу записаться на экскурсию по
    городу.**
*yah khahCHOO zahpeeSAHTsah nah
ehksKOORseeyoo pah GOHrahdoo*
What does a ticket cost?

Сколько стоит билет?
SKOHL'kah STOHeet beeLYEHT

When does the excursion leave?

На какое время она назначена?
*nah kahKOHyeh VRYEHmyah ahNAH
nahZNACHehnah*

When do we get back?

Когда мы вернёмся?
kahgDAH mih veerNYOHMsah

From where does the excursion leave?

Откуда отходит экскурсия?
ahtKOOdah ahtKHOHdeet ehksKOORseeyah

Tour guide.

Экскурсовод.
ehkskoorsahVOHT

Is there an English-speaking guide?

**Есть ли экскуросовод, говорящий
   по-английски?**
*yehst' lee ehkskoorsahVOHT gahvahRYAHshcheey
pahahngLEEYskee*

When should we be back on the bus?

**Во сколько мы должны вернуться к
   автобусу?**
*vahSKOHL'kah mih dahlzhNIH veerNYOOTsah
kahfTOHboosoo*

Taking a Walking Tour

Guided walking tours are available in most larger
museums. Most hotels can book tours of the major
sites.

When does it open/close?

Когда открывается/закрывается?
kahgDAH ahtkrihVAHeetsah/zahkrihVAHeetsah

SIGHTSEEING AND RELAXING

I want to sign up for a tour.

Я хочу записаться на экскурсию.
*yah khahCHOO zahpeeSAHTsah nah
ehksKOORseeyoo*
When does it start/end?

Когда она начинается/кончается?
*kahgDAH ahNAH nahchehNAHeetsah/
kahnCHAHeetsah*
What is the cost?

Сколько стоит билет?
SKOHL'kah STOHeet beeLYEHT
Free admission.

Вход бесплатный.
fkhoht beesPLAHTnihy
Do you sell guidebooks in English?

**У вас есть путеводитель на английском
    языке?**
*oo vahs yehst' pooteevahDEEteel' nah
ahngLEEYskahm yeezihkYEH*
Is there a map?

Есть у вас карта?
yehst' oo vahs KAHRtah
In front of...

Впереди...
vpeereeDEE
To the rear of...

Позади...
pahzahDEE
In the middle of...

Посередине...
pahseereeDEEnyeh
On the left of...

Слева...
SLYEHvah

SIGHTSEEING AND RELAXING

On the right of...

Справа...
SPRAHvah
Where can I buy postcards?

Где можно купить открытки?
gdyeh MOHZHnah kooPEET' ahtKRIHTkee
May I see what postcards you have for sale?

**Можно посмотреть, какие у вас
   открытки?**
*MOHZHnah pahsmahtRYEHT' kahKEEyeh oo vahs
ahtKRIHTkee*
Can I take pictures?

Можно здесь фотографировать?
MOHZHnah zdyehs' fahtahgrahFEErahvaht'
No cameras allowed.

Фотографировать воспрещается.
fahtahgrahFEEahvaht' vahspreeSHCHAHeetsah
Take a picture of me, please.

Сфотографируйте меня, пожалуйста.
sfahtahgrahFEErooytyeh meeNYAH pahZHALstah

Film Development

Western film and batteries are available for purchase
in Russia, but they can be more expensive and
sometimes difficult to find. It is best to stock up on
what you need before you leave home. Remember that
it is considered impolite to photograph people without
their permission.

Photography.

Фотография.
fahtahGRAHfeeyah

Camera.

Фотоаппарат.
fahtahahpahRAHT

Film.

Плёнка.
PLYOHNkah

Black and white film.

Чёрно-белая плёнка.
CHOHRnah-BYEHlahyah PLYOHNkah

Color film.

Цветная плёнка.
tsveetNAHyah PLYOHNkah

Thirty-six exposure.

Тридцать шесть кадров.
TREEtsaht' shehst' KAHDrahv

Battery.

Батарейка.
bahtehrEYkah

Slides.

Слайды.
SLAYdih

Videotape.

Видеокассета.
VEEdeeohkahSYEHtah

How much does processing cost?

Слолько стоит проявить плёнку?
SKOHL'kah STOHeet praheeVEET' PLYOHNkoo

When will they be ready?

Когда будут готовы фотографии?
kahgDAH BOOdoot gahTOHvih fahtahGRAHfeeee

SIGHTSEEING AND RELAXING

Taking in the Sights

I want to see the sights.

Я хочу осмотреть
достпримечательности.
yah khahCHOO ahsmahTRYEHT'
dahstahpremeeCHAHteel'nahstee

Let's go for a walk.

Давайте погуляем.
dahVAYtyeh pahgooLYAHeem

What kind of ... is that?

Что это за...?
shtoh EHtah zah

animal/bird/fish/flower/tree?

животное/птица/рыба/цветок/дерево?
zheeVOHTnahyeh/PTEEtsah/RIHbah/tsveeTOHK
deeRYEHvah

We don't have those at home.

У нас таких нет.
oo nahs tahKEEKH nyeht

What a beautiful view!

Какой прекрасный вид!
kahKOY preeKRAHSnihy veet

What's that building?

Что это за здание?
shtoh EHtah zah ZDAHneeyeh

When was it built?

Когда оно было построено?
kahgDAH ahNOH BIHlah pahstROHeenah

Who built it?

Кто его построил?
ktoh yeeVOH pahstROIleel

Who was the architect/artist?

Кто был архитектором/художником?
ktoh bihl ahrkheeTYEHKtahrahm/
khooDOHZHneekahm

When did he/she live?

Когда он/она жил(а)?
kahgDAH ohn/ahNAH zheel(AH)

Where's the house where ... lived?

Где дом, в котором жил(а)...?
gdyeh dohm fkahTOHrahm zheel(AH)

Can we go in?

Можно войти?
MOHZHnah vahyTEE

Very interesting.

Очень интересно.
OHcheen' eenteeRYEHSnah

It's...

Это...
EHtah

...beautiful.

...красиво.
krahSEEvah

...ugly.

...безобразно.
beezahbRAHZnah

...wonderful.

...прекрасно.
preeKRAHSnah

...horrible.

...ужасно.
ooZHAHSnah

...great.

...великолепно.
veeleekahLYEHPnah

…terrible.

…страшно.
STRAHSHnah

…amazing.

…удивительно.
oodeeVEEtyehl'nah

…strange.

…странно.
STRAHNnah

…cute.

…мило.
MEElah

…sinister.

…жутко.
ZHOOTkah

Let's rest.

Давайте отдохнём.
dahVAYtyeh ahtdahkhNYOHM

I'm tired. /(f.)

Я устал(а).
yah oostAHL(ah)

I'm bored.

Мне скучно/надоело.
mnyeh SKOOCHnah/nahdahYEHlah

Worship Services

Most places of worship do not mind visitors, as long as you observe their customs and do not disturb their services. In Orthodox churches there are no seats; worshippers are expected to stand for services which can last for several hours. Orthodox churches prefer that women wear skirts and cover their heads with a kerchief or hat. Men must remove their hats. Shorts

are not permitted. Taking pictures inside churches is
usually not permitted either.

Worship services.
Богослужения.
bahgahslooZHEHneeyah
Monastery.

Лавра.
LAHVrah
Cathedral.

Собор.
sahBOHR
Church.

Церковь.
TSEHRkahf'
Synagogue.

Синагога.
seenahGOHgah
Temple.

Храм.
khrahm
Mosque.

Мечеть.
meeCHEHT'
Orthodox.

Православный.
prahvahSLAHVnihy
Old-Believers.

Старообрядцы.
stahrahahbRYAHTtsih
Saint.

Святой.
sveeTOY

SIGHTSEEING AND RELAXING

Altar.

Алтарь.
ahlTAHR'

Iconostasis.

Иконостас.
eekahnahSTAHS

Icons.

Иконы.
eeKOHnih

Incense.

Ладан.
LAHdahn

Candle.

Свеча.
sveeCHAH

Contribution.

Пожертвование.
pahZHEHRTvahvahneeyeh

Prayers.

Молитвы.
mahLEETvih

Prayer book.

Молитвенник.
mahLEETveeneek

Rabbi.

Раввин.
rahVEEN

Priest.

Священник.
sveeSHCHEHNneek

When is the service?

Когда служба?
kahgDAH SLOOSHbah

SIGHTSEEING AND RELAXING

I want to look around the church.

Я хочу осмотреть церковь.
yah khahCHOO ahsmahtRYEHT' TSEHRkahf'
You must cover your head.

Вам надо покрыть голову.
vahm NAHdah pahKRIHT' GOHlahvoo
Are women allowed?

Женщины допускаются?
ZHEHNshcheenih dahpoosKAHyootsah
May I take a picture?

Можно здесь фотографировать?
MOHZHnah zdyehs fahtahgrahFEErahvaht'
No cameras allowed.

Фотографировать воспрещается.
fahtahgrahFEErahvaht' vahspreeSHCHAHeetsah
Cemetery.

Кладбище.
KLAHTbeeshcheh
Grave.

Могила.
mahGEElah
Tombstone.

Надгробный камень.
nahdGROHBnihy KAHmeen'

Outdoor Recreation

I enjoy...

Мне нравится...
mnyeh NRAHveetsah

…running.

…бегать.
BYEHgaht'

…cycling.

…велоспорт.
veelahSPOHRT

…playing tennis.

…теннис.
TYEHnees

…horseback riding.

…кататься верхом.
kahTAHTsah veerKHOHM

…swimming.

…плавание.
PLAHvahneeyeh

…sailing.

…катание на парусной лодке.
kahTAHneeyeh nah PAHroosnay LOHTkyeh

…mountain climbing.

…альпинизм.
ahl'peeNEEZM

…skiing.

…кататься на лыжах.
kahTAHTsah nah LIHzhahkh

…skating.

…кататься на коньках.
kahTAHTsah nah kahn'KAHKH

I want to play tennis.

Я хочу играть в теннис.
yah khahCHOO eegRAHT' FTYEHnees

Can we rent rackets?

Можно взять напрокат ракетки?
MOHZHnah vzyaht' nahprahKAHT rahKYEHTkee

SIGHTSEEING AND RELAXING

Are there courts here?

Есть ли здесь корты?
yehst' lee zdyehs' KOHRtih

Is there a swimming pool here?

Есть ли здесь бассейн?
yehst' lee zdyehs' bahsSEYN

Can one go swimming here?

Можно здесь купаться?
MOHZHnah zdyehs' kooPAHTsah

Is it safe to swim here?

Здесь не опасно купаться?
zdyehs' nee ahPAHSnah kooPAHTsah

Is the water here deep?

Здесь глубоко?
zdyehs' gloobahKOH

Is the water cold?

Вода холодная?
vahDAH khahLOHDnahyah

No swimming.

Купаться воспрещается.
kooPAHTsah vahspreeSHCHAHeetsah

I want to lie on the beach.

Я хочу полежать на пляже.
yah khahCHOO pahleeZHAHT' nah PLYAHzheh

I want to sunbathe.

Я хочу загорать.
yah khahCHOO zahgahRYAHT'

Can I rent...

Можно взять напрокат...
MOHZHnah vzyaht' nahprahKAHT

...a beach chair?

...шезлонг?
shehzLOHNG

…a sun umbrella?

…зонтик?
ZOHNteek

…a row boat?

…лодку?
LOHTkoo

…water skis?

…водные лыжи?
VOHDnihyeh LIHzhee

…skiing equipment?

…лыжное снаряжение?
LIHZHnahyeh snahreeZHEHneeyeh

…skates?

…коньки?
KOHN'kee

What's the charge per hour/per day?

Сколько стоит на час/день?
SKOHL'kah STOHeet nah chahs/dyehn'

Is there a skating rink here?

Есть ли здесь каток?
yehst' lee zdyehs' kahTOHK

Where can I go skiing?

Где можно кататься на лыжах?
gdyeh MOHZHnah kahTAHT'sah nah LIHzhahkh

Camping

Camping.

Кемпинг.
KYEHMpeeng

Camping equipment.

Оборудование для кемпинга.
ahbahROOdahvahneeyeh dlyah KYEHMpeengah

SIGHTSEEING AND RELAXING

Camping permit.

Разрешение на кемпинг.
rahzreeSHEHneeyeh nah KYEHMpeeng

Can we camp here?

Можно здесь устроить стоянку?
MOHZHnah zdyehs' oosTROHeet' stahYAHNkoo

What's the charge per day/per person?

Сколько стоит на день/на человека?
SKOHL'kah STOHeet nah dyehn'/nah
chehlahVYEHkah

Are there showers/toilets?

Есть душ/уборная?
yehst' doosh/oobOHRnahyah

Where are the toilets?

Где уборная?
gdyeh ooBOHRnahyah

Can we light a fire here?

Можно здесь разжечь костёр?
MOHZHnah zdyehs' rahzZHEHCH' kahsTYOHR

Is there electricity?

Есть электричество?
yehst' ehleekTREEchehstvah

Is swimming allowed?

Здесь можно купаться?
zdyehs' MOHZHnah kooPAHTsah

Can we fish here?

Здесь можно ловить рыбу?
zdyehs' MOHZHnah lahVEET' RIHBoo

Do we need a license to fish?

Надо ли иметь разрешение на рыбную
  ловлю?
NAHdah lee eemYEHT' rahzreeSHEHneeyeh nah
RIHBnooyoo LOHVlyoo

SIGHTSEEING AND RELAXING

Can we rent equipment?

Можно ли взять напрокат оборудование для кемпинга?
MOHZHnah lee vzyaht' nahprahKAHT ahbahROOdahvahneeyeh dlyah KYEHMpeengah

Where can we get (a) ...

Где можно достать...
gdyeh MOHZHnah dahsTAHT'

...corkscrew?

...штопор?
SHTOHpahr

...candles?

...свечки?
SVYEHCHkee

...can opener?

...консервный нож?
kahnSYEHRVnihy nohsh

...charcoal?

...древесный уголь?
dreeVYEHSnihy OOgahl'

...compass?

...компас?
KOHMpahs

...cooking utensils?

...кухонные принадлежности?
KOOkhahnnihyeh preenahdLYEHZHnahstee

...cooler?

...сумку-термос?
SOOMkooTYEHRmahs

...fire wood?

...дрова?
drahVAH

...first-aid kit?

...аптечку?
ahpTYEHCHkoo

…flashlight?

…карманный фонарь?
kahrMAHNnihy fahNAHR'

…groundsheet?

…подстилку под палатку?
pahdsTEELkoo paht pahLAHTkoo

…kerosene?

…керосин?
keerahSEEN

…lantern?

…фонарь?
fahNAHR'

…mattress?

…матрас?
mahtRAHS

…sleeping bag?

…спальный мешок?
SPAHL'nihy meeSHOHK

…tent?

…палатку?
pahLAHTkoo

…thermos?

…термос?
TYEHRmahs

Public Baths

The larger Russian public baths often have saunas and pools where you can relax Russian-style. After sitting for awhile in the sauna, it is a Russian custom to beat oneself lightly with dried birch switches.

SIGHTSEEING AND RELAXING

Public bath.

Баня.
BAHnyah

Men.

Мужчины.
mooshCHEEnih

Women.

Женщины.
ZHEHNshcheenih

What does admission cost?

Сколько стоит входной билет?
SKOHL'kah STOHeet fkhahdNOY beeLYEHT

I'd like to rent...

Я хотел(а) бы взять...
yah khahtYEHL(ah) bih vzyaht'

...a towel.

...полотенце.
pahlahTYEHNtseh

...a sheet.

...простыню.
prahstihNYOO

It's too hot/cold here.

Здесь слишком жарко/холодно.
zdyehs' SLEESHkahm ZHAHRkah/KHOHlahdnah

Shower.

Душ.
doosh

Pool.

Бассейн.
bahSEYN

Bathing cap.

Купальная шапочка.
kooPAHL'nahyah SHAHpahchkah

Bathing suit.

Купальный костюм.
kooPAHL'nihy kahsTYOOM

Soap.

Мыло.
MIHlah

Bucket.

Ведро.
veedROH

Steam room.

Парилка.
pahREELkah

Birch switches.

Берёзовый веник.
beerYOHzahvihy VYEHneek

SHOPPING

If you have a lot of money, you can buy anything your heart desires these days in Moscow and St. Petersburg. Moscow even sports Western-style shopping malls, but most Russians still prefer to shop at specialty shops like those listed below.

Shops and Stores

Where can I buy...?

Где можно купить...?
gdyeh MOHZHnah kooPEET'
Where can I find a...?

Где мне найти...?
gdyeh mnyeh nahyTEE
Is there a ... near here?

Есть ли поблизости...
yehst' lee pahbLEEzahstee
...bakery...

...булочная.
BOOlahchnahyah
...bookstore...

...книжный магазин.
KNEEZHnihy mahgahZEEN
...candy shop...

...кондитерская.
kahnDEEteerskahyah
...clothes store...

...одежда.
AhDYEHZHdah

...dairy...

...молочная.
mahLOHCHnahyah

...department store...

...универмаг.
ooneeveerMAHK

...drug store...

...аптека.
ahpTYEHkah

...farmers' market...

...рынок.
RIHnahk

...fish market...

...рыбный магазин.
RIHBnihy mahgahZEEN

...fruit and vegetable store...

...фрукты и овощи.
FROOKtih ee OHvahchshee

...furrier...

...меха.
meeKHAH

...gift shop...

...подарки.
pahdAHRkee

...grocery...

...продукты/гастронмом.
prahDOOKtih/gahstrahNOHM

...hat shop...

...магазин головных уборов.
mahgahZEEN gahlahvNIHKH ooBOHrahf

...jeweler...

...ювелирный магазин.
yooveelEERnihy mahgahZEEN

…liquor store…

…вино.
veeNAH

…newsstand…

…газетный киоск.
gahZYEHTnihy keeOHSK

…office supply store…

…канцелярские товары.
kahntsehLYAHRskeeyeh tahVAHrih

…record store…

…грампластинки.
grahmplahsTEENkee

…secondhand bookstore…

…букинистический магазин.
bookeeneestEECHehskeey mahgahZEEN

…secondhand store…

…комиссионный магазин.
kahmeeseeOHNnihy mahgahZEEN

…shoe store…

…обувный магазин.
OHboofnihy mahgahZEEN

…souvenirs…

…сувениры.
sooveeNEErih

…stationery…

…канцтовары.
kahntstahVAHrih

…tobacconist…

…табак.
tahBAHK

…toy store…

…магазин игрушек.
mahgahZEEN eegROOshehk

Looking Around

Service.

Обслуживание.
ahpsloozheeVAHneeyeh

Can you help me...

Будьте добры...
BOOT'tyeh dahbRIH

Where's the ... department?

Где находится отдел...
gdyeh nahKHOHdeetsah ahtDYEHL

Can I help you?

Слушаю вас.
SLOOshahyoo vahs

Do you have...

Есть ли у вас...
yehst' lee oo vahs

What kind of ... would you like?

Какой ... вы хотите?
kahKOY ... vih khahTEEtyeh

I'd like...

Я хотел(а) бы...
yah khahtYEHL(ah) bih

I'm sorry, we don't have any.

Простите, этого у нас нет.
prahsTEEtyeh, EHtahvah oo nahs nyeht

We're sold out.

Всё распродано.
vsyoh rahsPROHdahnah

Anything else?

Ещё что-нибудь?
yeeSHCHOH SHTOHneeboot'

Show me (this/that), please.

Покажите мне (это/то) пожалуйста.
pahkahZHEEtyeh mneyh (EHtah/toh)
 pahZHAHLstah

No, not that, but that there, next to it.

Нет, не это, а вот это рядом.
nyeht nee EHtah ah voht EHtah RYAHdahm

It's not what I want.

Это не то, что я хочу.
EHtah nee toh shtoh yah khahCHOO

I don't like it.

Это мне не нравится.
EHtah mnyeh nee NRAHveetsah

I'm just looking.

Я только смотрю.
yah TOHL'kah smahtRYOO

I prefer...

Я предпочитаю...
yah preetpahcheeTAHyoo

Something not too expensive.

Что-нибудь не очень дорогое.
SHTOHneeboot' nee OHcheen' darahGOHyeh

How much is it?

Сколько это стоит?
SKHOL'kah EHtah STOHeet

Repeat that, please.

Повторите, пожалуйста.
pahftahREEtyeh pahZHAHLstah

Please write it down.

Пожалуйста, напишите.
pahZHAHLstah nahpeeSHEEtyeh

Making a Purchase

Shopping in Russia used to be an adventure, but
not anymore. Many shops and stores are the self-
serve model, where you select what you want and
proceed to the checkout to pay for it.

Have you decided?

Вы решили?
vih reeSHEElee
Yes, I want this.

Да, я хочу это.
dah yah khahCHOO EHtah
I'll take it.

Я возьму это.
yah vahz'MOO EHtah
Will I have problems with customs?

**Будут ли у меня трудности на
таможне?**
*BOOdoot lee oo meeNYAH TROODnahstee nah
tahMOHZHnyeh*
Pay at the cashier.

Платите в кассу.
plahTEEtyeh FKAHsoo
Do you accept traveler's checks/credit cards?

**Вы принимаете дорожные чеки/
кредитные карточки?**
*vih preeneeMAHyehtyeh dahROHZHnihyeh
SHEHkee/kreeDEETnihyeh KAHRtahchkee*

Can I have a receipt, please.

Дайте, пожалуйста, квитанцию.
DAYtyeh pahZHAHLstah kveeTAHNtseeyoo

Wrap it up for me, please.

Заверните, пожалуйста.
zahveerNEEtyeh pahZHAHLstah

Please give me a bag.

Дайте мне сумку, пожалуйста.
DAYtyeh mnyeh SOOMkoo pahZHAHLstah

Gifts and Souvenirs

Souvenir stands can be found set up around all the major tourist attractions. In Moscow, you can find better quality and prices on arts, crafts, Soviet memorabilia and souvenirs at Izmailovsky Park on the weekends. Be careful when buying antiques or quality art made before 1945. To export items of value, you must get permission from the Ministry of Culture and pay an export tax of fifty percent of the antique's worth.

Amber.

Янтарь.
yeenTAHR'

Balalaika.

Балалайка.
bahlahLAYkah

Books.

Книги.
KNEEgee

Candy.
Конфеты.
kahnFYEHtih

Caviar.
Икра.
eekRAH

Ceramics.
Керамика.
keeRAHmeekah

Chess set.
Шахматы.
SHAHKHmahtih

Chocolate.
Шоколад.
shahkahLAHT

Cigarettes.
Сигареты.
seegahRYEHtih

Cigarette lighter.
Зажигалка.
zahzheeGAHLkah

Coins.
Монеты.
mahNYEHtih

CDs.
Компакт-диски.
kahmPAHKT-DEESkee

Fur hat.
Меховая шапка.
meekhahVAHyah SHAHPkah

Icon.
Икона.
EeKOHnah

Jewelry.
Драгоценности.
drahgahTSEHNahstee

Lace.
Кружева.
kroozhehVAH

Nested wooden doll.
Матрёшка.
mahtRYOHSHkah

Palekh boxes.
Палехские шкатулки.
PAHleekhskeeyeh shkahTOOLkee

Perfume.
Духи.
dooKHEE

Postcards.
Открытки.
ahtKRIHTkee

Posters.
Плакаты.
plahKAHtih

Records.
Пластинки.
plahsTEENkee

Samovar.
Самовар.
sahmahVAHR

Scarf.
Шарф.
shahrf

Shawl.
Платок.
PlahTOHK

Stamps.
Марки.
MAHRkee

Tapes.
Кассеты.
kahSYEHtih

Tea caddy.
Чайница.
CHAYneetsah

Toys.
Игрушки.
eegROOSHkee

Vodka.
Водка.
VOHTkah

Wine.
Вино.
veeNOH

Wood carvings.
Резьба по дереву.
rees'BAH pah DYEHreevoo

Wooden spoons and bowls.
Деревянные ложки и миски.
deereevYAHnihyeh LOSHkee ee MEESkee

Jewelry

Jewelry department.
Ювелирные изделия.
yooveelEERnihyeh eezDYEHleeyah

Jewelry.
Драгоценности.
drahgahTSEHnahstee

Bracelet.
Браслет.
brahsLYEHT

Brooch.
Брошь.
brohsh

Chain.
Цепочка.
tseePOHCHkah

Charm.
Брелок.
breeLOHK

Clips.
Клипсы.
KLEEPsih

Cufflinks.
Запонки.
ZAHpahnkee

Earrings.
Серьги.
SYEHR'gee

Money clip.
Денежная скрепка.
DYEHneezhnahyah SKRYEHPkah

Necklace.
Ожерелье.
ahzheeRYEHL'yeh

Pendant.
Кулон.
kooLOHN

Ring.
Кольцо.
kahl'TSOH

Tie pin.

Булавка для галстука.
booLAHFkah dlyah GAHLstookah

Watch.

Часы.
cheeSIH

Stones and Metals

What is it made of?

Из чего это сделано?
ees cheeVOH EHtah ZDYEHlahnah

Is it real silver/gold?

Это настоящее серебро/золото?
EHtah nahstahYAHshchehyeh seereebROH/ ZOHlahtah

How many carats is this?

Сколько здесь карат?
SKOHL'kah zdyehs' kahRAHT

What kind of metal/stone is it?

Что это за металл/камень?
shtoh EHtah zah meetAHL/KAHmeen'

Amber.

Янтарь.
yeenTAHR'

Amethyst.

Аметист.
ahmeeTEEST

Copper.

Медь.
myeht'

Crystal.

Хрусталь.
khroosTAHL'

Diamond.

Бриллиант.
breeleeAHNT

Ebony.

Чёрноедерево.
CHOHRnahyeh DYEHreevah

Emerald.

Изумруд.
eezoomROOT

Garnet.

Гранат.
grahNAHT

Gilded.

Позолоченный.
pahzahLOHCHehnihy

Glass.

Стекло.
steekLOH

Gold.

Золото.
ZOHlahtah

Ivory.

Слоновая кость.
slahNOHvahyah kohst'

Jade.

Нефрит.
NeefREET

Pearl.

Жемчуг.
ZHEHMchook

Pewter.
Олово.
OHlahvah
Platinum.
Платина.
PLAHteenah
Ruby.
Рубин.
rooBEEN
Sapphire.
Сапфир.
sahpFEER
Silver.
Посеребрённый
pahseereebRYOHnih
Silver plated.
Серебряный.
seeREEbreenihy
Topaz.
Топаз.
tahPAHS
Turquoise.
Бирюза.
beeryooZAH

Books and Stationery Supplies

Bookstore.
Книжный магазин.
KNEEZHnihy mahgahZEEN
Newsstand.
Газетный киоск.
gahZYEHTnihy keeOHSK

Secondhand bookstore.

Букинистический магазин.
bookeeneeSTEECHehskeey mahgahZEEN

Stationery store.

Канцтовары.
kahntstahVAHrih

Do you have any books in English?

**Есть ли у вас книги на английском
    языке?**
*yehst' lee oo vahs KNEEgee nah ahngLEEYskahm
yeezihKYEH*

Do you have any children's books/art books?

**Есть ли у вас детские книги/книги по
    искусству?**
*yehst' lee oo vahs DYEHTskeeyeh KNEEgee/
KNEEgee pah eesKOOSTvoo*

Where are the guidebooks/dictionaries?

Где находятся путеводители/словари?
*gdyeh nahKHOHdeetsah pooteevahDEEteelee/
slahvahREE*

How much is this book?

Сколько стоит эта книга?
SKOHL'kah STOHeet EHtah KNEEgah

Where do I pay?

Где мне платить?
gdyeh mnyeh plahTEET'

Have you got...

Есть ли у вас...
yehst' lee oo vahs

...calendars?

...календари?
kahleendahREE

...envelopes?

...конверты?
kahnVYEHRtih

...magazines in English?

...журналы на английском языке?
zhoorNAHlih nah ahngLEEYskahm yeezihKEE

...maps?

...планы/карты?
PLAHnih/KAHRtih

...paper?

...бумага?
booMAHgah

...pens?

...ручки?
ROOCHkee

...pencils?

...карандаши?
kahrahndahSHEE

...postcards?

...открытки?
ahtKRIHTkee

...stationery?

...почтовая бумага?
pachTOHvahyah booMAHgah

CDs, Tapes and Records

When shopping for music, be careful of counterfeit
copies and cheap knock-offs. Pirated CDs, CD-ROMs
and cassettes abound. The price may seem hard to
pass up, but the quality is usually substandard at best.

CDs.

Компакт-диски.
kahmPAHKT-DEESkee
Cassettes.

Кассеты.
kahSYEHtih
Records.

Пластинки.
plahsTEENkee
Have you got any records by...

Есть ли у вас пластинки...
yehst' lee oo vahs plahsTEENkee
Do you have any...

Есть ли у вас...
yehst' lee oo vahs
...Russian folk songs?

...русские народные песни?
ROOSkeeyeh nahROHDnihyeh PYEHSnee
...poets reading their work?

...поэты, читающие свои стихи?
pahEHtih cheeTAHyooshcheeyeh svahEE steeKHEE
...classical music?

...классическая музыка?
klahSEEchehskahyah MOOzihkah
...popular music?

...эстрадная музыка?
ehstRAHDnahyah MOOzihkah
...recordings of operas and plays?

...записи опер и спектаклей?
ZAHpeesee OHpeer ee speekTAHKley
...rock?

...рок?
rohk

Can I listen to this CD/cassette?

Можно прослушать этот компакт-
 диск/эту кассету?
*MOHZHnah prahsLOOshaht' EHtoht kahmPAHKT
deesk/EHtoo kahsSYEHtoo*

Toys

Toys./Games.

Игрушки./Игры.
eegROOSHkee/EEGrih

For a boy.

Для мальчика.
dlyah MAHL'cheekah

For a girl.

Для девочки.
dlyah DYEHvahchkee

Ball.

Мяч.
myahch

Blocks.

Кубики.
KOObeekee

Cards.

Игральные карты.
eegRAHL'nihyeh KAHRtih

Checkers.

Шашки.
SHAHSHkee

Chess.

Шахматы.
SHAHKHmahtih

Doll.

Кукла.
KOOKlah

Electronic game.

Электронная игра.
ehleekTROHNnahyah eegRAH

Stuffed animal.

Чучело.
CHOOchehlah

Teddy bear.

Мишка.
MEESHkah

Wooden toys.

Деревянные игрушки.
deereeVYAHnihyeh eegROOSHkee

Clothes

Clothes.

Одежда.
ahDYEHZHdah

Where can I find a...

Где мне найти...
gdyeh mnyeh nahyTEE

...bathing cap?

...купальную шапочку?
kooPAHL'nooyoo SHAHpahchkoo

...bathing suit?

...купальник?
kooPAHL'neek

...bathrobe?

...халат?
khahLAHT

…belt?

…пояс?
POHyees

…blouse?

…блузку?
BLOOSkoo

…bra?

…бюстгальтер?
byoozGAHL'teer

…children's clothes?

…детскую одежду?
DYEHTskooyoo ahDYEHZHdoo

…coat?

…пальто?
pahl'TOH

…dress?

…платье?
PLAHT'yeh

…fur coat?

…шубу?
SHOOboo

…fur hat?

…меховую шапку?
meekhahVOOyoo SHAHPkoo

…gloves?

…перчатки?
peerCHAHTkee

…handkerchief?

…носовой платок?
nahsahVOY plahTOHK

…hat?

…шляпу?
SHLYAHpoo

…jacket?

…куртку?
KOORTkoo

…panties?

…трусики?
TROOseekee

…pants?

…брюки?
BRYOOkee

…pyjamas?

…пижаму?
peeZHAHmoo

…raincoat?

…плащ?
plahshch

…scarf?

…шарф?
shahrf

…shirt?

…рубашку?
rooBAHSHkoo

…shorts?

…шорты?
SHOHRtih

…skirt?

…юбку?
YOOPkoo

…socks?

…носки?
nahsKEE

…stockings?

…чулки?
choolKEE

…suit?

…костюм?
kahsTYOOM

…sweater?

…свитер?
SVEEteer

…sweatsuit?

…тренироновый костюм?
treeneeROHvahchnihy kahsTYOOM

…swimming trunks?

…плавки?
PLAHFkee

…tie?

…галстук?
GAHLstook

…T-shirt?

…майку?
MAYkoo

Fit

I don't know my size.

Я не знаю мой размер.
yah nee ZNAHyoo moy rahzMYEHR

I take a size…

Мой размер…
moy rahzMYEHR

Is there a mirror?

Есть ли у вас зеркало?
yehst' lee oo vahs ZYEHRkahlah

Can I try it on?

Можно померить?
MOHZHnah pahMYEHreet'

Where is the fitting-room?

Где примерочная?
gdyeh preeMYEHrahchnahyah
Does it fit?

Вам годится?/Хорошо сидит?
vahm gahDEETsah/khahrahSHOH seeDEET
It fits well.

Очень хорошо сидит.
OHcheen' khahrahSHOH seeDEET
It doesn't suit me.

Не годится.
nee gahDEETsah
It's too...

Слишком...
SLEESHkahm
...big/small.

...велико/мало.
veeleeKOH/mahLOH
...long/short.

...длинно/коротко.
dleeNOH/KOHrahtkah
...loose/tight.

...широко/узко.
sheerahKOH/OOSkah

Women's sizes:

U.S.	6	8	10	12	14	16
Russ.	34	36	38	40	42	44

Men's sizes:

U.S.	34	36	38	40	42	44
Russ.	44	46	48	50	52	54

Colors

Color.
Цвет.
tsvyeht
What color is it?

Какого это цвета?
kahKOHvah EHtah TSVYEHtah
I don't like the color.

Мне не нравится этот цвет.
mnyeh nee NRAHveetsah EHtaht tsvyeht
Do you have other colors?

Есть ли у вас другие цвета?
yehst' lee oo vahs drooGEEyeh tsvyehTAH
I'd like *(f.)* something bright.

Я хотел(а) бы что-нибудь яркое.
yah khahtYEHL(ah) bih SHTOHneeboot' YAHRkahyeh
Do you have anything in red?

У вас есть что-нибудь красного цвета?
oo vahs yehst' SHTOH-neeboot' KRAHSnahvah TSVYEHtah
Red.

Красный.
KRAHSnihy
Pink.

Розовый.
ROHzahvihy
Violet.

Фиолетовый.
feeahLYEHtahvihy

Purple.

Пурпурный.
poorPOORnihy

Blue.

Синий.
SEEneey

Light blue.

Голубой.
gahlooBOY

Green.

Зелёный.
zeeLYOHnihy

Orange.

Оранжевый.
ahRAHNzhehvihy

Yellow.

Жёлтый.
ZHOHLtihy

Brown.

Коричневый.
kahrEECHneevihy

Beige.

Бежевый.
BYEHzhehvihy

Gray.

Серый.
SYEHrihy

Black.

Чёрный.
CHOHRnihy

White.

Белый.
BYEHlihy

Light-(+color).
Светло-...
SVYEHTlah-
Dark- (+color).
Тёмно-...
TYOHMnah-

Shoes

Shoes./Boots.
Обувь./Сапоги.
OHboof'/sahpahGEE
Felt boots.
Валенки.
VAHleenkee
Sandals.
Сандалии.
sahnDAHleeee
Slippers.
Тапочки.
TAHpahchkee
Children's shoes.
Детская обувь.
DYEHTskahyah OHboof'
Shoelaces.
Шнурки.
SHNOORkee
I take a size...
У меня номер...
oo meeNYAH NOHmeer
I don't know my size.
Я не знаю мой номер.
yah nee ZNAHyoo moy NOHmeer

Can I try these on in a size...

Я хочу примерить эти, номер...
yah khahCHOO preeMEEReet' EHtee, NOHmeer
These are too big/small/narrow/wide.

Они слишком большие/маленькие/
узкие/широкие.
ahNEE SLEESHkahm bahl'SHEEyeh/
mahLYEHN'keeyeh/OOSkeeyeh/sheeROHkeeyeh

Women's Shoes:

U.S.	5	6	7	8	9
Russ.	35	36	37	38	39

Men's Shoes:

U.S.	7	8	9	10	11
Russ.	41	42	43	44	45

Health and Beauty Supplies

Absorbent cotton.
Вата.
VAHtah
Antiseptic.
Антисептическая мазь.
ahnteeseepTEEcheeskahyah mahs'
Aspirin.
Аспирин.
ahspeeREEN
Ace-bandage.
Эластичный бинт.
ehlahsTEECHnihy beent

Band-Aids.

Пластырь.
PLAHStihr'

Bobby-pins.

Заколки.
zahKOHLkee

Comb.

Расчёска.
rahsCHOHSkah

Condoms.

Презервативы.
preezeervahTEEvih

Contraceptives.

Противозачаточные средства.
prahteevahzahCHAHtahchnihyeh SRYEHTstvah

Cough drops.

Таблетки от кашля.
tahbLYEHTkee aht KAHSHlyah

Curlers.

Бигуди.
beegooDEE

Deodorant.

Дезодорант.
deezahdahRAHNT

Diapers.

Пелёнки.
peeLYOHNkee

Disinfectant.

Дезинфицирующее средство.
deezeenfeeTSEErooyooshchehyeh SRYEHTstvah

Eardrops.

Ушные капли.
ooshNIHyeh KAHPlee

Eyedrops.

Глазные капли.
glahzNIHyeh KAHPlee
Eyeliner.

Тушь для век.
toosh' dlyah vyehk
Eye shadow.

Тени для век.
TYEHnee dlyah vyehk
Hairbrush.

Щётка для волос.
SHCHOHTkah dlyah vahLOHS
Hair dye.

Краска.
KRAHSkah
Hair spray.

Лак.
lahk
Hand cream.

Крем для рук.
kryehm dlyah rook
Insect repellent.

Средство от насекомых.
SRYEHTstvah aht nahseeKOHmihkh
Iodine.

Йод.
yoht
Laxative.

Слабительное.
slahBEEteel'nahyeh
Lipstick.

Губная помада.
goobNAHyah pahMAHdah

Makeup.

Косметика.
kahsMYEHteekah

Mascara.

Тушь для ресниц.
toosh' dlyah reesNEETS

Nail clipper.

Ножницы для ногтей.
NOHZHneetsih dlyah nahkTEY

Nail polish.

Лак для ногтей.
lahk dlyah nahkTEY

Nail polish remover.

Ацетон.
ahtseeTOHN

Pacifier.

Соска.
SOHSkah

Perfume.

Духи.
dooKHEE

Razor.

Бритва.
BREETvah

Razor blades.

Лезвия.
LYEHZveeyah

Rouge.

Румяна.
rooMYAHnah

Safety pins.

английские булавки.
ahngLEEYskeeyeh booLAHFkee

Sanitary napkins.

Гигиенические салфетки.
geegeeyehNEEchehskee sahlFYEHTkee

Shampoo.

Шампунь.
shahmPOON'

Shaving cream.

Крем для бритья.
kryehm dlyah breet'YAH

Soap.

Мыло.
MIHlah

Suntan lotion.

Крем для загара.
kryehm dlyah zahGAHrah

Tampons.

Тампоны.
tahmPOHnih

Throat lozenges.

Таблетки для горла.
tahbLYEHTkee dlyah GOHRlah

Toilet paper.

Туалетная бумага.
tooahLYEHTnahyah booMAHgah

Toothbrush.

Зубная щётка.
zoobNAHyah SHCHOHTkah

Toothpaste.

Зубная паста.
zoobNAHyah PAHStah

Vitamins.

Витамины.
veetahMEEnih

MEDICAL EMERGENCIES

Help

As in the West, Russia has set phone numbers for
calling emergency help. Dial 01 for fire, 02 for police
and 03 for ambulance. Most of the larger hotels have
their own doctor and medical services on the
premises. Contact your embassy or consulate when
the situation is serious.

Help!

Помогите!
pahmahGEEtyeh

Fire!

Пожар!
pahZHAR

Police!

Милиция!
meeLEEtseeyah

Stop!

Стоп!
stohp

I need help.

Мне нужна помощь.
mnyeh noozhNAH POHmahshch

There's been an accident.

Произошёл несчастный случай.
praheezahSHOHL neeSHAHSTnih SLOOchay

Please call the...

Вызовите, пожалуйста...
VIHzahveetyeh pahZHAHLstah

…American/British/Canadian embassy.

...американское/английское/канадское посольство.

ahmeereeKAHNskahyeh/ahngLEEYskahyeh kahNAHTskahyeh pahSOHL'stvah

…consulate.

...консульство.

KOHNsool'stvah

…ambulance.

...скорую помощь.

SKOHrooyooPOHmahshch

Please get...

Пожалуйста, вызовите...

pahZHAHLstah VIHzahveetyeh

…a doctor.

...врача.

vrahCHAH

…the police.

...милицию.

meeLEEtseeyoo

Please notify...

Пожалуйста, сообщите...

pahZHAHLstah sahahpSHCHEEtyeh

…my husband.

...моему мужу.

maheeMOO MOOzhoo

…my wife.

...моей жене.

mahYEHY zhehNYEH

…my family.

...моей семье.

mahYEHY seem'YEH

…my hotel.

…в мою гостиницу.
vmahYOO gahSTEEneetsoo
I've had my … stolen.

У меня украли…
oo meeNYAH ooKRAHlee
I've lost my…

Я потерял(а)…
yah pahteeRYAHL(ah)
…passport.

…паспорт.
PAHSpahrt
…wallet.

…бумажник.
booMAHZHneek
…purse.

…сумку.
SOOMkoo
…keys.

…ключи.
klyooCHEE
…money.

…деньги.
DYEHN'gee

Illness and Injury

He/She is hurt.

Он болен./Она больна.
ohn BOHleen/ahNAH bahl'NAH
He/She is bleeding badly.

У него/неё сильное кровотечение.
*oo neeVOH/neeYOH SEEL'nahyeh
krahvahteeCHEHneeyeh*

He/She is unconscious.

Он/Она потерял(а) сознание.
ohn/ahNAH pahteeRYAHL(ah) sahzNAHneeyeh
He/She is seriously injured.

У него/неё серьёзное повреждение.
oo neeVOH/neeYOH seer'YOHZnahyeh
pahvreezhDYEHneeyeh
I'm in pain.

Мне больно.
mnyeh BOHL'nah
My ... hurts.

У меня болит...
oo meeNYAH bahlEET
I can't move my...

Я не могу двинуть...
yah nee mahGOO DVEEnoot'
I'm ill. /(f.)

Я болен/больна.
yah BOHleen/(bahl'NAH)
I'm dizzy.

У меня кружится голова.
oo meeNYAH krooZHEEtsah gahlahVAH
I'm nauseous.

Меня тошнит.
meeNYAH tahshNEET
I feel feverish.

Меня лихорадит.
meeNYAH leekhahRAHdeet
I've vomited.

Меня вырвало.
meeNYAH VIHrvahlah
I've got food poisoning.

У меня пищевое отравление.
oo meeNYAH peeshchehVOHyehahtrahvLYEHneeyeh

I've got diarrhea.

У меня понос.
oo meeNYAH pahNOHS

I'm constipated.

У меня запор.
oo meeNYAH zahpOHR

It hurts to swallow.

Мне больно глотать.
mnyeh BOHL'nah glahTAHT'

I'm having trouble breathing.

Мне трудно дышать.
mnyeh TROODnah dihSHAHT'

I have chest pain.

У меня боль в груди.
oo meeNYAH bohl' fgrooDEE

I've got indigestion.

У меня несварение желудка.
oo meeNYAH neesvahRYEHneeyeh zheeLOOTkah

I've got a bloody nose.

У меня кровотечение из носа.
oo meeNYAH krahvahteeCHEHneeyeh ees NOHsah

I've got a sunstroke.

У меня солнечный удар.
oo meeNYAH SOHLneechnihy ooDAHR

I'm sunburned. /(f.)

я загорал(а).
yah zahgahrAHL(ah)

I have cramps.

У меня судороги/схватки.
oo meeNYAH SOOdahrahgee/SKHVAHTkee

I've broken my arm./(f.)

Я сломал(а) руку.
yah slahMAHL(ah) ROOkoo

I've sprained my ankle./*(f.)*

Я подвернул(а) ногу.
yah pahdveerNOOL(ah) NOHgoo

I've dislocated my shoulder./*(f.)*

Я вывихнул(а) лопатку.
yah VIHveekhnool(ah) lahPAHTkoo

I've been stung by a wasp/bee.

Меня укусила оса/пчела.
meeNYAH ookooSEElah ahSAH/pchehLAH

I've got...

У меня...
oo meeNYAH

...arthritis.

...артрит.
ahrtREET

...asthma.

...астма.
AHSTmah

...diabetes.

...диабет.
deeahBYEHT

...high blood pressure.

...высокое давление.
vihSOHkahyeh dahvLYEHneeyeh

...an ulcer.

...язва.
YAHZvah

Seeing a Doctor

I'd like an appointment...

Я хочу записаться на приём...
yah khahCHOO zapeeSAHTsah nah preeYOHM

…as soon as possible.

…как можно скорее.
kahk MOHZHnah skahRYEHyee
Where does it hurt?

Что у вас болит?
shtoh oo vahs bahLEET
Is the pain sharp/dull/constant?

Боль острая/тупая/постоянная?
bohl' OHStrahyah/ tooPAHyah/pahstahYAHnahyah
How long have you felt this way?

Вы давно так себя чувствуете?
vih dahvNOH tahk seeBYAH CHOOSTvooyehtyeh
I'll take your temperature.

Я измерю вашу температуру.
yah eezMYEHryoo VAHshoo teempeerahTOOroo
I'll measure your blood pressure.

Я измерю ваше давление.
yah eezMYEHryoo VAHsheh dahvLYEHneeyeh
I'll take your pulse.

Я пощупаю ваш пульс.
yah pahSHCHOOpahyoo vahsh pool's
Roll up your sleeve.

Засучите рукав.
zahsooCHEEtyeh rooKAHF
Undress to the waist.

Разденьтесь до пояса.
rahzDYEHN'tees' dah POHyeesah
Breathe deeply.

Сделайте глубокий вдох.
ZDYEHlaytyeh glooBOHkeey vdohkh
Open your mouth.

Откройте рот.
ahtKROYtyeh roht

MEDICAL EMERGENCIES

Cough.
Покашляйте.
pahKAHSHlyahtyeh
You will need an X-ray.

Надо сделать рентген.
NAHdah ZDYEHlaht' reenGYEHN
Is it serious?

Это серьёзно?
EHtah seer'YOHZnah
Do I need surgery?

Мне нужна операция?
mnyeh noozhNAH ahpeeRAHtseeyah
It's broken/sprained.

Это сломано/подвернуто.
EHtah SLOHmahnah/pahdVYOHRnootah
You need a cast.

Вам нужен гипс.
vahm NOOzhen geeps
You've pulled a muscle.

Вы растянули мышцу.
vih rahstyahNOOlee MIHSHtsoo
It's infected.

У вас заражение.
oo vahs zahrahZHEHneeyeh
Get well!

Поправляйтесь!
pahprahvLYAYtees'

Seeing a Dentist

Dentist.
Зубной врач.
zoobNOY vrahch

I need a dentist.

Мне нужен зубной врач.
mnyeh NOOzhen zoobNOY vrahch
What are the clinic's hours?

Когда приёмные часы в поликлинике?
kahgDAH preeYOHMnihyeh cheeSIH vpahleeKLEEneekeh
I want to make an appointment.

Я хочу записаться на приём.
yah khahCHOO zahpeeSAHTsah nah preeYOHM
Will I have to wait long?

Мне придётся долго ждать?
mnyeh preeDYOHTsah DOHLgah zhdaht'
I have...

У меня...
oo meeNYAH
...an abscess.

...нарыв.
nahRIHF
...a broken tooth.

...сломался зуб.
slahMAHLsah zoop
...a broken denture.

...сломался протез.
slahMAHLsah prahTEHS
...lost a filling.

...выпала пломба.
VIHpahlah PLOHMbah
...a toothache.

...болит зуб.
bahLEET zoop
...a cavity.

...дупло.
doopLOH

…sore and bleeding gums.

…дёсны очень воспалены и кровоточат.
*DYOHSnih OHcheen' vahspahLYEHnih ee
krahvahtahCHAHT*
Don't pull it out.

Не вырывайте его.
nee vihrihVAYtyeh yeeVOH
Can you fix it temporarily?

Можно ли его временно залечить?
*MOHZHnah lee yeeVOH VRYEHmeenhah
zahleeCHEET'*
When will my denture be ready?

Когда будет готов протез?
kahgDAH BOOdeet gahTOHF prahTEHZ
May I have an anesthetic?

Можно сделать обезболивание?
MOHZHnah ZDYEHlaht' ahbeezBOHleevahneeyeh

Treatment

I'm taking medication.

Я принимаю лекарство.
yah preeneeMAHyoo leeKAHRSTvah
What medicine are you taking?

Какое лекарство вы принимаете?
kahKOHyeh leeKAHRstvah vih preeneeMAHeetyeh
I'm taking antibiotics.

Я принимаю антибиотики.
yah preeneeMAHyoo ahnteebeeOHteekee
I'm on the Pill.

Я принимаю противозачаточные
    пилюли.
*yah preeneeMAHyoo prahteevahzah-
CHAHtahchnihyeh peeLYOOlee*

I'm allergic to penicillin.

У меня аллергия на пенициллин.
oo meeNYAH ahleerGEEyah nah peeneetseeLEEN

I'll prescribe an antibiotic/a painkiller.

**Я пропишу вам антибиотик/
   болеутоляющее средство.**
*yah prahpeeSHOO vahm ahnteebeeOHteek/
bohleeoootahLYAHyooshchehyeh SRYEHTstvah*

Where can I have this prescription filled?

**Где можно достать лекарство по этому
   рецепту?**
*gdyeh MOHZHnah dahsTAHT' leeKAHRSTvah pah
EHtahmoo reeTSEHPtoo*

When should I take the medicine?

Когда мне принимать это лекарство?
*kahgDAH mnyeh preeneeMAHT' EHtah
leeKAHRSTvah*

Take...

Принимайте...
preeneeMAYtyeh

...two pills.

...по две таблетки.
pah dvyeh tahbLYEHTkee

...three teaspoons.

...по три чайных ложки.
pah tree CHAYnihkh LOHSHkee

...every two/six hours.

...каждые два часа/шесть часов.
KAHZHdihyeh dvah cheeSAH/shehst' cheesOHF

...twice a day.

...два раза в день.
dvah RAHzah vdyehn'

…before meals.

…перед едой.
PYEHreet yeeDOY

…after meals.

…после еды.
POHSlee yeeDIH

…as needed.

…когда вам надо.
kahgDAH vahm NAHdah

…for five/ten days.

…пять/десять дней.
pyaht'/DYEHsyaht' dnyehy

I feel better/worse/the same.

Я чувствую себя лучше/хуже/также.
*yah CHOOSTvooyoo seeBYAH
LOOCHsheh/KHOOzheh/tagzheh*

Can I travel on Friday?

**Могу ли я отправиться в путь в
    пятницу?**
*mahGOO lee yah ahtPRAHveet'sah fpoot'
FPYAHTneetsoo*

At the Hospital

Hospital.

Больница.
bahl'NEEtsah

Clinic.

Поликлиника.
pahleeKLEEneekah

Doctor.

Врач.
vrahch

Surgeon.

Хирург.
kheeROORK

Gynecologist.

Гинеколог.
geeneeKOHlahk

Ophthamologist.

Офтальмолог.
ahftahl'MOHlahk

Pediatrician.

Педиатр.
peedeeAHTR

Nurse.

Медсестра.
myehdseesTRAH

Patient./(f.)

Пациент(ка).
pahtseeEHNT(kah)

Anesthesia.

Анестезия.
ahneesteeZEEyah

Bedpan.

Подкладное судно.
pahtklahdNOHyeh SOODnah

Injection.

Укол.
ookOHL

Operation.

Операция.
ahpeeRAHTSeeyah

Transfusion.

Переливание крови.
peereeleeVAHneeyeh KROHvee

MEDICAL EMERGENCIES

Thermometer.

Градусник.
GRAHdoosneek

I can't sleep/eat.

Я не могу спать/есть.
yah nee mahGOO spaht'/yehst'

When will the doctor come?

Когда придёт врач?
kahgDAH preeDYOHT vrahch

When can I get out of bed?

Когда я смогу вставать?
kahgDAH yah smahGOO fstahVAHT'

When are visiting hours?

Можно навестить больного?
MOHZHnah nahvehsTEET' bahl'NOHvah

Parts of the Body

Ankle.

Лодыжка.
lahDIHSHkah

Appendix.

Аппендикс.
ahPYEHNdeeks

Arm.

Рука.
rooKAH

Back.

Спина.
speeNAH

Bladder.

Мочевой пузырь.
mahchehVOY pooZIHR'

Blood.
Кровь.
krohf'
Body.
Тело.
TYEHlah
Bone.
Кость.
kohst'
Breasts.
Грудь.
grood'
Calves.
Икра
eekRAH
Cheek.
Щека.
shchehKAH
Chest cavity.
Грудная полость.
groodNAHyah POHlahst'
Ear/Ears.
Ухо/Уши.
OOkhah/OOshee
Elbow.
Локоть.
LOHkaht'
Eye.
Глаз.
glahs
Face.
Лицо.
leeTSOH

Finger.

Палец.
PAHleets

Foot.

Нога.
nahGAH

Gall bladder.

Жёлчный пузырь.
ZHOHLCHnihy pooZIHR'

Genitals.

Половые органы.
pahlahVIHyeh OHRgahnih

Glands.

Железы.
ZHEHlehzih

Hand.

Рука.
rooKAH

Heart.

Сердце.
SYEHRttseh

Heel.

Пятка.
PYAHTkah

Hip.

Бедро.
beedROH

Intestines.

Кишки.
keeshKEE

Jaw.

челюсть.
CHEHlyoost'

Joint.
Сустав.
soosTAHF
Kidney.
Почка.
POHCHkah
Knee.
Колено.
kahLYEHnah
Leg.
Нога.
nahGAH
Lip.
Губа.
gooBAH
Liver.
Печень.
PYEHchehn'
Lungs.
Лёгкие.
LYOHKHkeeyeh
Mouth.
Рот.
roht
Muscle.
Мышца.
MIHSHtsah
Neck.
Шею.
SHEHyah
Nerve.
Нерв.
nyehrf

Nose.

Нос.

nohs

Rib.

Ребро.

reebROH

Shoulder.

Плечо.

pleeCHOH

Skin.

Кожа.

KOHzhah

Spine.

Позвоночник.

pahzvahNOHCHneek

Stomach.

Живот./Желудок.

zheeVOHT/zheeLOOHdahg

Teeth.

Зубы.

ZOObih

Tendon.

Сухожилие.

sookhahZHEEleeyeh

Throat.

Горло.

GOHRlah

Thumb.

Большой палец.

bahl'SHOY PAHleets

Toe.

Палец ноги.

PAHleets nahGEE

Tongue.
Язык.
yeeZIHK

Tonsils.
Миндалины.
meenDAHleenih

Vein.
Вена.
VYEHnah

Wrist.
Запястье.
zahPYAHST'yeh

NUMBERS & TIME EXPRESSIONS

Cardinal Numbers

Russian numbers are highly irregular. The number "one" agrees in gender with the noun it modifies, so that it can be masculine, feminine or neuter. The number "two" has two forms: one serves as both masculine and neuter, while the other form is reserved for feminine subjects. All the remaining numbers have only one form.

0		Ноль/Нуль	*nohl'/nool'*
1	*m.*	Один	*ahDEEN*
	f.	Одна	*ahDNAH*
	n.	Одно	*ahDNOH*
2	*m.,n.*	Два	*dvah*
	f.	Две	*dvyeh*
3		Три	*tree*
4		Четыре	*chehTIHree*
5		Пять	*pyaht'*
6		Шесть	*shehst'*
7		Семь	*syehm'*
8		Восемь	*VOHseem'*
9		Девять	*DYEHveet'*
10		Десять	*DYEHseet'*
11		Одиннадцать	*ahDEEnahtsaht'*
12		Двенадцать	*dveeNAHtsaht'*
13		Тринадцать	*treeNAHtsaht'*
14		Четырнадцать	*chehTIHRnahtsaht'*
15		Пятнадцать	*peetNAHtsaht*
16		Яестнадцать	*sheesNAHtsaht'*
17		Семнадцать	*seemNAHtsaht'*

NUMBERS & TIME EXPRESSIONS

18	Восемнадцать	*vahseemNAHtsaht'*
19	Девятнадцать	*deeveetNAHtsaht'*
20	Двадцать	*DVAHtsaht'*
21	Двадцать один	*DVAHtsaht' ahDEEN*
22	Двадцать два	*DVAHtsaht' dvah*
23	Двадцать три	*DVAHtsaht' tree*
24	Двадцать четыре	*DVAHtsaht' chehTIHree*
25	Двадцать пять	*DVAHtsaht' pyaht'*
26	Двадцать шесть	*DVAHtsaht' shehst'*
27	Двадцать семь	*DVAHtsaht' syehm'*
28	Двадцать восемь	*DVAHtsaht' VOHseem'*
29	Двадцать девять	*DVAHtsaht' DYEHveet'*
30	Тридцать	*TREEtsaht'*
31	Тридцать один	*TREEtsaht' ahDEEN*
40	Сорок	*SOHrahk*
41	Сорок один	*SOHrahk ahDEEN*
50	Пятьдесят	*pee'deesYAHT'*
60	Шестьдесят	*sheezdeesYAHT'*
70	Семьдесят	*SYEHM'deeset*
80	Восемьдесят	*VOHseem'deeset*
90	Девяносто	*deeveeNOHstah*
100	Сто	*stoh*
200	Двести	*DVYEHstee*
300	Триста	*TREEstah*
400	Четыреста	*chehTIHreestah*
500	Пятьсот	*peet'SOHT*
600	Шестьсот	*sheesSOHT*
700	Семьсот	*seem'SOHT*
800	Восемьсот	*vahseem'SOHT*
900	Девять сот	*deeveet'SOHT*
1,000	Тысяча	*TIHseechah*

2,000	Две тысячи	*dvyeh TIHseechee*
5,000	Пять тысяч	*pyaht' TIHseech*
100,000	Сто тысяч	*stoh TIHseech*
1,000,000	Миллион	*meeleeOHN*

Ordinal Numbers

Since they act as adjectives grammatically, ordinal numbers have masculine *(-ый, -ой)*, feminine *(-ая)* and neuter forms *(-ое)*, which can be identified by their endings. The number "three" has irregular ("soft") endings.

1st	Первый (-ая, -ое)	*PYEHRvihy (-ahyah, -ahyeh)*
2nd	Второй (-ая, -ое)	*vtahROY (-ahyah, -ahyeh)*
3rd	Третий (-ья, -ье)	*TRYEHteey (-'yah -'yeh)*
4th	четвёртый	*chehtVYOHRtihy*
5th	Пятый	*PYAHtihy*
6th	Шестой	*sheesTOY*
7th	Седьмой	*seed'MOY*
8th	Восьмой	*vahs'MOY*
9th	Девятый	*deeVYAHtihy*
10th	Десятый	*deeSYAHtihy*
11th	Одиннадцатый	*ahDEEnahtsahtihy*
12th	Двенадцатый	*dveeNAHtsahtihy*
13th	Тринадцатый	*treeNAHtsahtihy*
14th	Четырнад-цатый	*chehTIHRnaht-sahtihy*
15th	Пятнадцатый	*peetNAHtsahtihy*
16th	Шестнадцатый	*sheesNAHtsahtihy*

17th	Семнадцатый	*seemNAHtsahtihy*
18th	Восемнадцатый	*vahseemNAH tsahtihy*
19th	Девятнадцатый	*deeveetNAHtsahtihy*
20th	Двадцатый	*dvahTSAHtihy*

Quantities and Measurements

Quantity.
Количество.
kahLEEchehstvah
A lot./Much.
Много.
MNOHgah
A little./Few.
Мало./Несколько.
MAHlah/NYEHskahl'kah
More./Less.
Больше./Меньше.
BOHL'sheh MYEHN'sheh
Most/least/best/worst of all.
Больше/меньше/лучше/хуже всего.
*BOHL'sheh/MYEHN'sheh LOOCHsheh/KHOOzheh
vseeVOH*
Majority./Minority.
Большинство./Меньшинство.
bahl'sheenstVOH/meen'sheenstVOH
Enough./Too much.
Достаточно./Слишком много.
dahsTAHtahchnah/SLEESHkahm MNOHgah
A third.
Треть.
tryeht'
A quarter.
Четверть.
CHEHTveert'

NUMBERS & TIME EXPRESSIONS

A half.
Половина.
pahlahVEEnah
Three-quarters.
Три четверти.
tree CHEHTveertee
The whole.
Целое.
TSEHlahyeh
Once.
Раз.
rahs
Twice.
Два раза.
dvah RAHzah
Three times.
Три раза.
tree RAHzah
Five times.
Пять раз.
pyaht' rahs
Early./Late.
Рано./Поздно.
RAHnah/POHZnah
Now.
Сейчас.
seeCHAHS
Still.
Ещё.
yeeSHCHOH
Never.
Никогда.
neekahgDAH
Seldom.
Редко.
RYEHTkah

Sometimes.
Иногда.
eenahgDAH
Usually.
Обычно.
ahbIHCHnah
Often.
Часто.
CHAHStah
Always.
Всегда.
FSYEHGdah
In the past.
В прошлом.
FPROHSHlahm
In the future.
В будущем.
VBOOdooshchehm
A long time ago.
Давным давно.
dahvNIHM dahvNOH
A short while ago.
Не так давно.
nee tahk dahvNOH

Days and Weeks

Sunday.
Воскресенье.
vahskreeSYEHN'yeh
Monday.
Понедельник.
pahneeDYEHL'neek

Tuesday.
Вторник.
FTOHRneek
Wednesday.
Среда.
sreeDAH
Thursday.
Четверг.
chehtVYEHRK
Friday.
Пятница.
PYAHTneetsah
Saturday.
Суббота.
sooBOHtah
On Wednesday.
В среду.
FSRYEHdoo
On Monday.
В понедельник.
fpahneeDYEHL'neek
Last Saturday.
В прошлую субботу.
FPROHSHlooyoo sooBOHtoo
Next Thursday.
В будущий четверг.
FBOOdooshcheey chehtVYEHRK
From Monday to Friday.
С понедельника до пятницы.
spahneeDYEHL'neekah dah PYAHTneetsih
What day is it today?
Какой сегодня день недели?
kahKOY seeVOHdnyah dyehn' neeDYEHlee
It's Tuesday.
Сегодня вторник.
seeVOHdnyah FTOHRneek

Week.
Неделя.
neeDYEHlyah
Last week.
На прошлой неделе.
nah PROHSHlay neeDYEHlyeh
This week.
На этой неделе.
nah EHtay neeDYEHlyeh
Next week.
На следующей неделе.
nah SLYEHdooyooshchey neeDYEHLyeh
In two weeks.
Через две недели.
CHEHrees dvyeh neeDYEHlee
In five weeks.
Через пять недель.
CHEHrees pyaht' neeDYEHL'
Every week.
Каждую неделю.
KAHZHdooyoo neeDYEHlyoo
For three weeks.
На три недели.
nah tree neeDYEHlee
Two weeks ago.
Две недели назад.
dvyeh neeDYEHlee nahZAHT

Months

Month.
Месяц.
MYEHseets

This month.
В этом месяце.
VEHtahm MYEHseetseh
Last month.
В прошлом месяце.
FPROHSHlahm MYEHseetseh
Next month.
В следущем месяце.
VSLYEHdooyooshchehm MYEHseetseh
Every month.
Каждый месяц.
KAHZHdihy MYEHseets
In a month.
Через месяц.
CHEHrees MYEHseets
January.
Январь.
yeenVAHR'
February.
Февраль.
feevRAHL'
March.
Март.
mahrt
April.
Апрель.
ahpRYEHL'
May.
Май.
Mahy
June.
Июнь.
eeYOON'
July.
Июль.
eeYOHL'

August.

Август.

AHVgoost

September.

Сентябрь.

seenTYAHBR'

October.

Октябрь.

ahkTYAHBR'

November.

Ноябрь.

nahYAHBR'.

December.

Декабрь.

deeKAHBR'

In July...

В июне...

veeYOONyeh

Since January...

С января...

syeenvahRYAH

In the beginning of October...

В начале октября...

vnahCHAHlyeh ahkteebRYAH

In the middle of December...

В середине декабря...

fseereeDEEnyeh deekahbRYAH

In the end of April...

В конце апреля...

fkahnTSEH ahpRYEHlyah

We'll be here from June to August.

Мы здесь будем с июня до августа.

*mih zdyehs' BOOdeem seeYOOnyah dah
   AHVgoostah*

NUMBERS & TIME EXPRESSIONS

We'll be here from the third of May through the nineteenth of July.

Мы здесь будем с третьего мая по девятнадцатое июля.

mih zdyehs' BOOdeem STRYEHT'eevah MAHyah pah deeveetNAHtsahtahyeh eeYOOl'yah

I've been here since October fourteenth.

Я здесь с четырнадцатого октября.

yah zdyehs' schehTIHRnahtsahtahvah ahktee-bRYAH

What's the date?

Какое сегодня число?

kahKOHyeh seeVOHdnyah cheesLOH

It's January twenty-second.

Сегодня двадцать второе января.

seeVOHdnyah DVAHtsaht' vtahROHyeh yeen-vahRYAH

When did he come?

Когда он приехал?

kahgDAH ohn preeYEHkhahl

He arrived on May twentieth.

Он приехал двадцатого мая.

ohn preeYEHkhahl dvahTSAHtahvah MAHyah

Years

Year.

Год.

Goht

Decade.

Десятилетие.

deeseeteeLYEHteeyeh

Century.

Век.

vyehk

This year.
В этом году.
VEHtahm gahDOO
Next year.
В будущем году.
FBOOdooshchehm gahDOO
Last year.
В прошлом году.
FPROHSHlahm gahDOO
In a year.
Через год.
CHEHrees goht
For a year.
На год.
NAH goht
Three years ago.
Три года назад.
tree GOHdah nahZAHT
Year-round.
Круглый год.
KROOGlihy goht
In the 19th century.
В девятнадцатом веке.
vdeeveetNAHtsahtahm VYEHkyeh
In the twentieth century.
В двадцатом веке.
vdvahTSAHtahm VYEHkyeh
In the twenty-first century.
В двадцать первом веке.
VDVAHtsaht' PYEHRvahm VYEHkyeh
In 2010.
В две тысячи десятом году.
vdvyeh TIHseechee deeSYAHtahm gahDOO

In 1991.

В тысяча девятьсот девяносто первом
году.

*FTIHseechah deeveetSOHT deeveeNOHstah
PYEHRvahm gahDOO*

In 1985.

В тысяча девятьсот восемьдесят пятом
году.

*FTIHseechah deeveetSOHT VOHseem'deeseet
PYAHTahm gahDOO*

How old are you?

Сколько вам лет?

SKOHL'kah vahm lyeht

I'm forty/sixty-three years old.

Мне сорок лет/шестьдесят три года.

*mnyeh SOHRahk leht/shezdeeSYAHT tree
GOHdah*

When was he/she born?

Когда он родился?/Когда она
родилась?

*kahgDAH ohn rahDEELsah/kahgDAH ahNAH
rahdeeLAHS'*

He was born in 1936/1960.

Он родился в тысяча девятьсот
тридцать шестом году/тысяча
девятьсот шестидесятом году.

*ohn rahDEELsah VTIHseechah deeveet'SOHT
TREEtsaht' shehsTOHM gahDOO/ TIHseechah
deeveetSOHT sheezdeeSYAHtahm gahDOO*

Other Time Expressions

Today.

Сегодня.

seeVOHdnyah

Tomorrow.
Завтра.
ZAHFtrah
Yesterday.
Вчера.
fchehRAH
Day after tomorrow.
Послезавтра.
pahsleeZAHFtrah
Day before yesterday.
Позавчера.
pohzahvchehRAH
The next day.
На следующий день.
nah SLYEHdooyooshcheey dyehn'
Three/Five days ago.
Три дня/Пять дней назад.
tree dnyah/pyaht' dnyey nahZAHT
Morning.
Утро.
OOTrah
In the morning.
Утром.
OOTrahm
This morning.
Сегодня утром.
seeVOHdnyah OOTrahm
Yesterday morning.
Вчера утром.
fchehRAH OOTrahm
Tomorrow morning.
Завтра утром.
ZAHFtrah OOTrahm
All morning.
Всё утро.
fsyoh OOTrah

Every morning.
Каждое утро.
KAHZHdahyeh OOTrah
Day.
День.
dyehn'
In the afternoon.
Днём./После обеда.
dnyohm/POHSlee ahBYEHdah
This afternoon.
Сегодня после обеда.
seeVOHdnyah POHSlee ahBYEHdah
Yesterday afternoon.
Вчера после обеда.
fchehRAH POHSlee ahBYEHdah
Tomorrow afternoon.
Завтра после обеда.
ZAHFtrah POHSlee ahBYEHdah
All day.
Весь день.
vyehs' dyehn'
Every day.
Каждый день.
KAHZHdihy dyehn'
Evening.
Вечер.
VYEHchehr
In the evening.
Вечером.
VYEHchehrahm
This evening.
Сегодня вечером.
seeVOHdnyah VYEHchehrahm
Yesterday evening.
Вчера вечером.
fchehRAH VYEHchehrahm

Tomorrow evening.
Завтра вечером.
ZAHFtrah VYEHchehrahm
All evening.
Весь вечер.
vyehs' VYEHchehr
Every evening.
Каждый вечер.
KAHZHdihy VYEHchehr
Night.
Ночь.
nohch'
At night.
Ночью.
NOHCH'yoo
Tonight.
Сегодня ночью.
seeVOHdnyah NOHCH'yoo
All night.
Всю ночь.
fsyoo nohch'
Every night.
Каждую ночь.
KAHZHdooyoo nohch'
Holiday.
Праздник.
PRAHZneek
Vacation.
Отпуск.
OHTpoosk
School holiday.
Каникулы.
kahNEEkoolih
Birthday.
День рождения.
dyehn' rahzhDYEHneeyah

NUMBERS & TIME EXPRESSIONS

Telling Time

Moscow and St. Petersburg are eight hours ahead of Eastern Standard Time.

Time.
Время.
VRYEHmyah
Half hour.
Полчаса.
pahlcheeSAH
Hour.
Час.
chahs
Minute.
Минута.
meeNOOtah
Second.
Секунда.
seeKOONdah
Early./Late.
Рано./Поздно.
RAHnah/POHZnah
I'm sorry, I'm late.
Простите за опоздание.
prahsTEEtyeh zah ahpahzDAHneeyeh
On time.
Вовремя.
VOHvreemyah
What time is it?
Сколько времени?
SKOHL'kah VRYEHmeenee

NUMBERS & TIME EXPRESSIONS

It's...
Сейчас...
seeCHAHS
...one o'clock.
...Час.
chahs
...five past three.
...пять минут четвёртого.
pyaht' meeNOOT chehtVYOHRtahvah
...ten past six.
...десять минут седьмого.
DYEHseet' meeNOOT seed'MOHvah
...quarter after four.
...пятнадцать минут пятого.
peetNAHtsaht' meeNOOT PYAHtahvah
...twenty past twelve.
...двадцать минут первого.
DVAHtsaht' meeNOOT PYEHRvahvah
...twenty-five after two.
...двадцать пять минут третьего.
DVAHtsaht' pyaht' meeNOOT TRYEH T'ehvah
...seven thirty.
...половина восьмого.
pahlahVEEnah vahs'MOHvah
...twenty-five to nine.
...без двадцати пяти девять.
byehs dvahtsahTEE peeTEE DYEHveet'
...twenty to eleven.
...без двадцати одиннадцать.
byehs dvahtsahTEE ahDEEnahtsaht'
...quarter to one.
...без четверти час.
byehs CHEHTveertee chahs
...ten of eight.
...без десяти восемь.
byehs deeseeTEE VOHseem'

…five of two.

…без пяти два.

byehs peeTEE dvah

…twelve o'clock midnight/noon.

…двенадцать часов ночи/дня.

dveeNAHtsaht' cheeSOHF NOHchee/dnyah

A.M.

Утра.

ootRAH

P.M.

Вечера.

VYEHchehrah

At what time?

В котором часу?

fkahTOHrahm cheeSOO

At one.

В час.

fchahs

At 3:05.

В пять минут четвёртого.

fpyaht' meeNOOT chehtVYOHRtahvah

At 2:10.

В десять минут третьего.

VDYEHsyaht' meeNOOT TRYEHT'ehvah

At 5:30.

В половине шестого.

fpahlahVEEnyeh sheesTOHvah

At 7:40.

Без двадцати восемь.

byehs dvahtsahTEE VOHseem'

At 12:50.

Без десяти час.

byehs deeseeTEE chahs

Seasons

Seasons.
Времена года.
vreemeeNAH GOHdah
Spring./In the spring.
Весна./Весной.
veesNAH/veesNOY
Summer./In the summer.
Лето./Летом.
LYEHtah/LYEHtahm
Fall./In the fall.
Осень/Осенью.
OHseen'/OHseen'yoo
Winter./In the winter.
Зима./Зимой.
zeeMAH/zeeMOY

REFERENCE

Some Russian National Holidays

New Year's Day: Jan. 1.
Новый год.
novihy goht
Orthodox Christmas: Jan. 7-8.
Рождество.
rahzhehstVOH
International Women's Day: Mar. 8.
Международный день женщин.
myehzhdoonahROHTnihy dyen' ZHEHNshcheen
Russian Orthodox Easter: March-April.
Пасха.
PAHskah
May Day: May 1.
Праздник весны и труда.
PRAHZDneek vehsNIH ee trooDAH
V-E Day: May 9.
День Победы.
dyehn' pahBYEHdih
Russian Independence Day: 12 June.
День независимости.
dyehn' nyehzahVEEseemahstee

Weather

The weather.
Погода.
pahGOHdah

What is it like outside?

Какая сегодня погода?
kahKAHyah seeVOHdnyah pahGOHdah
What's the forecast (for tomorrow)?

Какой прогноз погоды (на завтра)?
kahKOY prahgNOHS pahGOHdih (nah ZAHFtrah)
Tomorrow it will rain.

Завтра будет дождь.
ZAHFtrah BOOdeet dohsht'
Today it's...

Сегодня...
seeVOHdnyah
...sunny.

...солнечно.
SOHLneechnah
...overcast.

...пасмурно.
PAHSmoornah
...cool.

...прохладно.
prahKHLAHdnah
...warm.

...тепло.
teepLOH
...hot.

...жарко.
ZHAHRkah
...cold.

...холодно.
KHOHlahdnah
...humid.

...влажно.
VLAHZHnah

…windy.

…ветрено.
VYEHTreenah

It's raining/snowing.

Идёт дождь/снег.
eeDYOHT dohsht'/snyehk

What a beautiful day!

Какой прекрасный день!
kahKOY preeKRAHSnihy dyehn'

What awful weather!

Какая ужасная погода!
kahKAHyah ooZHAHSnahyah pahGOHdah

Directions

North.	Север.	*SYEHveer*
In the north.	На севере.	*nah SYEHveeryeh*
To the north.	На север.	*nah SYEHveer*
Northward.	К северу.	*KSYEHveeroo*
South.	Юг.	*yook*
In the south.	На юге.	*nah YOOgyeh*
To the south.	На юг.	*nah yook*
Southward.	К югу.	*KYOOgoo*
East.	Восток.	*vahsTOHK*
In the east.	На востоке.	*nah vahsTOHKyeh*
To the east.	На восток.	*nah vahsTOHK*
Eastward.	К востоку.	*kvahsTOHkoo*
West.	Запад.	*ZAHpaht*
In the west.	На западе.	*nah ZAHpahdyeh*
To the west.	На запад.	*nah ZAHpaht*
Westward.	К западу.	*KZAHpahdoo*

Family

Family.
Семья.
seem'YAH
Relatives.
Родственники.
ROHTSTveeneekee
Children.
Дети.
DYEHtee
Adults.
Взрослые.
VZROHSlihyeh
Wife./Spouse. *(f.)*
Жена./Супруга.
zhehNAH/soopROOgah
Husband./Spouse.*(m.)*
Муж./Супруг.
moosh/soopROOK
Mother.
Мать.
maht'
Father.
Отец.
ahTYEHTS
Baby.
Ребёнок.
reeBYOHnahk
Daughter.
Дочь.
dohch'
Son.
Сын.
sihn

Sister.

Сестра.
seesTRAH

Brother.

Брат.
braht

Grandmother.

Бабушка.
BAHbooshkah

Grandfather.

Дедушка.
DYEHdooshkah

Granddaughter.

Внучка.
VNOOCHkah

Grandson.

Внук.
vnook

Aunt.

Тётя.
TYOHtyah

Uncle.

Дядя.
DYAHdyah

Niece.

Племянница.
pleemYAHneetsah

Nephew.

Племянник.
pleemYAHneek

Cousin. *(m./f.)*

Двоюродный брат/Двоюродная сестра.
dvahYOOrahdnihy braht/dvahYOOrahdnahyah
seesTRAH

Husband's mother.

Свекровь.
sveekROHF'

Husband's father.

Свёкор.
SVYOHKahr

Wife's mother.

Тёща.
TYOHshchah

Wife's father.

Тесть.
tyehst'

Signs

Information.

Справки./Справочное бюро.
SPRAHFkee/SPRAHvahchnahyeh byooROH

Bathroom *(M/W)*

Туалет (М/Ж)
tooahLYEHT

Don't touch.

Не прикасаться.
nee preekahSAHT'syah

Push./Pull.

От себя./К себе.
ahtseeBYAH/ kseeBYEH

No admittance.

Не входить.
neefkhahDEET'

Entrance.

Вход.
fkhoht

Exit.

Выход.
VIHkhaht

No entry.

Нет входа.
nyeht FKHOHdah

No exit.

Нет выхода.
nyeht VIHkhahdah

Emergency exit.

Запасной выход.
zahpahsNOY VIHkhaht

Employees' entrance.

Служебный вход.
slooZHEHBnihy fkhoht

Elevator.

Лифт.
leeft

Stairs.

Лестница.
LYEHSneetsah

Up./Down.

Вверх./Вниз.
vvyehrkh/vnees

Keep to the left/right.

Держитесь левой/правой стороны.
deerZHEEtyehs LYEHvay/PRAHvay stahrahNIH

Don't lean against.

Не прислоняться.
nee preeslahNYAHTsah

Stop.

Стоп.
stohp

Wait.

Стойте.
STOYtyeh

Go.

Идите.
eeDEEtyeh

Careful!

Осторожно!
ahstahROHZHnah

Attention!

Внимание!
vneeMAHneeyeh

Prohibited.

Воспрещается.
vahspreeSHCHAHeetsah

Danger!

Опасно!
ahPAHSnah

Police.

Милиция.
meeLEEtseeyah

Quiet!

Не шуметь.
nee shooMYEHT'

Self-service.

Самообслуживание.
sahmahahpSLOOzheevahneeyeh

Occupied.

Занято.
ZAHneetah

No smoking.

Не курить.
nee kooREET'

Closed for lunch/repairs/cleaning.

**Закрыто на обед/ремонт/санитарный
день.**

*zahKRIHtah nah ahBYEHT/
reeMOHNT/sahneeTAHRnihy dyehn'*

Closed for a break from one to two.

Перерыв с часу до двух.
peereeRIHF SCHAHsoo dahDVOOKH

Office hours.

Приёмные часы.
preeYOHMnihyeh cheeSIH

Men working.

Ремонтные работы.
reeMOHNTnihyeh rahBOHtih

Watch out for cars.

Берегись автомобиля.
beereeGEES' ahftahmahBEElyah

Metric Conversions

Temperature:

To convert Celsius into Fahrenheit, multiply degree Celsius by 1.8 and add 32. To convert Fahrenheit into Celsius, subtract 32 from degree Fahrenheit and divide by 1.8.

Distance:

To convert miles into kilometers, divide miles by 5 and multiply by 8. To convert kilometers into miles, divide kilometers by 8 and multiply by 5.

1 km = 5/8 mile
1 centimeter = 0.39 inches
1 meter = 3.28 feet
1 kilometer = .675 mile
1 inch = 2.54 centimeters
1 foot = 30.5 centimeters
1 mile = 1609 meters

Weight:
1 kilogram = 2.2 pounds
1 gram = 0.0352 ounces
1 ounce = 28.35 grams
1 pound = 453.60 grams

Volume:
1 liter = 0.264 gallons
1 liter = 1.06 quarts
1 quart = .95 liter
1 gallon = 3.8 liters

FROM HIPPOCRENE'S RUSSIAN LIBRARY

Mastering Russian
Erika Haber
The Hippocrene Mastering Series offers contemporary foreign language instruction designed for individual or classroom use. Everyday situations and local customs are explained and used in dialogues, which expand vocabulary and encourage practice.
0-7818-0270-9 • $14.95 • (11)
Audio: 0-7818-0271-7 • $12.95 • (13)

Hippocrene Children's Illustrated Russian Dictionary
Ages 5-10
English-Russian/Russian-English
500 entries • 0-7818-0892-8 • $11.95pb • (216)

Russian-English Comprehensive Dictionary
Oleg Benyuch
40,000 entries • 0-7818-0560-0 • $35pb • (689)

Russian-English Comprehensive Dictionary
Oleg Benyuch
40,000 entries • 0-7818-0506-6 • $60hc • (612)

English-Russian Comprehensive Dictionary
Oleg Benyuch
50,000 entries • 0-7818-0442-6 • $35pb • (50)

Russian-English/English-Russian Standard Dictionary
Revised Edition with Business Terms
Oleg and Ksana Benyuch
The common-sense system of phonetics provides romanization of Russian words as well as the Cyrillic version of English words to help Russian speakers pronounce American English. An extensive appendix of Russian-English/English-Russian business terms has been added to aid Americans conduct business with Russians and vice versa. It also contains detailed menu terms, especially helpful for travelers to Russia.
32,000 entries • 0-7818-0280-6 • $18.95pb • (322)

Russian-English/English-Russian
Concise Dictionary
Oleg and Ksana Benyuch
Compact and totally modern, this dictionary contains over 10,000 entries with transliteration provided for each word.
10,000 entries • 0-7818-0132-X • $11.95pb • (262)

Russian-English/English-Russian
Compact Dictionary
10,000 entries • 0-7818-0537-6 • $9.95pb • (688)

Beginner's Russian
Nonna H. Carr & Ludmila V. Rodionova
The Beginner's Series was designed to meet the bilingual needs of the businessperson, tourist or student traveling in Eastern Europe. The language lessons are developed around common situations like going through customs, checking into a hotel, making phone calls, going to the post office, and extending and accepting invitations.
0-7818-0232-6 • $9.95pb • (61)

Dictionary of Russian Verbs
Daum and Schenk
This highly acclaimed dictionary featuring 20,000 fully declined verbs has already become the indispensable companion of thousands of Russian language students, who call it the most helpful guide of its kind.
20,000 fully declined verbs • 0-88254-420-9 • $35.00pb • (10)

Dictionary of Russian Proverbs
Bilingual
Edited by Peter Mertvago
A comparable or literal translation is provided for 5,335 entries, with references to similar English proverbs or sayings. Ample cross-referencing for proverbs on related subjects is included, as is a handy English proverb index. The dictionary serves as a valuable reference and learning tool for students, scholars, businessmen, travelers, translators, and anyone interested in Russian culture, attitudes, and lifestyle, of which proverbs are the quintessential embodiment.
5,335 proverbs • 0-7818-0424-8 • $35pb • (555)

Dictionary of 1000 Russian Proverbs

Edited by Peter Mertvago

This collection of the most commonly used and understood proverbs of the day is designed for a broad readership composed of students of both language and culture, from secondary school level to post-graduate, as well as teachers, travelers, and linguists. A comparable or literal translation is provided for the thousand proverbs, which are organized alphabetically by key words. The index is organized by English subject.

0-7818-0564-3 • $11.95pb • (694)

Treasury of Russian Love Poems, Quotations & Proverbs

in Russian and English
Edited by Victoria Andreyeva
0-7818-0298-9 • $11.95hc • (591)
Audio: 0-7818-0364-0 • $12.95 • (586)

Russia: An Illustrated History

Joel Carmichael

Encompassing one-sixth of the earth's land surface—the equivalent of the whole North American continent—Russia is the largest country in the world. Renowned historian Joel Carmichael explores Russia's rich and expansive past—upheaval, reform, social change, growth—in an easily accessible and concentrated volume. From the Tatar's reign to the present, this book spans seven centuries of Russian history, highlighting the major political events, cultural accomplishments, military conflicts and economic developments that have helped to shape the tradition of modern-day Russia. Over 50 photographs and illustrations bring Russia's history to life for readers.

50 photos/maps/illus. • 0-7818-0689-5 • $14.95hc • (154)

Moscow: An Illustrated History

Kathleen Berton Murrell

As capital of the largest country in the world, Moscow has experienced glorious and turbulent times. Home to the tsars and a center of the Bolshevik Revolution, it also has persisted as a thriving hub for culture and the arts. This volume succinctly recounts the city's political, economic, and cultural history, spanning the rise and fall of Imperial Russia and the Soviet Union up to today's era of democracy. Special attention is given to changes in the city's size and architecture during different historical periods. Featuring over 50 illustrations and photographs, this is the perfect introduction to a city that continues to play a major role in world event.

50 photos/illus. • 0-7818-0945-2 • $14.95pb • (419)

The Best of Russian Cooking

Expanded Edition

Alexandra Kropotkin

From *zavtrak* (breakfast) to *uzhin* (dinner), Russians love to eat heartily. Originally published in 1947, The Best of Russian Cooking is a treasured classic that combines authentic Russian recipes with culinary tips and invaluable cultural insights. This expanded edition features a concise list of menu terms, sections on Russian table traditions and mealtimes, and a guide to special cooking utensils. It includes 300 recipes for popular dishes such as beef stroganoff and borscht, as well as many lesser-known dishes that are daily fare in Russia—*kotleti* (meatballs), *piroshki* (dumplings with meat or vegetables) and *tvorojniki* (cottage cheese cakes).

0-7818-0131-1 • $12.95pb • (251)

Cuisines of the Caucasus Mountains
Recipes, Drinks, and Lore from Armenia, Azerbaijan, Georgia, and Russia

Kay Shaw Nelson

People of the Caucasus Mountains, a region comprising Armenia, Azerbaijan, Georgia and Russia, are noted for a creative and masterful cuisine that cooks evolved over the years by using fragrant herbs and spices and tart flavors such as lemons and sour plums. The 184 authentic recipes featured in Cuisines of the Caucasus Mountains offer new ways of cooking with healthful yet delectable ingredients like pomegranates, saffron, rose water, honey, olive oil, yogurt, onions, garlic, fresh and dried fruits, and a variety of nuts. The literary excerpts, legends, and lore sprinkled throughout the book will also enchant the reader-chef on this culinary journey to one of the world's most famous mountain ranges.

0-7818-0928-2 • $24.95hc • (37)

All prices subject to change without prior notice. To purchase Hippocrene Books contact your local bookstore, call (718) 454-2366, visit www.hippocrenebooks.com, or write to: Hippocrene Books, 171 Madison Avenue, New York, NY 10016. Please enclose check or money order, adding $5.00 shipping (UPS) for the first book and $.50 for each additional book.